THE GODS OF
GREECE AND ROME

I. ZEUS.

Marble Bust from Otricoli in the Vatican Museum, Rome.

THE GODS OF GREECE AND ROME

Talfourd Ely

DOVER PUBLICATIONS, INC.
Mineola, New York

Bibliographical Note

This Dover edition, first published in 2003, is an unabridged republication of *Olympos: Tales of the Gods of Greece and Rome,* which was originally published by G. P. Putnam's Sons, New York, and H. Grevel & Co., London, in 1891. That work was based on, and partly translated from, *Der Olymp* by Hans Dütschke (n.d.).

Library of Congress Cataloging-in-Publication Data

Ely, Talfourd
    [Olympos]
    The gods of Greece and Rome / Talfourd Ely.
        p. cm.
    Includes bibliographical references and index.
    ISBN 0-486-42798-6 (pbk.)
     1. Mythology, Classical. I. Title.

BL730 .E52 2003
292.2'11—dc21

2002041126

Manufactured in the United States of America
Dover Publications, Inc., 31 East 2nd Street, Mineola, N.Y. 11501

PREFACE.

SOME knowledge of Classical Mythology is needed to understand even our own literature from Dan Chaucer to Shelley and Swinburne ; nor are mythological books wanting, from the *Lemprière* of our youth to the *Golden Bough* of last year and Mr. Dyer's *Studies of the Gods* published only a month or two ago. Of these works, however, few are systematic treatises, and of these few still fewer are readable.

The present volume claims then a right to exist. It is based on, and partly translated from, Dr. Dütschke's *Der Olymp ;* but several chapters (as that on Athena) are my own work, and none are without some addition or alteration by me.

Virginibus puerisque canto ; in a book intended for the youth of both sexes much must be passed over in silence. Nor is there place here for cumbrous learning ; and in a volume of avowedly popular character no list of authorities need be given. Suffice it to say that in ancient literature I have borrowed most from the Homeric Poems and from Apollodoros ; while, among the moderns, Roscher's *Ausführliches*

Lexikon has proved of the greatest value. Nor have I failed to draw on my notes of the lectures on *Griechische Kunstmythologie*, delivered at Berlin by Professor Ernst Curtius in the Summer Semester of 1887.

The renderings of passages from the Classics are mostly taken from standard translations ; the few to which no name is attached are my own. I have added references to the originals, which may be of service to students.

Old-fashioned people will not perhaps easily bring themselves to recognise the Olympian family as composed, for the most part, of deities, each originally the supreme god of one of the many branches of the Hellenic stock.[1] Nor will they be pleased with the constant suggestion of the elemental origin of heathen worship. Yet the elemental idea is constantly cropping up in such stories as those of Danaë and Semele. Moreover, Pausanias has preserved many hints of early " beast " stories ; to say nothing of the well-known disguises of Zeus as bull, swan, etc., and the metamorphoses of Io and Kallisto.

These earlier views underwent a redaction at the hands of the poets. It was Homer and Hesiod, according to the Greek historian,[2] who put the stories of the gods into poetic shape, provided the means of distinguishing between the various deities, and

[1] Egyptian religion has been described as " a confederacy of local cults " (Frazer, *The Golden Bough*, vol. i., p. 313).

[2] Herodotus, ii., 53.

assigned to each his special functions. Not only were the forms of these gods described as those of mortal men, but their passions and their moral weaknesses closely reflected those that had full play among their earthly counterparts. The gods of Olympos, originally twelve in number, were in such respects no better than their humbler fellows who peopled every glade and every sparkling spring. Yet their special powers and characters, distinctly marked out for all time in Grecian poetry and Grecian art, entitle them to a precedence over the rank and file of supernatural folk.

Dr. Dütschke has well observed that the Roman differed from the Greek in nothing more widely than in religion. The Romans were essentially a practical people ; and this was reflected in their religious ideas. Eventually, however, foreign conquest brought them into contact with new forms of belief ; *Græcia capta ferum victorem cepit ;* and Apollo and Athena elbowed out the old homely deities of the Italian husbandman.

TALFOURD ELY.

HAMPSTEAD,
August, 1891.

TABLE OF CONTENTS.

CHAPTER II.

HERA—JUNO.

CHAPTER III.

POSEIDON—NEPTUNUS.

CHAPTER IV.

HESTIA—VESTA.

CHAPTER VIII.

ARTEMIS—DIANA.

CHAPTER IX.

HEPHAISTOS—VOLCANUS.

PART II.

THE LESSER GODS.

CHAPTER XVI.

THE DIOSCURI.

CHAPTER XVII.

HERAKLES—HERCULES.

CHAPTER XVIII.

RHEA KYBELE—MAGNA MATER.

CHAPTER XIX.

ASKLEPIOS—ÆSCULAPIUS; HYGIEIA.

LIST OF ILLUSTRATIONS.

PLATES.

ILLUSTRATIONS.

PART I.

THE GREATER GODS AND THEIR FOLLOWING.

CHAPTER I.

ZEUS—JUPITER.

(A) ZEUS.

1. Zeus Lykaios; the Cretan Zeus; Kronos.

When earth in springtime clothed herself afresh with herbage and with flowers; when summer's glow withered alike the foliage and the grass; when the refreshing storm burst forth from the hills, or winter's grim tempests wrapped the land in snow,—then knew the Greeks full well that a mightier power than man's guided nature on her path,—a heavenly power, whose name was Zeus. Unseen of mortal eye, he yet was known by his works; and his presence was often felt very near,—aye! nearer and nearer the higher men climbed the mountain-side. For there on the mountain-top he mostly had his dwelling. So lofty and so awful did the nature of Zeus appear in olden time that in such places ordinary men cared not to draw too nigh to him. So, amidst Arcadia's mountains the lonely towering "Wolf's Peak," or Lykaios, was a specially sacred abode of the god of heaven; Lykaios, from which men gazed over the whole Peloponnese, and in whose forests wolves, bears, and wild boars had their home. Here the pious of olden times had established a holy place for Zeus, the wolf-god (Lykaios).

For was it not a destructive frenzy as of a ravening
wolf, if in mid-summer the scorching heat of heaven
blasted nature's blossoming life, and spread death and
barrenness over the fields ? So raged, then, Zeus
Lykaios against nature and against man.   Him to
appease, nought else but human sacrifice availed, and
thus horrid rites lingered here on the lonely peak of
Arcadia's highlands, perhaps even till Christian times.
He who tasted of the victim's flesh, that the god alone
had a right to taste, was changed for nine years' space
into a were-wolf, wandering in loneliness, and shunning
the company of human kind.   He who, unbidden, burst
into this holy place of Zeus lost his shadow ; that is,
he vanished from the number of the living, for the
disembodied dead alone no shadows cast.

Yet the god's wrath was not without end ; nay,
'twas the same Zeus that sent, too, the refreshing
shower.   The priest need only stir with an oak twig the
waters of the mountain-stream, and mists came forth
and rolled together into the cloud teeming with rain.

And as on Arcadia's Wolf-mount, so, too, in Crete
men had to tell of a god of heaven, destroying what
he had brought into being ; only here such deeds were
portioned out between two persons, and it was not
Zeus that was regarded as the destroyer, but his
father Kronos.   He devoured, so ran the tale, all the
children his wife Rhea bore him, save the youngest,
Zeus.   In his stead shrewd Rhea gave her husband
a stone, wrapped in swaddling clothes, to swallow,
while she carried the young Zeus, fair as springtime,
to a cave on Mount Ida, where he was reared by
honey-laden bees, and by the nymph Amaltheia, who

nurtured the boy with goat's milk. But when the little fellow cried, then the youths (Kouretes) would begin their war-dance, and by striking together spears and shields raised such a din that the father heard not his child's cries, and could do him no harm. Long did they in Crete celebrate this festival of the birth of Zeus with such armed dances, and struck upon their shields as though they would frighten away evil spirits, and keep them off from the child awakening with the spring.

Here, then, there was divided between two persons that which really belonged to one and the same. For Kronos also might have originally been a god of heaven, as Zeus, the giver of growth and bloom. So in honour of him too, as god of the harvest, was celebrated the festival of Kronos in Greece about the time of the winter solstice, when the seed had been sown and the farmer rested from his toil. In like fashion the Romans, who recognised Kronos in their own god of the sowing, Saturnus, celebrated at the same season the Saturnalia, the farmer's merry feast, at which men sought to keep green in general jollity the memory of a golden age long past and gone. It was about our Yuletide. Then all gave themselves up to sports and feasting, and at table the master served the slave.

For a short time, then, it seemed as though all men were brothers and all wealth was shared alike. But the festival passed, and those happy days were never to return! They had long since passed away ; hence Kronos (or Saturnus) stood for the representative of the most ancient time. The poets too told of the

transitoriness of his rule. When the stripling Zeus
had grown up in Crete he forced his father Kronos
to disgorge the devoured children, and thrust him
from the throne deep down into the murky abyss of
Tartaros, the lowest deep. Later, indeed, the Greeks
would hear nothing of this story that told of such
misdeed of a son against his father; for men had
gradually learnt to see in Zeus a milder being; and
so from the old greedy Kronos cast out from his throne
there was made a mild god of the Dead, who in restful
peace held sway over the Islands of the Blest.

2. Revelations of Zeus in Nature; Olympos; Dodona.

If, however, men had ceased to see in the god of
heaven the wild destroyer of what he himself had made,
yet knew they full well that Zeus ruled earth and the
realms above, and let this power be known in many
a sign of heaven. Should tempests rage, and the
storm burst over the fields, and terrify feeble man
with gloomy cloud, or flashing bolt, or with sheet
lightning, or should heaven's azure gleam and tranquil
air attune to a like calm the soul of man,—'twas ever
at the bidding of Zeus that this befell.

And how could he have more clearly displayed his
majesty? If the storm-cloud drew nigh dark a n
gloomy, till the furious shock of the tempest shattered
it with the din of thunder, then it was known that
Zeus had grasped that wondrous armour which he
could throw round him as a cloak or brandish as a
shield. Then quaked all on earth; then there was

clattering on high, as when the thunder-god of the old
Teuton race drove over the clouds on his chariot
drawn by steeds of flame.

To that storm-mantle of Zeus the Greeks gave the
name of *Aigis*, or goat skin; a skin believed to have been
that of the goat that had nurtured the god as a child.

Wondrous was the look of this ægis, now dark as
if a cloud were passing over the mountains, now varied
with a hundred tassels of twisted gold that sparkled as
the lightning.   How must the dread cloud have appeared from which Zeus, to punish men's brutal deeds,
poured forth the mighty deluge on the earth, when the
waters rose above the mountains so that fish lodged
in the tops of elms, and gazelles swam on the surface
of the flood?[1]   Then Zeus delivered but one pair of
mortals from destruction, Deukalion and Pyrrha, the
ancestors of the human race; and Deukalion in turn
raised the first altar in his honour, and built at Athens
the first temple of the Olympian Zeus.

The rain-streams of Zeus, however, not only flood
the fields to the harm of men and crops, but bestow
on rivers their water and on earth her fruitfulness.
"Golden" was the name the Greek gave to such rain,
and into such golden rain could the god transform
himself when secretly he made his way into Danaë's
dark prison, where her father had immured her through
fear of what might be born.   All in vain! for Zeus
gave her a son Perseus, sprung from a god.   But the
Greeks also called Zeus "The Down-comer,"[2]   so

---

[1] Horace, *Odes*, i., 2, 9-12.

[2] καταιβάτης; but perhaps this refers rather to the descent of the
lightning.

closely was the belief in the god's nature bound up with the idea of falling rain.

Yet not only rain, but hail and snow did Zeus hurl with his right hand over the earth. Nobly does Homer mirror for us this might of the god :—

> " As falls a snow-shower all a winter's day,
>   When Zeus in his high purpose hath ordain'd
>   Snow-fall on man, and speeds his feathery shafts ;
>   He lulls the winds to slumber, and sheds down
>   Snow upon snow, enfolding every peak,
>   Mountain and headland, hill and dale alike,
>   Meadows of lotos, and the fruitful works
>   Of man, the shore, and harbours to the brink
>   Of heavy ocean, where the washing wave
>   Gives it the limit which it shall not pass ;
>   But else the face of all the world is wrapp'd
>   Within that heavy mantle from above." [1]

There are no phenomena of the heavens that do not proceed from Zeus, and therefore he is called also "The Cloud-Gatherer," "The Ægis-Bearer," "The Rejoicer in Thunder," and "The Far-Resounding."

The rainbow, too, with its many colours, has he placed in the clouds as a token of his might for mortal men. Above all, however, his favourite weapons are the lightning and the thunderbolt, companions of the storm.

Thunder and lightning the Kyklopes are bound to forge for him, those mighty beings, each with one round eye, the smithy-god's helpful comrades in the dark forge of fire-vomiting Ætna. With such lightning did Zeus dash down the giants when they threatened to scale heaven. Who is not reminded of the Teutonic thunder-god, that with his lightning-hammer in like fashion dashes down the giants of mountain and of

---

[1] *Iliad*, xii., 278-86, Cordery's translation.

frost? But as the lightning, so too the wind is a sign of the might of Zeus. We hear, indeed, also, of a king of the winds, Aiolos, who, cut off from all the world, dwells on a floating island in the distant sea.[1] Steep rises the island from the water, and a bronze wall cuts off his realm from the outer world, that the wild winds may not burst forth. But so much the more comfortable is it within with the king, who, in the midst of his twelve married children, takes his pleasure in a richly-decked table and the sound of wind-instruments. Of his winds he lets forth which he will, and coops up the rest; so to Odysseus, who had come to see him, he gave the west wind as guide for his voyage, and, that the other winds might not drive him back, gave them into his keeping in a leather sack, which he, by way of precaution, had tied up tight with a silver thread. In vain! The imprudent companions of Odysseus unloosed the thread, the winds blustered forth, and drove the unlucky hero back again to Aiolos.[2]

Aiolos, however, is merely the manager of the winds, and has no power to rouse or calm them without the consent of Zeus.

Lightning and storm, then, are the tokens of the power of Zeus, and are his weapons. When the god came to battle with the serpent-footed giants the eagle first brought him the lightning; hence the eagle, king of birds, circling high in air, has become his armour-bearer. When he roams alone round the mountain peaks, then is he nearest to the throne of Zeus. Here

---

[1] See the beginning of the tenth book of the *Odyssey*.
[2] Cf., Hugh Miller's *Scenes and Legends*, p. 278.

first gather together the rain-giving clouds, and here bursts forth the storm at its wildest. While the battle between Greeks and Trojans was raging, Zeus let his voice be heard in thunder from the Trojan Ida's snow-capped peak. His most famous abode, however, was Mount Olympos in Thessaly, whose summit is for the most part veiled in mysterious cloud; and because men forthwith fancied the homes of the other gods allotted on the mountain-slopes, the gods were generally styled the "Olympians," and their dwelling-place "Olympos."

In many parts of Greece the lofty oak, the special "lightning-tree" of the forest, served as a sanctuary of Zeus, and especially renowned were the holy oaks in the grove of Dodona. On this spot were the thoughts of Achilles fixed when, far from his home, he was warring round Troy, and with ardour he prayed to Zeus of Dodona, the god of his race. Unseen and depicted by no mortal hand, here in the oak grove Zeus held sway; only in the rustling of the trees and the plashing of the sacred rill that rippled adown the forest glade did men believe they heard his voice. Bronze bowls hung on the boughs, and, blown hither and thither by the wind, chimed in wondrously with these murmurs of air and water. To lay folk it was but an empty sound; but the god's learned priests, the "Selloi," and with them grey-haired priestesses, knew how to explain from this the will of Zeus, so that this oracle of Dodona soon gained great repute. It was perhaps the oldest of all in Greece, and old-fashioned and peculiar seemed the ways of these priests of the Dodonæan Zeus to the Greeks of a later age. They had to sleep on the bare earth, and were not allowed to wash their feet; though perhaps this applied only to the water of the spring at Dodona, so as not to profane its sanctity. For such were the powers of this water, that while burning torches were quenched in it, yet when quenched they took fire once more if dipped therein. So wondrously here did Zeus hold sway over air and water alike.

Lastly, however, Dodona was noteworthy in the eyes of the Greeks on account of this also, because here was maintained the worship of a spouse of Zeus, Dione. Poets called her later the mother of Aphrodite, goddess of love.

3. ZEUS, KING OF GODS AND MEN; ZEUS, THE COUNSELLOR.

Zeus then made his will known to men through signs, and sent his divine sons to declare to them his pleasure. Apollo, the god of prophecy at Delphi, is only "the mouth" of his father Zeus; he is the servant, Zeus the king. For only a king can make his will known and claim obedience.

Assuredly there was no need for each man who would learn to know him first to go to Delphi and ask Apollo. There were interpreters outside Delphi who understood the will of the gods, and among many a portent the heart itself told mortal man whether the god approved his undertaking or not.

Of especial importance was it if the eagle of Zeus appeared, and it was auspicious if he came from the right hand. When King Priam set forth on his journey to the Grecian camp, to beg for his son Hektor's body

from the tents of Achilles, his bitterest foe, he prayed
first thus to Zeus :—

> " Father, who from thy throne on Ida rul'st,
>   Great Zeus, most glorious ! grant me that I find
>   Favour and grace before Achilles' sight.
>   So send thy wingèd messenger, best-loved
>   By thee, and mightiest of the fowls of air,
>   A sign on my right hand, that, when I see
>   The sign, my heart being strengthen'd, I may go
>   Bold through the ships and chariots of my foes." [1]

And in fact the old man gained what he wished. But
the interpreters of omens seem not to have enjoyed a
particularly good reputation, and in any case it was
more important if the god himself set in man's heart
the true perception. Thus it was when Hektor was
preparing to cast the firebrand on the ships of the
Greeks ; there appeared to him from the left hand, as
boding ill, the eagle of Zeus, with a blood-red serpent
in his claws ; still writhing, it twisted round and bit the
eagle's breast, and the eagle, with a loud shriek of pain,
let the creature fall to earth.

> " The Trojans, shuddering, in their midst beheld
>   The spotted serpent, dire portent of Jove." [2]

But brave Hektor was not to be disheartened by the
qualms of his comrades, for Zeus had placed in his
heart courage for battle, and so he could shout
aloud :—

> " Surely the gods have reft thee of thy mind ;
>   Who bidd'st abandon the commands of Zeus,
>   His word, and pledge, and nod, as things forgotten,
>   To follow the behests of feather'd fowls !

---

[1] *Iliad*, xxiv., 308-13, Cordery's translation.
[2] *Ib.*, xii., 208, 209, Lord Derby's translation.

For whom I swerve not from my course one jot,
Whether their flight be toward the gates of Dawn,
Or westward to the cradle of the mist.

    *   *   *   *   *

Best of all omens is a country's cause." [1]

Nor did this feeling lead him astray, for victorious he forced his way into the Grecian camp.

But not only the eagle and other birds of prey were sent by Zeus; lightning also and thunder could warn men from an undertaking, or give them courage for it; clear above all were the terrible portents of heaven, if blood-red dew had fallen, or light from moon or sun turned suddenly to darkness. In general, all tokens from unknown distance that filled the heart with uneasy foreboding, all such came from Zeus; so, too, the mysteriously rising rumour, the " Ossa," which can spread further and further with furious haste, and fill a whole host with dread; this too is called the messenger of Zeus.

Yet the kingly might of the highest god shows itself not only in the counsel and the warning with which he gives help to man through wondrous signs. Zeus is also the actual giver of all good. 'Tis he that ordains the course of the moon and all the phenomena of heaven; he that sends the sailor the favouring breeze, and loads such nations as he will with wealth.

On his palace threshold stand two vessels, filled, the one with bad gifts, the other with good. From these Zeus assigns to men what he thinks right—now joy and sorrow mingled, now one without the other. But because he rules freely over the fate of gods and men,

---

[1] *Iliad*, xii., 234-40, and 243, Cordery's translation.

he is in very truth a king.   Therefore earthly kings also are styled his sons and "descended from Zeus," and the oldest kings of ancient story, as Aiakos of Aigina, and Minos of Crete, were also his priests, who spread abroad his worship ; and because they on earth ruled powerful and wise as Zeus himself, they were set after death in the world below, as judges of the dead.

Kingly, too, is the whole appearance of Zeus in Olympos.   If in his graciousness he nods assent to a suppliant, moves his dark eyebrows, and shakes his wavy locks (*cf.* Pl. I.), then quakes the whole hall of the gods, and the heavenly ones rise with reverence from their seats as soon as he sets foot within his golden palace hall.   Not even his brother Poseidon would venture to remain seated.   Nay, this god himself, who once on a time, in league with the spouse and the daughter of Zeus, had plotted to throw him into chains, does not refuse, when the god drives in his chariot to Olympos, to take out the horses and put the chariot away.   For thus says Zeus himself derisively in the consciousness of his power, "If all ye gods pulled at a golden rope fastened to heaven, still ye could not draw me to the earth : yet I can draw to me all of you together if I choose, and earth and sea as well."   In Fig. 1 we see him enthroned as a king, holding in his left hand the sceptre and the winged lightning, and with his right stretching forth the bowl to receive the libations of his worshippers.   A bunch of laurel adorns the back of his artistically-wrought seat, and laurel wreathes the god's long wavy locks.

To a king, however, there belong servants and messengers to do his will.   The fair youth Ganymede, whom his eagle had carried off for him from Troy, had

Fig. 1.—Zeus, the King.
On a vase from Gela in Sicily, now in Rome.

not only to give drink to the bird of Zeus, but also handed to the king of the gods the cup of nectar.

As messenger of Zeus and agent between heaven

and earth, we see the " wind-footed," " gold-winged" Iris flying past. Really her name denoted the many-coloured rainbow, with its span like a bridge from earth to heaven ; but this meaning was forgotten, and men thought only of the messenger, so that even the over-weening suitors of Penelope could derisively use the name " Iros" for the ragged beggar whom they employed for their errands.

4. ZEUS, THE GUARDIAN OF RIGHTS AND OATHS.

If, however, the king of the gods was invested with supreme power in heaven and on earth, yet his power was not lawless and tyrannical, but mild, as that of a father. And because Zeus exercised a fatherly care he was called the " Father of gods and men."

Wise and prudent, but above all righteous, was the rule of Zeus. Therefore the goddesses Themis and Dike (Law and Right) stand at his side ; and it is Themis also who, as his messenger, summons the gods to council. But right and justice again cannot exist without the oath and good faith, and so Zeus, under the name Herkeios, was also the guardian of oaths. He who took an oath on a specially solemn occasion called Zeus to witness; for Zeus punished perjury most severely. What he has once decided remains unalterable ; right is not curtailed, and justice maintains its course. Zeus, therefore, is the protector of every arrangement, especially of that of the house and the family. In his honour an altar is erected in every courtyard, and it stands under his special protection. On this altar the head of the house offers sacrifice to Zeus Herkeios (*i.e.*,

Zeus of the courtyard) on behalf of his people, and it was this altar that first met the stranger's eye when he set foot within the premises. Were he wandering in unknown parts, distressed by many a danger, he now saw safety before him; for he knew that here right and clemency prevailed, and the nearness of the highest god would protect him against lawless wrong. Therefore the honest swineherd could truly tell the beggar Odysseus that he received him in his hut, not out of curiosity, but from reverence for Zeus, the protector of strangers. All the more wanton and atrocious was it that the savage Neoptolemos, after the fall of Troy, did not hesitate to dash to pieces on the altar of Zeus Herkeios the little son of the fallen Hektor, and then to slay the old man Priam himself. Such crime, however, Zeus did not leave unpunished, for Neoptolemos, too, met his death later at the hands of an assassin.

5. Zeus, the Conqueror and Subduer of the Titans.

Strict then, and righteous, yet mild and peaceable, was the king of the gods. Such, too, was the conception that the great sculptor Pheidias formed for his statue which the Greeks, after the Persian wars, dedicated in the temple of Zeus at Olympia. This statue was so sublime and beautiful that it was esteemed a great piece of good fortune in a man's life to have looked on it if but for once.

The ruins of the temple are still to be seen, but the statue is gone. And yet, from the descriptions of ancient authors we can form a fairly clear notion of it. On a throne richly adorned with figures of all kinds

sat Zeus in a flowing robe of gold ; head, hands, and
feet, in fact all the naked parts, were of ivory ; in his
left hand he held a sceptre, and on its top the eagle
sat ; his right hand supported the winged goddess of
victory.[1] For victory belongs necessarily to the complete image of a king.

For the same reason the hair falling plainly down

Fig. 2.—Head of the Zeus of Olympia.   From a coin of Elis.

(Fig. 2) was adorned with a wreath of the same kind
as that received by the victor in the Olympian games.

But this peaceful and simple type of the king of
gods became gradually more and more haughty and
bold (*cf.* Pl. I.), and at the time of the world-conquering
Alexander the Great the god was conceived of rather
as the triumphant victor.   On the curly hair rested the

[1] See Pausanias, v., 11, 1.

broad and splendid oak wreath of Dodona ; there was a
bold backward turn of the head, and over the shoulder
was cast the scaly war-dress of the ægis (Fig. 3).
Thus had Zeus himself appeared in fierce warfare
when the giants essayed to storm heaven (Fig. 4).

FIG. 3.—HEAD OF ZEUS, WITH OAK-WREATH AND ÆGIS.
From the Julian cameo from Ephesos, now at Venice.

Yet still fiercer must the fight of gods have raged
when Zeus had thrust his father Kronos from the
throne and seized the reins to lord it o'er the world.
For the ancient line of Titans, descended from the gods,
did not so easily yield to him, and the rent uplands of

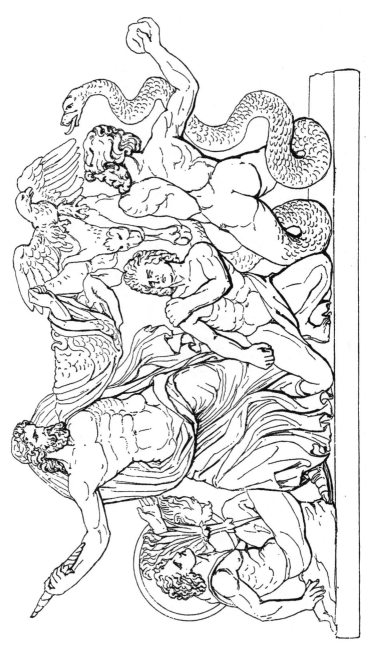

Fig. 4.—Zeus and the Giants.

Restoration of part of the frieze from the Altar of Zeus at Pergamos, now at Berlin.

Thessaly, through which the swift-rolling stream of Peneios makes its way into the sea (*cf.* p. 47), bore testimony to a strife that had convulsed even the solid earth itself.

Not till Zeus had summoned to his aid the "hundred-armed" giants and the round-eyed Kyklopes whom his father had imprisoned did complete victory fall to his lot. Now with his thunderbolts he hurled the Titans into the murky abyss of Tartaros that springs as deep beneath the earth as heaven above; thither never breath of air nor ray of sun can make its way, and there Kronos and the Titans were fain to dwell as gods of the world below, till at length the wrath of Zeus was calmed (*cf.* p. 6). In a four-horsed chariot he rode after his victory to Olympos, attended by the gods, whose abode heaven or Olympos was henceforth destined to be, and who now, to distinguish them from the "infernal" deities, receive the title "Heavenly," or "Ouraniones." Moreover in commemoration of his victory (as some say) the games were established at Olympia. Now Zeus shared the lordship of the universe with his brothers who had helped him. Hades received the realms of the dead beneath the earth, Poseidon the water, Zeus the heavens and the supreme command, while the surface of earth and of Olympos was common to all.

6. Zeus and Fate; the Weakness of the King of the Gods.

Brilliant as may be the picture of a victorious king from an outside point of view, still a king has enough

and to spare of cares. Truly it was said that Zeus
"spins the web of fate" for mortals; yet a little consideration would show that, however wisely he might
ordain and guide the fate of men, he himself was
fettered by a necessity, and a power still higher stood
above him. When once on a time the other gods and
men slept fast the whole night through, then Zeus lay
restless on his couch, and pondered how he could bring
honour to the goddess-born hero Achilles, who had
been so sorely wronged by Agamemnon. As one who
inclines this way and that, and cannot decide, he
takes the balance and casts the lots of the Greeks and
Trojans into the scales, to see which lot of the two will
rise the higher. Once again, with the same purpose,
he placed in the scales the death-lots of Achilles and
Hektor; Hektor's lot sank deep down to earth, and
Zeus knew that to the hero speedy death was decreed.
So Zeus was not fully free, and had to bow to the
destiny and power of Fate.

This power was called by the Greeks Moira, that is
"Portion," and when they imagined the action of this
Moira they conceived it to be, not a single person, but
three—Klotho, Lachesis, and Atropos; for the fate of
mankind is defined by birth, life, and death. Klotho,
"the Spinner," span the thread of life; Lachesis apportioned it to men; and Atropos, "the Inevitable," cut the
thread.[1] The Romans also believed in such a power of
fate which fixed at birth the lot of mortals, and named
it Parca; out of this Parca, however, or goddess of birth,

---

[1] "Comes the blind fury with the abhorred shears,
  And slits the thin-spun life."
                              MILTON, *Lycidas*.

they soon made, like the Greeks, three Parcæ, who had in their hands the fate of men.

Zeus, then, cannot always act as he chooses. Many of his favourite sons and heroes fall before Troy without his being able to rescue them, and what misery had not his son Herakles and his loved Io to endure from the plots and jealousy of his wife Hera! This wife, indeed, once managed by stratagem to lull her spouse to sleep, because she wanted behind his back to aid the Greeks in war against the Trojans. Such weakness did the poets attribute to their highest god; and it seemed as if he must demean himself in all things as a mortal. Zeus was no longer a moral and pure being, for he was very often faithless to his wife, and fell in love with goddesses and mortal women, whence again arose ground for quarrels and discord in the family of the gods.

With so little reverence did the Greeks of later times think of the king of the gods. How different had Zeus seemed to their pious forefathers, when they only with anxious dread looked up to the lord of life and death, and none but the initiated ventured to draw nigh to his sanctuary on the mountain-peak, or beneath the rustling oaks!

(B) JUPITER.

1. The Italian God of Heaven; the Heavenly Phenomena, and the Augurs.

The nations of Italy also, like the Greeks, honoured a god of heaven as the highest being, and they gave him the name of Jupiter, that is, Father of Heaven, or Light. But they never attributed to him mortal weaknesses that could degrade his divine dignity. Jupiter remained for the Romans a pure, spotless being, who ruled in the brightness of light, and guided the phenomena of the heavens. Therefore the day of full-moon, "Idus" (*cf.* p. 41, note 1), was sacred to him, when the light of day was continued alike in the night. Shining white must be the colour of victims well pleasing in his sight, and when the victorious general rode in triumph, as an earthly Jupiter, his car too was drawn by four snow-white steeds. The bright gleam that started from heaven was his work—the thunder-bolt, the summer lightning ; but also thunder and rain. Various names expressed his activity ; people spoke of Jupiter Pluvius [1] when the rain poured down; of Jupiter Tonans when the clouds dashed thundering on one another ; of Jupiter Fulminator when the lightning struck peaks and trees, and of Jupiter Summanus, (properly *Submanus*) if it lightened in the night towards morning. These signs of heaven might be beneficent or ruinous, especially to the countryman, whose well-being depended so completely on them. And so it was the more important to discover the grounds of their occurring so unexpectedly. Was the god angry, or did he wish only to warn mankind ?

A spot struck by lightning became sacred, and might not be meddled with by mortals. A flint was usually buried in it, for this could produce sparks, and represented Jupiter's missile fallen in the lightning, as his thunderbolt ; then the spot was fenced in, and an altar erected over it, round in shape, like a well, the so-called Puteal, and this altar was sacred to Jupiter. Madness

[1] See the figure on the column of M. Aurelius.

seized the wretch who desecrated such a spot. If a person was killed by lightning it was a sure sign he had deserved it ; if, however, he was only touched by lightning without being killed, as in the case of Anchises, father of Æneas, then Jupiter had marked him out, and destined him for high fortune.

Yet it was not easy to ascertain Jupiter's will in these wondrous tokens, and only the initiated were in a position to do so. For not only in lightning and storm, but also through all sorts of other signs, could the god declare himself,—in the flight and cry of birds, in their way of eating, in the appearance of various quadrupeds, especially of the wolf, but also when unexpected sounds and noises were heard. The founder of the Roman rites, King Numa, had first established the rules by which all these phenomena were to be interpreted, not arbitrarily, but according to the holy command of Jupiter himself. He had managed to induce the god to descend in lightning and impart everything to him, and then, in gratitude for his instruction, had dedicated a temple to Jupiter Elicius, that is, the enticed Jupiter. This, however, happened once and once only, for the god did not allow people to trifle with him. When, on a later occasion, King Tullus Hostilius wanted to induce Jupiter to descend, the lightning came down and slew the king. It was a secret lore according to which the tokens were to be interpreted, and this lore had to be learned by study. Only the Augurs, literally the " Birdseers," possessed this knowledge, and on that account they were very important in the Roman state, for without previously ascertaining the will of Jupiter it was impossible to enter upon any important undertaking.

2. JUPITER, THE PROTECTOR OF PROPERTY.

Between the temple of Jupiter and the citadel which lay on the two summits of the Capitoline Hill at Rome there was a hollow overgrown with oaks. In this grove stood an ancient image of a youthful god, who had in one hand a bundle of arrows and by his side a goat. The Romans called the god Veiovis, and thought it a representation of the youthful Jupiter. In remote antiquity, while wild force still prevailed, such an image of a god alone could ensure protection to the fugitive; and therefore Romulus invited the criminals and the outcasts with whom he proposed to people his new city of Rome to flee to this place for refuge. Here was protection guaranteed them. As generally in antiquity, in place of human sacrifice a goat was offered in atonement to the god; so the goat stood here beside the god's image, and a goat was actually sacrificed here every month in honour of Jupiter. The presence of Jupiter, then, is salutary, and every house stood in need of his protection. So every enclosure was dedicated to him, and under the name "Terminus," or god of boundaries, he became the protector of each man's property. Only with those beasts that were dedicated to him and his consort Juno, namely, a white steer and a white cow, was the boundary generally fixed for each possession, whether it was a whole city or merely a single homestead, both beasts were harnessed to a plough, and the furrow which the plough made represented the boundary ordained by Jupiter. On each side of the furrow a sacred space was left, and when an entrance had to be indicated the plough was lifted and carried over. There only was it permitted to enter the property, and Romulus killed his brother Remus because he had ventured to leap over the wall of the newly-founded city. In like manner it was held an offence worthy of death to remove or to plough up the boundary stone. Each single homestead was called by the Romans an "island," for through the sacred space on both sides of the furrow it was separated like an island from all other homesteads. On the last day of every year, therefore on the boundary of the old year —this was in early Rome the 23rd of February—the neighbours assembled at the boundary, placed wreaths on the boundary stone, and offered to Jupiter Terminus at first a bloodless sacrifice, later also a lamb ; and while they indulged in the meat from the sacrifice, they found pleasure at their feast in living at peace with their neighbours.

3. JUPITER, THE GOD OF GOOD FAITH AND THE OATH ; THE FETIALES.

So old was the worship of this Jupiter of Boundaries that it was said that King Numa Pompilius had built the first temple to Terminus. When the foundations of the Capitoline temple were being laid, the stone of Terminus refused to be removed from its position, and had to be left for ever within the area of the temple of Jupiter. But good faith also was inseparably bound up with Jupiter ; all property rests on good faith and covenants. To the god who dwelt in the clear brightness of the heavens nothing was more hateful than lying and a cunning disposition. Frank and open, pure and guiltless, should be also the intercourse of man. Shining white was the hue of the garments of his servants, and above all should his priest, the Flamen Dialis, with his wife, the Flaminica, be a human pattern of purity and holiness.

No ring nor knot might there be on his apparel; nay, his very eye was to shrink from fixing on any object that might bear the semblance of a fetter. Should a prisoner make his way into his house he was freed of his fetters. But when the priest of Jupiter visited the ancient sanctuary of Good Faith to offer his sacrifice, then was he completely veiled in his white robe, even to the finger-tips, to show that good faith had to guard against all contact with unholy things, and only the fingers might be ready to shake hands. Neither family nor state were without the bond of the faith of stability; therefore Jupiter also had to watch over good faith. His priest was present at the solemnisation of marriage. The stranger and the wayfarer took refuge in the protection of Jupiter, and the allies of Rome invoked on the coins the good faith of the Roman state. The Sabines, too, the old neighbours of the Romans, had made their god of heaven, Dius Fidius, lord of oaths. He, however, as a god of light, could be invoked only under the open sky. With this object his temple had in its midst an open space to admit the light of day, and the Romans took to swearing by Dius Fidius, just as by their own Jupiter. If, however, the matter in hand were a public treaty or alliance of the state, men turned again to Diespiter, the father of day as he was called. For light and clearness were unexceptionable witnesses for every act. The Fetiales, servants of Jupiter, probably twenty in number, were required to arrange the conclusion of an alliance with a foreign people under the protection of the highest god. Just so was it at the declaration of a war. Then was the grass, as it grew on the Capitoline Hill, pulled up with roots and earth, and brought to the actual spot where the oath was to be taken. Thus were people, to some extent at least, aware of Jupiter's presence, since Jupiter's spirit, as it held sway in the Capitoline temple, floated also unseen over the turf which surrounded it. Similarly, at the taking of an oath, the first of the Fetiales held the holy sceptre, or the lance of Jupiter, and the holy flint. At the ratification of the sworn agreement, the pig which was usually sacrificed on the conclusion of a treaty was killed with this sacred flint. For the flint was an image of the thunderbolt, and the lightning was the due punishment of perjury. How many splendid examples the history of Rome affords to show that in the estimation of the true-born Roman the keeping of his word stood higher than even life itself; and, indeed, the betrayer of his fatherland merited nothing else than to be hurled from the declivity of the temple of Jupiter on the Capitol, the so-called Tarpeian Rock.

4. Jupiter, the God of Victory and Ruler of the Roman State.

Through this manly firmness did the Romans become lords of the earth, as Jupiter was the ruler of the universe. Therefore he was also the bestower of victory. Victoria, goddess of victory, dwelt near him in the Capitoline temple ; men dedicated to him gold

and silver images of the goddess of victory (as once
Hiero, tyrant of Syracuse, did, in order to make the
god favourable to his own hoped-for victories), and on
his hand was placed the goddess of victory, as was
done by the Greeks in the case of Zeus at Olympia.
So we see in a Pompeian wall-painting Victory herself
flying to crown the god with a wreath (*cf.* Fig. 5).
When King Romulus, in a bloody battle against the
Sabines, could not gain the victory, he vowed in his
anxiety a temple to Jupiter if he stayed the pursuing
foe ; and lo ! the onward rush of the Sabines was
checked, and the Romans were victorious.　To Jupiter
Stator (*i.e.*, to the god who stops the enemy) Romulus
built a temple.　If, however, the commander had killed
the leader of the enemy and stripped him of his armour
with his own hand, the glorious spoils (*spolia opima*)
were offered on a bier (*feretrum*) to Jupiter Feretrius.
Twice only after Romulus could Roman history point
to such heroic deed.　The noblest exploit, then, that
the victorious Roman could perform in fight he owed
to Jupiter's favour.　Was it strange if Jupiter was
generally recognised as the gracious protector of the
Roman state ?　From the Capitoline temple in Rome
originated all power with which the world was governed,
and as long as the temple of Jupiter stood the power
and sovereignty of Rome also could not pass away.
Twice did it sink in flames, and twice rose more lordly
and more brilliant from its ashes.　It was in the
Capitoline temple that the general departing for war
offered the victim to Jupiter, and on his knees laid the
laurel wreath when he returned in triumph as a conqueror.　But also the youth, when entering on manhood

FIG. 5.—JUPITER, LORD OF THE UNIVERSE.
Restoration of a Pompeian wall-painting at Naples.

and the service of the state, raised his prayer to the Capitoline Jove. The god held in his hand the fate of the entire commonwealth. Yearly on the day of full moon in September, the anniversary of the dedication of the Capitoline temple, a magistrate of the highest rank, specially chosen for that purpose, drove a nail into the right hand wall of the temple, and thereby was it to be testified that the iron fate which has power over all, has that power only through the will and under the support of Jupiter; with the blow of the hammer on the nail Jupiter impressed his seal on fate.

That dedication festival of his temple was the most brilliant of Roman spectacles save the ostentatious triumphal processions of victorious generals, who, disguised as the Capitoline Jupiter, their faces coloured red like the god's image in the temple, rode on their four-horsed cars. But the "Roman games" on the dedication day of the temple were reckoned among the greatest delights which regularly recurred every year. They began with the sacrifice of a white bull in the Capitoline temple, whose horns were gilded; with this were connected a banquet of the highest magistrates and a feast for the people. The next day there was a trial of the horses destined for the races, and then the solemn procession of the deities, and above all of Jupiter, Juno, and Minerva, on costly vehicles, to the *Circus Maximus*, and lastly the races held there. And well had Jupiter, whom they called *Optimus Maximus*, or "Best and Greatest,"—well had he deserved that all this splendour should be displayed at his chief festival, for with the existence of his temple was bound up the existence of the Roman state.

CHAPTER II.

HERA—JUNO.

(A) HERA.

I. DIONE, THE HEAVEN-GODDESS; AND HERA, THE EARTH-GODDESS.

BESIDE the heaven-god Zeus, there was worshipped at Dodona, from time immemorial, his wife also, Dione, whose name corresponds to that of Zeus (gen. *Di-os*), and means "Goddess of Heaven"; for it was to be expected that women would prefer to address their prayers to a female being rather than to a male.

But it was not every Grecian tribe that held exactly the same religious views as the people of Dodona, and so it came about that gradually the chief female deity of another and a more powerful tribe usurped Dione's place. Dione then faded almost completely out of the remembrance of the people, and the poets boldly asserted that she was the mother of Aphrodite, goddess of love. They might just as well have called her the mother of any other goddess.

The new deity, however, was called Hera, and was the chief goddess of the chivalrous tribes of the Æolians and Achæans. Wherever these had settled, there was spread abroad also the belief in Hera; and the Achæan

33

cities—as Argos, Mykenai, and Sparta—remained also in later times the favourite abodes of the goddess.

Hera was, perhaps, originally the goddess of earth, and stood, therefore, in opposition to the heaven-god Zeus. So the poets recounted that the wedded pair often fell out with each other; indeed, there is a story in Homer that Zeus had, in his anger, given Hera a beating. Who is not reminded by this of the icy hail-stones and the darting lightning that the enraged god of heaven hurls down upon the earth? But we find, also, that Hera was honoured as the mourning goddess. In a city of Arcadia, a district of Greece in which so many old-fashioned usages were kept up, people prayed, for example, to the "widowed" Hera, who had lost her husband, Zeus. And is there not also a mourning of the earth, when she lies torpid in wintry chill, and sends forth nor grass nor flower? But poets knew another ground for this torpidity or enchaining of the earth-goddess. Homer, for instance, tells how Hera's own son, Hephaistos, had prepared for his mother so wondrous a seat that she could not rise up when once she had seated herself thereon; only Hephaistos could free her from these bonds.

The earth, however, wakes again from her torpor; then is it springtide, the cuckoo sounds his note, the crocus and the hyacinth burst forth, and the wrath of the clouded heaven gives place to the cheerful blue. Then are the mighty gods reconciled once more; then is celebrated the holy marriage of Zeus and Hera. When the great sculptor Polykleitos carved at Argos the far-famed image of Hera, he placed on her shoulder the cuckoo, harbinger of spring. Later, too, the artists

II. HERA.

Marble Bust in the Villa Ludovisi, Rome.

loved to deck the diadem of the goddess with budding spring-flowers (see Plate II.).

It was on the lofty mountain-peak, above all, that Zeus and Hera met; and as Zeus was honoured on the summits of the mountains, so these were in many places consecrated to Hera. Thus she was connected with Mount Ida near Troy, and Kithairon in Bœotia; and in the district of Corinth, Hera had the distinct title " Goddess of the Heights." Now Earth decked herself with fresh verdure, and spread forth the most lovely couch for the goddess,—clover and the dainty blossoms of the spring. Yet not alone plants that joy the eye did the earth-goddess send forth, but fruits as well that serve for nourishment, as the golden apples of the Hesperides, an image of inexhaustible blessings and a souvenir of the marriage of Zeus and Hera. For earth nourishes all. Therefore the cow, as a giver of nourishment, was sacrificed to Hera, just as it was offered to Nerthus, the Teutonic mother-earth. And just as this goddess rode on a car drawn by sacred cows, so it was the rule that the priestess of Hera at Argos should be drawn by cows to the sanctuary on the mountain-side. With this usage is connected the beautiful story of Kleobis and Biton, sons of the priestess of Hera. These harnessed themselves to their mother's chariot in place of the cows that were not to be found; and when she, with thankful heart, besought the goddess to reward them, her gracious mistress, as they slumbered in her sanctuary after their labours, turned their sleep to painless death. But death is in his hand to give who gave life as well; and is not Earth mother of all mankind?

2. Hera, Queen of the Gods and Guardian of Marriage.

This, indeed, was not always the view as to Hera in the belief of the Greeks. As Dione had once been forgotten for Hera, so men's belief passed on to another earth-mother, Demeter. Yet Hera remained the powerful bride of the king of the gods, and shared his honours. She, like Zeus, was a child of Kronos (Saturnus) and Rhea, and so the Roman poets were wont to name her Saturnia; and in Homer she calls herself "the noblest daughter of wily Kronos." She grew up in the home of Okeanos, god of the great sea, and next to Zeus she is the most important among the Olympians. When these two are united, the others all together cannot stand against them. Superhuman is her power and her activity. When she swoops down from Olympos, she speeds over the snowclad mountains of Thrace, touching only the highest peaks; she treads not with her feet the level earth, but the forest resounds beneath her. When her war-chariot flies between earth and starry heaven, then the lashed steeds spring at each stride as far as a man seated on a high watch-tower can look over the sea into the misty distance. Of giant size then does Homer picture to himself the goddess; and when she once took a solemn oath to Hypnos, the god of sleep, he thus addressed her :—

> "With one hand grasp earth that gives food to many,
> And with the other grasp the glistening sea."[1]

Broad Olympos quaked if Hera moved in anger on

----

[1] *Iliad*, xiv., 272-7

her throne; and when she entered the halls of the gods, all rose from their seats to do her honour, or saluted her with the brimming cup.

She appears among the others as a queen. Her chariot sends forth rays of gold and silver; a hundred golden tassels hang from her girdle down. As a queen, too, is she served by the other goddesses. Athena herself has woven her the beautiful robe of state, adorned with patterns of many a varied hue; she is surrounded by a princely throng. The three goddesses of the Seasons, the Horai, who open and shut the gates of heaven, serve not Zeus alone, but they harness horses for Hera too; in Hera's train is seen as well her daughter Hebe, goddess of eternal youth, who pours out nectar at the banquet of the Immortals; or the three Charites (Graces), the goddesses of charms, who at all times appear when nobility and beauty are united. And beauteous indeed is the queen of the gods; "white-armed," "large-eyed," "adorned with fair braids of hair," are epithets applied to her by Homer; and as stately and majestic did the artists also represent her, always in long robes falling in many a fold, at times with the veil, at times with the high sceptre and a cup in her outstretched hand, as if she awaited a libation from those who drew near her with prayer (Fig. 6).

As queen of the gods, however, Hera partook not only of all the honours of Zeus, but also of his power over heaven and earth and the whole of nature. Like Zeus, she had power to wield the thunder and the lightning, to rouse storm and spread forth cloud; nay, she can hasten into the sea the course of the unresting chariot of the sun. And of this power she is so con-

Fig. 6.—Hera, the Queen of the Gods.
Marble statue in the Vatican Museum at Rome.

scious that opposition often provokes her to the greatest
violence. When, in the war before Troy, Artemis met
her in hostile guise, she did not hesitate to hold fast with
her left hand both the hands of the youthful goddess,
and with her right to tear her bow and quiver from her
shoulders; then, scornfully laughing, she struck her with
these about the ears, so that the arrows flew out. And
can one blame a mother for falling into a passion if
a daughter dares to oppose her? For Hera stands at
the head of the family of gods as a mother ; all power
rests, then, in her hands as in those of her husband. So
Hera was also the guardian of marriage and of conjugal
fidelity. In the island of Samos she was worshipped
in the form of a very ancient wooden image, which was
veiled as a bride ; and in Athens, February, the so-called
" wedding-month," was dedicated to her. That conjugal morals should not be harmed, but kept pure and
chaste, that was what Hera had most at heart. Every
amorous creature was hateful to her in the depths of
her soul; and therefore she remained an implacable
enemy to the effeminate Paris, who had adjudged the
prize to the goddess of love, and through his artifices
had carried off a noble woman from her husband, little
recking that for the sake of one woman his own fatherland was doomed to destruction. And as she pursued
the effeminate Paris, so she pursued with equal fury the
Trojans also, his countrymen, and never rested till Troy
had sunk in flames. Nay, indeed, the pious Trojan
Aineias, son of the goddess of love, she drove in her
implacable enmity over sea and land ; and she would
have utterly destroyed him, together with his companions, had not the will of Zeus from the beginning

determined it otherwise. But woe to him who ventured to approach her herself! Ixion, to punish him for daring to covet her in marriage, was stretched out in the infernal regions on an ever-revolving wheel of fire.

But she was also unsparing in pursuing the faithlessness of her own husband. What troubles Herakles had to endure, who was son of Zeus and Alkmene! How Hera persecuted Io, the poor favourite of Zeus! Hera changed her into a cow, and appointed a keeper for her, the hundred-eyed Argos, in order to frustrate all the stratagems of her husband. Zeus sent the messenger of the gods, his son Hermes, to slay Argos. He by his flute-playing lulled the watcher to sleep, and killed him ; but Hera struck Io with frenzy, and had her hunted through every land by a stinging gadfly. But the eyes of the slain Argos were placed on the tail of the peacock, Hera's favourite bird. He stalked as proudly among his mates as Hera among the goddesses, and showed by the coronet on his head that he belonged to the retinue of a queen.

(B) JUNO.

1. JUNO, THE GODDESS OF LIGHT AND GUARDIAN OF WOMEN.

The goddess of heaven, Dione, who at Dodona was honoured as wife of Zeus, was called Juno among the nations of Italy ; it was the same name, for originally Juno had the sound of Diuno.

When, however, the Greeks ceased to esteem Dione

among deities, Juno remained among the Italians the highly honoured goddess of heaven and wife of Jupiter. Like him, she had power to rouse thunder and lightning, and therefore in some Italian cities, as Lavinium, her image appeared in warlike equipment, armed with shield and spear.

But while the bright gleam of day was ascribed to Jupiter above all, the moon's gentle light was esteemed one of Juno's works. Especially was the new moon consecrated to Juno, as the day of full moon, that divided the month and was called *Idus*,[1] was held sacred to Jupiter.

There was, of course, no kalendar in use among the earlier Romans ; nay, they could not have profited by one, since reading and writing were very rare accomplishments. So each new moon had to be announced to the people by the crier, and on this account received the name of *Kalendæ*,[2] whence we get our word "kalendar." Most important, however, seemed the Kalends of March,—a month named after Juno's son, Mars. For the Roman year originally began with March, and on the first of March was the birthday of Mars. The Kalends of March was ever afterwards the principal festival of Juno, mother of Mars.

This festival was entitled "*Matronalia*," because it was celebrated by all matrons. Only married women of good reputation and virgins were permitted to take part in it ; husbands made presents to their wives, and the latter entertained their domestics ; so that the

---

[1] From the Latin word *iduare = dividere =* divide.
[2] From *kalare =* call.

unmarried poet Horace could with good reason exclaim
on this day despairingly—

"Wonderest thou, learned friend, what I, a bachelor, am doing on
the Kalends of March ? " [1]

To no other goddess, indeed, had women so intimate
a relation as to Juno.   According to Roman belief, each
man was attended by a *genius*; this was the power
that lived in each man, maintained his life, and as his
guardian angel left him at death only to pass over into
blissful and purer regions.   But women also had their
guardian angel, who lived in them and accompanied
them unseen ; this guardian angel was Juno.   A woman
therefore, naturally enough, prayed first to her Juno,
and swore by her, and offered to her also on her birthday a special sacrifice.

2. JUNO, THE PROTECTRESS OF MARRIAGE AND QUEEN OF THE STATE.

As, however, matrimony is the most important occur-
rence in woman's life, Juno also kept guard over each
conjugal tie.   Her marriage with Jupiter was for the
Roman the fairest type of wedlock,—honourable and
chaste ; and the presence of the high priest of Jupiter
was required at every solemn celebration of the nuptial
tie.   Conjugal fidelity was a charge of Juno *Pronuba;*
hence the frequent adorning of the Roman sarcophagus
with Juno's figure, who, with outspread arms, brings
together the affianced pair, as a token that the union
effected beneath her eyes is not broken even by death
(Fig. 7).

[1] *Carm.*, iii., 8, 1.

On the other hand, it is again Juno who avenges the
breach of the marriage tie ; and therefore, in Vergil's
Æneid, it is she who, together with Mother-Earth,
when Dido and Æneas approach each other in unlawful

Fig. 7.—Juno Pronuba
From a Roman sarcophagus now at St. Petersburg.

love, expresses through lightning and fiery tokens her
indignation at their wanton deeds.

The ancient Romans knew well that lawful wedlock
was the foundation of well-ordered family life and of
the State as a whole. In some cities of Italy—as, for
example, in Veii—Juno, under the title of " Queen," was

esteemed guardian of the Commonwealth. After the
conquest of Veii, this "Queen Juno" was also invited
to take up her abode in Rome, and was worshipped
with Jupiter in the Capitoline temple.

This was a distinction shared only with Minerva;
and these three deities became, accordingly, the special
guardians of the Roman State. On occasion of the
public games, their images were carried in procession
on splendid chariots; and Juno's care for the preservation of the Capitol had been shown when the savage
hordes of Gauls were on the point of surprising it one
night. Then it was the cackling geese that roused the
Roman sentinels and frustrated the attempts of the Gauls.
But the geese were sacred to Juno, for these domestic
animals were cherished as pets also by the women of
antiquity; and after that time, in commemoration of the
deliverance from the Gauls, Juno's sacred geese were
kept on the Capitol at the public expense. Later,
when an Empire had taken the place of the Roman
Republic, the Emperor's person was almost as important for the State as the Capitoline temple; and as
prayers for the Emperor's life had to be offered in
the temple of the Capitoline Jove, so also Juno, queen
of heaven, was invoked on the Capitol as the special
guardian of the Empresses of Rome.

CHAPTER III.

POSEIDON—NEPTUNUS.

(A) POSEIDON.

1. POSEIDON, THE GOD OF THE WATER; POSEIDON, THE DESTROYER, AND THE SEA-MONSTERS.

BEFORE the worship of Poseidon was established among the Greeks, there were a number of water deities, as Nereus and Triton. Gradually, however, the belief in Poseidon as a deity superior to these spread throughout the Hellenic world. He was not, however, exclusively a water-god. We hear of Poseidon "Phytalmios," as the fosterer of plants. He thus came into contact with various other deities, and sometimes had to give way to them, as to Apollo at Delphi. Occasionally a compromise was effected, as at Athens, where Poseidon shared a sanctuary with Athena.

Poseidon was held to be god of the sea. But in earlier times he was god of water in general, of springs and rivers, as well as of the sea. The Dorians pronounced his name, not as Poseidon, but Poteidan. This word reminds us of the Greek word for river (*rotamos*) and marks the god as lord of streams and water in general. If winter's chill cast the lively, gushing

45

water into bonds of ice, so that it lay stiff as though dead, then was the god Poseidon in distress and fettered. Legend actually tells of Poseidon's slavery. This god, together with Apollo, was compelled to serve for a year the grim Trojan king Laomedon, and built for him the walls of Troy. Laomedon, however,—literally, "Sub-duer of the People,"—is only another name for the god of death. But if the god Poseidon is in fetters, we must think of his rule extending only over springs and streams. Again, springs gush out of the earth; and if Poseidon sends them up, must we not look for his habitation in the depth of the earth? The ancients actually believed that the earth rested like a disk on the water, and so Poseidon had also the name of "The Earth-Holder." So, too, the giant Atlas, who "knew all the depths of the sea," and, therefore, was also really a sea-god, supported the pillars of the world; that is to say, the disk of the earth, with the hemisphere of the heavens above it, rested on solid pillars, and Atlas supported these pillars on his shoulders. It was the later poets who identified this sea-god with the mountain-giant in Africa, whose head, covered with snowy locks, towers up into heaven. Poseidon was supposed to have closed Tartaros with doors of bronze,—Tartaros, the lowest space of the universe, lying as deep beneath the earth as heaven above it. The roots of the earth rested on Tartaros; and so the god who holds in his power the firm foundations can also cause them to quake. Hence he is called "Earth-Shaker," as well as "Earth-Holder"; and he tears down strong walls as quickly as he builds them. For the Trojan king Laomedon he built the stout walls of Troy; but he tore

down the rampart that the Greeks had raised before
the city, because they had neglected to offer to him
the victims that were his due.

> "Neptune's self,
> His trident in his hand, led on the stream,
> Washing away the deep foundations, laid,
> Laborious, by the Greeks, with logs and stones,
> Now by fast-flowing Hellespont dispersed.
> The wall destroyed, o'er all the shore he spread
> A sandy drift." [1]

Wherever men saw mighty masses of rock torn
asunder, there they were ready to trace Poseidon's
power. Thus in Thessaly, where he was worshipped
as the "Render of Rocks," he cleft with his trident
a passage for the river Peneios through the Vale of
Tempe by tearing the mountains asunder [2]; wherever
else earthquakes have occurred, there they were his
doing. Once on a time, when a Spartan king invading
Argolis (B.C. 390) was terrified by an earthquake, all
the Spartans, in anxious dread, addressed in prayer
"Poteidan," as they called him in the Dorian speech.

Especially when insolent outrage had to be punished,
the god appears unexpectedly with his terrible weapon,
the rock-shattering trident. When the Grecian fleet
was wrecked on its return from Troy, and Poseidon
had placed the hero Aias safe on the rocks of Euboia,
the boaster presumed to say that it was by his own
strength that he had escaped the hurricane; but
Poseidon marked his words,—

> "This heard the raging ruler of the main;
> His spear, indignant for such high disdain

---

[1] *Iliad*, xii., 27-32, Lord Derby's translation.
[2] See Herodotus, vii. 129.

> He launch'd, dividing with his forky mace
> The aërial summit from the marble base:
> The rock rush'd seaward with impetuous roar
> Ingulf'd, and to th' abyss the boaster bore." [1]

Almost more clearly still did the god's wrath show itself when he sent mighty waves over the lands and flooded them, as though he would seize full possession of them. Then it was said he was contending for the land with the gods who dwelt there; and on many a spot could people tell of a struggle between Poseidon and the deities of the land. So floods he Argos, and falls to strife with Hera, the goddess worshipped there; so contends he at Corinth with the sun-god Helios, in Naxos with Dionysos, at Delphi with Apollo, and in Attica with Athena. Everywhere he has at last to give way and be reconciled with his opponents. But the legend of his contest for the soil of Attica held its ground as most famous of all. Here had he created the horse and the spring of salt water, while Athena created the olive. Kekrops, however, the king of the land, decided that the olive was more valuable for Attica, and the land belonged of right to Athena.

Enraged at this decision, Poseidon covered the plain of Eleusis once more with water, and even in later times men were fain to recognise the traces of this flood in small salt-water lakes between Eleusis and Athens.

Besides this, when there is talk of mighty floods suddenly bursting forth, and threatening mortals with death and destruction, we hear of gigantic monsters rising from the sea. These too are sent of course by

---

[1] *Odyssey*, iv., 505-10, Pope's translation.

Poseidon, and generally to punish the presumption of men. When King Laomedon refused him the stipulated reward for building the walls of Troy, he sent a sea-monster, to whom was given up the king's daughter Hesione. The wife of the Æthiopian king Kepheus boasted herself more beautiful than the Nereids, daughters of the sea; and therefore Kepheus, to propitiate Poseidon's anger, had to make up his mind to abandon his daughter Andromeda to a sea-monster till Perseus set the unhappy maiden free. Hippolytos, too, that bold but chaste hunter, falsely denounced to his father Theseus, by his stepmother Phaidra,—Hippolytos met his death through Poseidon. For on his father's begging of the god vengeance for the supposed outrage, Poseidon sent up from the waves a huge bull, whereby the horses drawing the chariot of Hippolytos were frightened, the chariot was upset, and Hippolytos killed.

2. POSEIDON, CREATOR OF THE HORSE; HORSE-MANSHIP; RACES.

Well might the belief of the people see in the bellowing, heaving waves a wild bull that swept away all that stood in his path; but when from the sea there rose clouds, that the tempest chased as a wild herd before it, then it was fancied that a herd of horses had sprung from the sea; and so Poseidon was esteemed the creator of the horse (see p. 48). So, for example, he had created the divine horse Pegasos, that carried for Zeus his thunderbolts, and with the blow of his hoof caused fountains to spring up from the earth; such was the "horse-fountain" Hippokrene, on Parnassos. But because fountains often have to do with inspiration, people in a later age made of this a " poets'-well." Originally the Greeks had no such idea about it, but Pegasos was to them only the horse of the cloud or of the spring; Zeus took the lightning-flash from the back of the cloud ; the cloud with its rain, too, moistens the earth, so that she can send forth the joyous springs.

As, however, Poseidon is the creator of the horse, so he, as god of water, changed himself into a horse ; and in Attica he was for this reason often designated Poseidon Hippios, or "The Horse-Poseidon." Some, however, would explain this of Poseidon on horseback, as on the coins of Potidaia.[1] Besides his altar in Athens, Pausanias also found an altar of Athena Hippia.[2]

Poseidon, as creator of the horse, teaches heroes the art of horsemanship, and his sons are held to be masters of this art. To Peleus he gave horses as a marriage gift, and his son Bellerophon alone was able to bridle the divine horse Pegasos. A counterpart of Poseidon, some say, is Erichthonios,[3] a king of Attica, whose name means "Earth-Breaker." This Erichthonios was held to be the inventor of the four-horse team, and was afterwards placed among the constellations as the " Charioteer."

As creator of the horse, Poseidon is patron of the equestrian games with horse and chariot, and his protection is invoked by charioteers on the racecourse. Thus, before Troy, Antilochos, holding in one hand the whip and with the other touching the horses of his

---

[1] Head, *Coins of the Ancients*, p. 9.
[2] Paus., i., 30, 4.
[3] For a different account of Erichthonios, see p. 161.

chariot, had to swear by Poseidon that he had acted
fairly towards Menelaos in the race. Not only Antilochos, however, showed himself a skilful driver, but
also his father, the aged Nestor, son of Neleus. He too
was reputed a descendant of Poseidon, and is commonly
designated "the horseman Nestor." On the Isthmus
of Corinth equestrian games with horse and chariot
were celebrated every third year in honour of Poseidon.

3. POSEIDON, GOD OF SEAFARING MEN AND KING OF THE SEA.

When Telemachos, the unhappy son of the wandering
Odysseus, came on his travels to the realms of aged
Nestor, 'he found the old man on the shore surrounded
by his kinsfolk, and about to offer up to the god
Poseidon a solemn sacrifice of a hundred steers as
black as night; for Nestor's clan was a tribe of hardy
seamen, and for this reason Nestor was called a grand-
son of Poseidon.

Of such seafaring tribes there were many on the
coasts of Greece. Seven ancient cities of the Peloponnese, whose power reached over the sea, had founded
on the island of Kalauria in the Saronic Gulf, a
sanctuary of Poseidon, in which the confederates held
regular meetings. To the revered sanctuary of this
Poseidon of Kalauria the orator Demosthenes at a later
time fled from his pursuers, and finally put an end to
his life there by poison.

But all these tribes of Peloponnesos were surpassed
in naval skill by the Ionians of Asia Minor, who also
naturally looked upon Poseidon as their principal deity.
His temple at Mykale, in Asia Minor, was specially the

pledge of his divine protection ; and hither came the envoys of the Ionians every year to take counsel together in common. The ships of these Ionians sailed in all directions ; their colonies lay on every shore, and wealth and prosperity were the result of their bold traffic on the sea. Was not then Poseidon clearly the appropriate deity of their race ?

Certainly it was among these Ionians that the charming story arose of the Phæacians, the favourites of Poseidon. They were all his descendants, and through his blessing had become great. Their " oar-loving" men were at home on every sea ; skilfully and speedily could they carry to his home each stranger that approached their shores, for quick as thought and as a bird their ships flew over the waves. Riches and comfort filled their homes ; they passed their day in feasting and the dance ; at their board the singer gladdened their hearts with songs of times past and gone ; and the young men took delight in the race, while the women were skilled in weaving and the making of gorgeous stuffs. Of prosperity and good order their city gave full proof, whose spacious harbour was alive with masts, while in the market-place rose Poseidon's stately fane.

Such was the favour Poseidon showed to those who honoured him, and so powerful a god deserved a place among the highest. If he could not supplant the heaven-god of the other Grecian tribes, he was at least esteemed as his brother, almost his equal in power and honour. After the overthrow of his father Kronos, heaven fell to the lot of Zeus as his province, while the lordship of the waters became the portion of

Poseidon. Matched with Zeus, indeed, he is the weaker, if at times he rages in anger against him, and ventures to resist him, if Hera, the haughty consort of Zeus, leads him astray; in the presence of Zeus, however, he is officious and submissive; and when Zeus comes to Olympos, Poseidon takes out his horses, and spreads a linen cover carefully over the beautiful chariot.

Over the sea alone does Poseidon hold unlimited sway as a monarch. The means of destroying the poor seafarer on the high seas, if he has in aught offended, await Poseidon's will. The winds with which he lashes the waves to fury owe him obedience. Terrible as the sea and incalculable is Poseidon's wrath. Naught could appease his hatred against Odysseus, who had blinded his son, Polyphemos. It was only behind his back, when he was gone to a sacrificial feast among the pious Æthiopians, that Athena could win from Zeus the permission for Odysseus to return to his home. Though this decision of Zeus could not be contested, yet Poseidon sought at least to throw difficulties in the way of its fulfilment, and to postpone it.

Odysseus, on his raft, was already near the land of the Phæacians, that rose from the sea before his eyes like the top of a fig tree, when Poseidon caught sight of him; wildly he drove the clouds together and roused up the sea.

> " He spake, and high the forky trident hurl'd,
> Rolls clouds on clouds, and stirs the wat'ry world,
> At once the face of earth and sea deforms,
> Swells all the winds, and rouses all the storms.
> Down rush'd the night: east, west, together roar;
> And south, and north, roll mountains to the shore." [1]

---

[1] *Odyssey*, v. 292–96, Pope's translation.

Powerful and mighty is the aspect of the god. When he strides swiftly, the heights and the forests quake. As a hawk speeds his flight that soars from the crag to chase another bird, so swoops Poseidon on his prey. Broad is his chest, dark locks float around his head. Thus has art depicted him ; never in the delicate form of a boy, or lying at his ease, but either striding with long steps, grasping a fish, or gazing into the distance, hand on hip and foot raised on some support. So gazes the sailor over the sea to scan both cloud and wave. His weapon, the trident, is seldom wanting, through a blow of which he can cause land and sea alike to quake and totter from their foundations (see Fig. 8).

On the other hand, the king of the sea appears also at times girt with magnificence and pomp, just as the sea is not ever roaring wild and troubled. In the depths of the water stands his lordly palace, glittering with gold, and imperishable. There he yokes his bronze-hoofed steeds, that swiftly fly with fluttering golden manes.

> " Refulgent arms his mighty limbs infold,
> Immortal arms, of adamant and gold.
> He mounts the car, the golden scourge applies,
> He sits superior, and the chariot flies :
> His whirling wheels the glassy surface sweep ;
> Th' enormous monsters rolling o'er the deep
> Gambol around him on the wat'ry way,
> And heavy whales in awkward measures play ;
> The sea subsiding spreads a level plain,
> Exults, and owns the monarch of the main ;
> The parting waves before his coursers fly ;
> The wond'ring waters leave his axle dry." [1]

---

[1] *Iliad*, xiii., 25-30, Pope's translation.

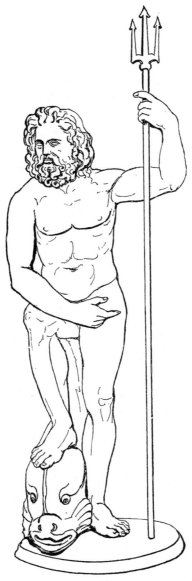

Fig. 8.—Poseidon.

Marble statue in the Royal Museum, Dresden.

Still more brilliant, however, is the sea-king's train
when his consort Amphitrite sits beside him.   At first
she would not listen to the god's wooing, and fled his
presence ; but he rested not till he could call her his
own ; through a dolphin's help he found out where she
had hidden, and led her home as a goddess.   Now she
too enjoyed due royal honours.   All monsters of the
deep owed her vassal service.   She was the fairest of

FIG. 9.—POSEIDON AND AMPHITRITE.
From a frieze now in the Glyptothek at Munich.

the Nereids, daughters of the sea-god Nereus ; but her
son, Triton, a god of the waters, had a form half man,
half fish.   'Twas in truth a merry company—these droll
spirits of the waters, who with the human parts of their
forms rising above the waves, sporting and blowing shell
trumpets, swarmed round the car of Poseidon and
Amphitrite (see Fig. 9).

The Loves often held the bridles of the sea-horses,
on which the sea-nymphs floated in blissful reverie.

Thus the ancients would adorn their stone coffins with the procession of sea-gods, and looked on it as a sort of consoling promise of a happy existence after death.

(B) NEPTUNUS.

NEPTUNUS, GOD OF HARBOURS AND OF SEA-VOYAGES.

The Romans were not such seafarers as the Ionians, or the coast tribes of the Peloponnesos. It was not till late that they learnt seamanship from the Etruscans and the Greeks, and ventured on the wild sea. There was therefore no god in their creed who, like the Greek Poseidon, appeared in the character of the mighty master of the wildly raging sea. They were much more prone to think of the god who granted return to the peaceful harbour, and this god of the harbour was called among them Portunus. At the little port of the Tiber, near the wooden bridge in Rome, a festival was held yearly in his honour; but he enjoyed no special consideration. His image bore in its hand a key, and pointed therewith to the place of peaceful security which the Roman sailor yearned for most.

When indeed, in B.C. 399, the Romans began to introduce into the religion of the State a whole series of Greek gods, the attributes which the Greeks assigned to their god Poseidon were transferred, on the advice of the sacred Sibylline books, to a Roman god who bore the name Neptunus or Nevtunus, and was properly the god of flowing water. The difference, however, between the Greek Poseidon and the Roman Neptunus, was considerable enough. For example, when the Greeks

in Rome saw that races were held in honour of a
Roman earth-god, called Consus, they believed their
own god Poseidon, the god of equestrian games, was to
be recognised in him rather than in any other Roman
deity; and so the Romans too gave this Consus the
name of the " Equestrian Neptune."

The Roman Neptune, however, did not arrive at
especial honour till the Romans themselves attained to
a certain superiority in naval tactics, and this was not
till a comparatively late period.   Sextus Pompeius, on
account of his victories at sea, claimed to be regarded
as a son of Neptune; but Agrippa, the admiral of
Augustus, was the first who could pass for a distinguished naval hero among the Romans, and it was not
till his time that Neptune rose into high estimation.
Agrippa, who allowed himself to be represented as
Poseidon-Neptune, with a dolphin beside him, erected
in honour of the god in the Campus Martius a splendid
hall, what was called a basilica, in commemoration of
his glorious sea-fight off Actium against Antonius and
Cleopatra.   From this time forward the Roman poets,
too, depicted Neptune exactly as the Greek Poseidon;
hence he also became a fit reflection of the inconstant
sea,—now wildly raging, now in joyous brilliancy
speeding ships on their way.

CHAPTER IV.

HESTIA—VESTA.

(A) HESTIA.

THOUGH the original view of religion among the Greeks may have been the honouring of Zeus alone, there soon sprang up among them the idea of a number of deities united in the form of a *family*, an idea which was not so much the work of religious belief as of poetry. It was the poets who represented the Olympian gods in that close relationship in which they appear in the sculptures of the Parthenon, and in their war against the giants. Of this family life Hestia, goddess of the hearth, was the central point among the gods, as the domestic hearth is among men.

I. HESTIA, GODDESS OF THE SACRIFICIAL FIRE.

Who loves not to peer into the blazing flame, that darts up flickering and crackling, and pours forth clouds of smoke to heaven ? Yet how much grander a thing it must have appeared to primæval man, who could not explain by what natural laws flame takes its form ! If day by day he made fire serve his purpose, to warm himself and prepare his food, yet he could not tell whence flame came or whither it vanished. But was not this the mystic virtue of a deity who, consuming all that man threw into the fire, changed it to cloud-like air, and bore it up to heaven, where the gods dwelt? To this power the Greeks gave the name of Hestia. The goddess Hestia, then, was the agent between man and the gods, when he wished to offer them sacrifice as a thanksgiving. It was to Hestia that he handed his sacrifice; and thus every sacrifice began, as was commonly said, with Hestia.

Often, however, as men turned to Hestia, still the goddess was to them a being wrapped in mystery. The power of the sacrificial flame remained ever alike, and in that alone did mortals see the rule of Hestia. As all other deities assumed human shape, and united in a divine family under Zeus as their head, so Hestia too received a dignified form; she became sister of Zeus and daughter of Kronos. The poets, however, and minstrels had nothing to tell of her actions and attributes. Hestia was the only goddess that remained without mortal frailties; alone she exercised her power as the means of communication between men and gods. From all community with other deities she shrank coyly back. Poseidon wished once to gain her love, and so did Apollo; but she held aloof sternly, and, touching the head of Zeus, swore the mighty oath to live in perpetual virginity. The flame was a true picture of brilliant purity, that consumed and destroyed all that was vicious and impure. Hence Zeus gave Hestia the privilege to sit in the midst of the house, and "to receive fat,"[1] *i.e.*, her place of honour was the

---

[1] Others render this "the fat of the land," *i.e.*, "what is choicest and best." See *Homeric Hymn to Aphrodite* (III. 30).

altar found in all premises, the sacrificial flame of which
consumed with crackling the fat of the animals sacrificed. Here ruled the goddess unseen with her blessing, and therefore at the beginning and at the end of
a feast men poured libations of wine into the flame in
her honour.

2. HESTIA, THE GODDESS OF THE HEARTH AND OF THE STATE.

As, however, men in general enjoyed nothing without
throwing a share into the flame for the gods, so the
idea of the sacrifice gradually blended with that of the
meal, and so it came about that the Greeks called every
hearth in general Hestia. But if Hestia had her place
on every hearth, so too the hearth itself was a consecrated place, a blessing for the house, and Hestia
the guardian of the house in general.

When a child was seven days old, it was carried
round the flame of the house-altar; for this had a
cleansing power, and purified it as it were on its
entrance into the world. It was not till the child had
thus been placed under the protection of Hestia that
it received its name. We know, to be sure, that the
feeling for family life and domesticity among the Greeks
was not very lively, and so Hestia, as goddess of the
hearth, obtained among them no great importance; at
least, she met with less immediate regard than the other
deities, who shared the feelings of ordinary mortals.
Hence it happened that an image of the goddess was
rarely made. She belonged indeed to the circle of the
Olympian gods, and when that circle was represented
Hestia was not forgotten, in her dress that concealed

her form, and in her veil; separate images of Hestia, however, are not known with certainty. She does not appear among the gods on the east frieze of the Parthenon, for she could not leave Olympos.

Hestia stood in much the same relation to the State as a whole that she did to the family. The father of the family, when he wished to invoke the protection of the gods in the name of his household, began each sacrifice with Hestia; in the same way the king, or the prytanis who took his place, if he addressed the gods in the name of the whole people had first to address himself to Hestia. Accordingly there was in each town hall or prytaneion, a public hearth, dedicated to Hestia. This was Hestia Prytanitis. A perpetual fire burned on this hearth, and from this fire citizens going to a foreign land took a portion, that in new colonies they might still keep up the old method of communion with the gods. But exactly as the domestic altar had originally been the hearth of the house, so also the altar in the town hall was the hearth of the state. Ambassadors and guests of the state were entertained here, and it was, of course, a special mark of distinction if a citizen were invited to take his meals in the prytaneion. Sokrates, when on trial for his life, being challenged himself to name a penalty, had the boldness to demand the honour of being supported at the public expense beside the Hestia of the town hall. Thus Hestia dispensed also the highest honours of the State; yet she was no nearer the hearts of the Greeks on that account, for the bright enjoyment of life too often stood higher in their estimation than the feeling for family and for the State.

(b) VESTA.

1. VESTA AND HER HANDMAIDS.

The idea of the sanctity of the sacrificial flame is of the remotest antiquity. When the tribes of Greece and Italy still formed a single nation, they must already have worshipped in common this goddess of the sacrificial fire; for we find also among the Romans a goddess pretty closely corresponding to the Greek Hestia. This was Vesta, whose name too has the same meaning. As, however, the two nations developed in different ways after their separation, Vesta meant to the Romans something special and altogether different. The peoples of Italy had a purer and nobler idea of the family life. They knew that their individual desires must yield to the will of the father as to that of the State, if family and State in general were to prove a blessing to human society; and that both without religion would be a failure. But how could the requisite blessing be secured if Vesta's flame were not protected and cherished? To watch over Vesta's fire seemed thus one of the most important duties of the State, and Vesta was without exception the holiest and most highly esteemed of all Roman goddesses.

Every earthly fire was impure. It was necessary that the fire through which Vesta brought to the gods the gifts of men should be spontaneously kindled; therefore the holy fire of sacrifice was lighted by rubbing together two pieces of wood. Thus alone was the flame produced that was pleasing to the gods, a flame that the pure hands of a virgin alone could duly tend. For this purpose, six so-called vestals were chosen by the Pontifex Maximus, the chief priest of the State. They had to devote themselves entirely to their sacred office. Their chief task was to watch over the fire in its purity, and to provide clean, running water for the purification of the sanctuary. All other duties of life were postponed during this time of service. The new vestal's hair was cut off, and she appeared in public clad in white from head to foot, and closely veiled, the veil being clasped under the chin. Even the guilty criminal who met her became through her look free from his guilt and pardoned. Not even a suspicion of having broken her vow of chastity must weigh on her. The goddess herself came to the assistance of the falsely accused. The Vestal Tuccia, whose character was thus attacked, carried water up from the Tiber in a sieve in proof of her innocence ; and another vestal in like position re-kindled the extinguished fire with the corner of her white garment. Consequently, these vestals met with honours actually greater than those enjoyed by the highest officers of the State. Even the consul himself had respectfully to give way to the vestal he met in the street.

A vestal generally assumed her office between the sixth and tenth years of her age. If she had performed her duties faithfully she was allowed to return to the life of the ordinary citizens and to marry ; but woe to her if she had done ill ! Scourging was the punishment of her who had let the sacred fire die out, and through whose carelessness the intercourse between gods and men had been interrupted. But for her who had broken the vow of chastity no sufficient punishment could be inflicted. Even to touch the polluted person would have been an offence. The wretched woman was buried alive in a vault, and the state had to seek, by every kind of expiation, to appease the wrath of the offended goddess.

2. Vesta, the Goddess of the Hearth, and the Domestic Spirits called Lares and Penates.

Just as among the Greeks Hestia became the goddess of the hearth, so also among the Italian tribes the same thing happened. In proportion, however, as the latter valued more highly the comfortable place from which not only in the cold season of the year the salutary warmth streamed forth, but where every day the food for the family was prepared, the higher rose the sacred dread of the goddess of the hearth who bestowed such blessings. Here was so clearly the central point of the family, and here the comfortable place in which everybody was glad to linger, and where the happiness of a peaceful domesticity could be felt by all.

Vesta of the hearth, then, was the protectress of all the friendly little spirits of the house, who, like our Kobolds—Milton's "lubbar fiend"[1]—worked in the dark, and took thought above everything for a rich store of provisions. These were the Lares and Penates The name Penates has the meaning of "those who rule within;" they were spirits who filled the storeroom with food and drink. So their share was given them at each meal. For them there stood on the table, even

[1] See *L'Allegro*.

in a poor man's house, a small salt-cellar, frequently of silver, and a plate of fruit or cakes.

Very much like the Penates were the Lares, who also were the friendly guardians of the family, and who were under the protection of Vesta, and delighted to dwell unseen on the domestic hearth. Here stood too the little cupboard in which were kept their images, pretty dolls in short dresses. On birthdays and other family festivals these cupboards were opened, and the images of the Lares were adorned with flowers. Among the Romans, however, the laws of the family and those of the State were equally sacred. There were therefore Lares of the State as well as Lares of the house. In the temple of Vesta, near the old stronghold of the kings and the dwelling of the chief priest, were deposited the most venerated relics belonging to the commonwealth; for example, what was called the Palladium of Troy, a pledge for the existence of the State as a whole, and other similar objects, of which an ordinary eye never caught sight. Only the chief priest and the vestals had the right of entrance to this holy of holies in the temple of Vesta, and here were placed the images of the Lares and Penates of the Roman people. They watched over the prosperity of the whole community, just as the Penates of the house watched over that of the family.

As, however, Vesta through the Lares and Penates provided for the daily requirements of mankind, she soon came to be regarded as the nurturer of the people, almost as the corn-goddess Ceres. Thus Vesta became the patroness of millers and bakers. On the 9th of June, her special festival, when the harvest began, and

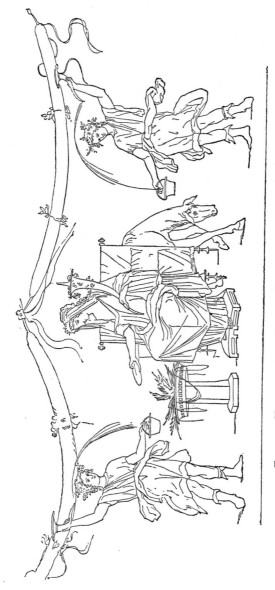

Fig. 10.—Vesta and the Lares. From a Pompeian wall-painting.

the millers and bakers could rejoice in the new supply,
the whole people joyfully paid homage to Vesta.
Women brought her offerings of all sorts of cakes;
but also the miller's industrious beast was not forgotten,
the ass, that was sacred to Vesta. Now he had his
holiday, and was decked out in garlands and rolls of
bread strung together. Quite in opposition to the
Greeks, who had not learned to prize the blessings of
the goddess of the hearth so highly, the inhabitants
of Italy delighted to adorn their houses with images of
Vesta; and especially in the meal stores and bakers'
shops of Pompeii we frequently come across a picture of Vesta with her sacred attributes (see Fig. 10).
We see the food-giving goddess sitting on a throne,
and pouring a libation on an altar strewn with ears of
corn. Behind her is seen the mule, and both on her
right and left is the elegant figure of a Lar, who from
an uplifted drinking-horn pours into a cup a stream of
sparkling wine.

CHAPTER V.

HERMES—MERCURY.

(A) HERMES.

HERODOTUS tells us that while the Thracians in general recognised as gods only Ares, Dionysos, and Artemis, their kings, on the other hand, worshipped Hermes as their special deity and regarded him as their ancestor. This was, no doubt, the original bearded type of Hermes found in older specimens of Grecian art, but afterwards superseded by the ideal of youthful strength and agility, the prototype and model of Hellenic youth.

In the earlier poetry he figures as the messenger of Zeus. He conducts the dead to their abode in the shades; and is equally at home there and in the realms above. Himself given to sportive thefts, he becomes the god of thieves. We find him, too, presiding over the wrestling ground, and the patron of eloquence.

Almost alone among the Olympians he has a kindly feeling for weak mortals, and is ever ready to lend a helping hand.

1. HERMES, THE SLAYER OF ARGOS AND GIVER OF FRUITFULNESS.

When one thinks of Hermes as the swift-flying messenger of the gods, that with his herald's staff skims

over sea and land on the errands of Zeus, one finds
some difficulty in grasping the idea that this handy
deity, so ready to serve his fellows, was once worshipped
as king of the gods. Yet such was the case. Nay,
not only as king of the gods, but as the mighty ruler
of universal nature who, like Zeus, can destroy and
can create as well.

But in truth this belief was a thing of many centuries
past, and so only vague remembrances survived as to
this power. Above all, however, the tale of Hermes
the Argos-slayer had its rise in this idea.

This Argos, the watcher and attendant of Io (p. 40)
was the sun-god; hence he is called the "all-seeing," and
it is fabled of him, either that he had one single eye in the
middle of his head (the light of the sun), or that his body
was entirely covered with eyes. This Argos the mighty
Hermes slew; that is, he overpowered the light of the
sun, and brought on the unfruitful season of the year
instead of the warm one. The ancients, however, loved
to think of the all-nourishing earth under the form of
an ox or cow ; and so Io with her cow's horns may be
called an image of the earth. And so, too, men had
a tale to tell of a theft of oxen committed by Hermes,
a tale which probably had the same meaning as that
of Hermes killing the sun-god Argos. For the oxen
belonged to Apollo, and Apollo was essentially a god
of the sun. But Hermes drove the oxen into a dark
cave near Pylos, where lay, it was generally supposed,
the entrance to the world below. He was, therefore,
at the same time, a god of death that cuts off life in its
bloom.

This attribute of his, however, was little known in

Greece; only in Argos, where he had been worshipped from time immemorial as chief deity of the land, where also the legend laid the scene of the slaying of Argos, there existed, even in later times, the usage of offering a sacrifice to Hermes, as god of death, thirty days after the death of a relation.

But the god who destroys life can also create life, for out of the depth of the earth springs the fruitfulness that wakes new life and growth. So Homer calls the god also the "Luck-bringer" and the "Giver-of-good." For the simple wants of early man, however, the best thing was wealth in flocks and herds.[1] To King Atreus legend assigns a ram with a golden fleece, to indicate his wealth. Wealth, however, is power, and so the god Hermes is said to have given him the sceptre of his sovereignty, that passed in turn to his brother and successor, Thyestes, "rich in lambs." If Hermes is fond of a man he increases his flocks, as in the case of the son of the Trojan rich in sheep, Phorbas. So the son of Hermes and the nymph Eumele (*i.e.*, "with fine sheep") is called Eudoros, or "rich in gifts." As god of the herdsmen Hermes dwells of choice in meadow or in forest, where he sports and dances with the nymphs.

To their fostering care he brings new-born babes, as the little god Dionysos or the infant hero Herakles, that they may grow up strong in Nature's freedom. None the less faithfully, however, does he take thought for the flocks and for the lambs that go astray, which he, as the good shepherd, brings home on his shoulders. Thus we see him depicted on one side of an altar

---

[1] So the Latin word *pecunia* = money is connected with *pecus* = cattle.

preserved at Athens (Fig. 11).   But in the small town
of Tanagra, in Bœotia, Hermes had an annual festival,
with a procession in which the handsomest boy had to
carry a ram on his back.   So it came about that the
Arcadian shepherd folk who specially worshipped the
goat-footed Pan made him out to be a son of Hermes,

FIG. 11.—HERMES THE GOOD SHEPHERD.
Fragment in relief from an altar at Athens.

and maintained that the god was born on the range of
Kyllene in Arcadia : the guardian of their flocks should
be a native of their own country.   That Hermes really
was one of the oldest Grecian gods is shown by the
simple, almost rude, shape of his oldest images, a
quadrangular pillar with the god's head put upon it

(Fig. 12). When this form was at a later time adopted for the representation of other gods and mortals, it was still always called a *Herm*, or image of Hermes.

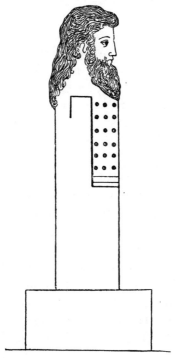

FIG. 12.—ARCHAIC IMAGE OF HERMES. (Vase-painting.)

2. HERMES, THE MESSENGER OF THE GODS AND CONDUCTOR OF THE DEAD.

When the chivalrous tribes of Achæans had placed themselves at the head of the Grecian people, if a bard, as Homer, were extolling the heroic deeds of their war-like ancestors, and inspiring them themselves to like

exploits, then the god of the shepherds and country folk
gave place to the warlike deities of the nobility. Now
Hermes himself had to come down to the position of
servant to the other deities; he became their messenger.
The heroes warring before Troy pay little heed to the
god, but the swine-herd Eumaios offers sacrifice to him
as to the nymphs, the herdsman's special guardians.

Still there remained for Hermes honours enough.
He was no ordinary messenger as the goddess Iris
(p. 16), who only as an outsider executes the commissions of the Olympians. Hermes is in the service of
the highest god, Zeus, and is employed even by him
only on errands, out of the difficulties of which others
could hardly be expected to see their way. Thus it
is Hermes that warns Aigisthos against murdering
Agamemnon and marrying his wife Klytaimnestra; and
how cleverly he executes his difficult commission with
regard to the nymph Kalypso, and induces her to set
free the hero Odysseus whom she loved! But cleverness
and promptness are the qualifications most important
for such a mission. Hardly has Zeus uttered his
command, when Hermes is binding on to his feet his
golden sandals (later the Greeks made them into
winged shoes); for these sandals carried him, like the
blast of the wind, over the waters of the sea and over the
immeasurable earth. Over the waves he hastens,—

> "As when the sea-gull swiftly chasing fish,
>   O'er the dread bosom of the barren brine,
>   Wets in the waves her thickly-feathered wing." [1]

So obliging and shrewd a messenger of the gods
might well be invoked by mortals, too, to rescue them

[1] Homer, *Odyssey*, v., 51-3.

from the perils of a journey. The traveller stood, therefore, under his special protection, and the stone-heaps on the wayside, on which a Hermes-pillar was often raised, could not fail to remind the passer-by that the god was close at hand. On these symbols of Hermes information as to the way was often placed ; and the traveller readily threw on such a landmark a fresh stone that lay in his path ; thus contributing his mite, not only to the improvement of the road, but also to the honour of Hermes. This usage, however, must have been of remote antiquity, since as early as the time of the Odyssey the swine-herd Eumaios mentions the " Hermes-hill " to Telemachos as a land-mark above the city of Ithake.

It was the trader who on his travels peculiarly stood in need of the protection of Hermes, and with his efforts after gain was devoted to the god that dealt out blessings. But the most dangerous of all travelling for men was the journey into the other world. It was here especially that the protection of Hermes was most to be desired. Thus Aias, in an impressive monologue of the tragedy by Sophokles that bears his name, when departing from this world, prays Hermes, the conductor and god of the dead, to lead him safely down. So, too, as he descends into the gloomy cavern of the Eumenides, King Oidipous, weary of life, believes he already feels the guidance of Hermes when he cries,—

> " This way are leading me
> Hermes th' escorter, and th' infernal queen." [1]

It was accordingly among the Greeks a very usual

---

[1] Soph., *Oid. Kol.*, 1547-48.

custom to place images of Hermes on burial-mounds ; often, indeed, the deceased themselves were represented on tombs in the form of Hermes. It was, as it were, a pious wish that the departing spirit might pass as easily and securely as Hermes into the darkness of the world below. For dreadful, indeed, was the idea of this terrible journey. Let us hear how Homer describes it, in the passage in which he recounts that Hermes summoned the souls of the slain suitors out of the palace of Odysseus :—

"He held in his hand his wand that is fair and golden, wherewith he lulls the eyes of men, of whomso he will, while others again he even wakens out of sleep. Herewith he roused and led the souls who followed gibbering. And even as bats flit gibbering in the secret place of a wondrous cave, when one has fallen down out of the rock from the cluster, and they cling each to each up aloft, even so the souls gibbered as they fared together, and Hermes, the Helper, led them down the dark ways." [1]

From these verses, however, we recognise, at the same time, Hermes as the sender of sleep to man. It was, indeed, in connection with this belief that Hermes, as we saw, had in the earliest times power over life and death. But in later days Sleep took the place of Death, Sleep the gentle twin-brother of Death, as men had gradually become accustomed to believe naught but good of Hermes himself. Whomsoever he touches with his magic wand of gold, him he lulls to sleep, as he lulled Argos, the watcher of Io, before he slew him. But whomsoever he once more touched with his wand,

---

[1] *Odyssey*, xxiv., 2-10, Butcher and Lang's translation.

him could he rouse from slumber. He who laid him down to sleep prayed Hermes to send him gentle slumber and pleasing dreams. Thus Odysseus found the Phæacian princes busied in offering from their cups libations to the " clear-sighted slayer of Argos,"—

"To whom last they poured their libations what time they bethought them of slumber."[1]

Nay, " Hermes " was actually the name given to the last libation.

3. What the Poets Sang of Hermes.

We have already seen how the character of Hermes became milder and more gentle. But the artists and poets who depicted his image and sang of his deeds suppressed completely the time-honoured peculiarities of the god, and represented him almost as an ordinary mortal. Homer, indeed, when describing Hermes, thinks of him still as a dignified, stately person, with long hair and beard. So it is a transformation that Hermes undergoes, when he chooses to appear in the guise of a youth with beard just beginning to sprout, in order to escort Priam into the hostile camp of the Greeks. It was as a man no longer young that the older painters, too, depicted him, with long beard, and with hair fastened up high on the back of his head in old-fashioned way. But this was soon altered when the poets began to represent the god as a child, and imputed to him a number of sly tricks which could not fail to delight through their roguishness. Thus an ancient hymn[2] relates as follows :—

---

[1] *Odyssey*, vii., 138.
[2] Homeric *Hymns*, ii., *To Hermes*.

When the boy, who was a son of Zeus and Maia, had hardly seen the light, his cradle seemed already too small for him, and he leaped out. In front of the cave in which he was born he found a tortoise. Of this he at once made use to form the body of a lyre. Towards evening, feeling hungry, he crept, under cover of darkness, to where the herds of oxen belonging to the Sun-god Apollo were grazing. Fifty oxen he drove secretly thence along ways where it would be difficult to track them. He fastened bundles of brushwood to the tails of the beasts, to efface their traces. Thus he arrived at the cavern at Pylos already mentioned, where he slaughtered two oxen and roasted their flesh. Then he carefully effaced all traces of the cooking and the fire, and went back to the mountain Kyllene, the home of his mother. Crouching he slipped like a breath of wind through the lock of the door, placed himself hastily in his cradle, drew the coverlet round his shoulders, and lay there a picture of innocence, while touching with one hand the chords of the lyre he had invented.

It was not long, indeed, before Apollo observed the fraud, and hastened to Maia and her little son. But Hermes hid himself deeper in the swaddling clothes, and pretended to be asleep. Apollo, however, was not to be so outwitted, but threatened Hermes that he would throw him into murky Tartaros if he did not give back his oxen. The boy's sly looks softened his anger, and even made him laugh. At last Hermes, when all his arts of opposition were unsuccessful, was obliged to go, just as he was, wrapped up in his bed-clothes, to his father Zeus, to explain the state of affairs between them. Here, too, was the gravity of the supreme judge put to a severe trial by the child's mendacious defence; still the culprit was in the end compelled to give back the oxen. He made Apollo a present, too, of his lyre, in order to appease his anger once for all: so that the two brothers were at peace with each other. Hermes retained the care of the herds, and obtained from Apollo the marvellous wand, with which he could produce good fortune and wealth. He received, too, the privilege of visiting the lower world.

4. Hermes, the Prototype of the Grecian Youth.

If, through such stories as those given above, the belief in the old slayer of Argos was pretty well suppressed, still we see that Hermes was regarded as of equal birth with the Olympian gods. It was now that people found out that Hermes was a son of Zeus, invented also the name of his mother Maia (which itself again only means " mother "), and made her a daughter of the powerful Titan Atlas. Thus the minister of the gods was, at any rate, sprung from an ancient and honourable family. Next to his brother Apollo, he was the most helpful divine mediator between Zeus and mortal man; and the latter the more readily sought his aid, as he himself had thoughts and feelings akin to those of men. Now the artists forgot the old type of Hermes as a grown-up man, and made him into a beauteous youth. For youth and beauty seemed more calculated to inspire confidence, and therefore more suited to the "Helper in time of need."

Hermes, the conductor of the dead, was now no longer the stern driver of the herd of ghosts whom he chased on before him with the whip like squeaking

FIG. 13.—HERMES CONDUCTING EURYDIKE.
Relief in the National Museum, Naples.

bats ; nay, he now rather sympathizes with the fate of the individual. Who could fail to recognise this if he glanced at the charming composition shown in Fig. 13 ?

Hermes in friendly fashion escorts the minstrel Orpheus, to whom it was granted to raise his wife Eurydike from the realms of the dead, on condition that he should not turn to gaze on her.

Yet the longing of Orpheus is too strong ; he looks

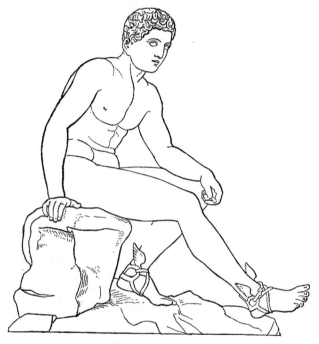

FIG. 14.—HERMES.
Bronze statue in the National Museum, Naples.

round, and then Hermes lays his left hand on the right hand of Eurydike to lead her gently back with him. Sorrowfully, however, does his right hand grasp the folds of his robe ; and one sees by his pensively-bending head how hard it is for the god to perform his melan-

choly task. Yet who would not find more consolation
in thinking of the gentle, sympathetic escorter than
of him that with scourge in hand drives on the dead
before him ?

Henceforth Hermes was for artists the model of
a beauteous youth. The old-fashioned long hair and
the beard gave place to a smooth face and short curly
hair, and his powerful frame remained the type of
the Grecian youth that grew wiry and supple in the

gymnasium and the pa-
læstra. Such we see him
in a fine statue (Fig. 14),
as, wearied with his flight,
he rests for a moment
seated on a rock. Such,
too, is the beautiful image
of Hermes (see Fig. 15)
which the master-hand of
Praxiteles has shaped,
lately recovered by the
Germans from Olympia's
soil. Close to every gym-
nasium stood an image of

FIG. 15.—HERMES.
From the statue by Praxiteles at
Olympia.

Hermes, so that boys and young men might know to
whom they had to pray for bodily vigour and activity.

The Greek, however, demanded from youth far more
than the activity of the body. No less high in his
estimation stood a modest yet unwearying readiness to
serve, together with corporeal adroitness ; but, above
all, ready activity of the mind. All these advantages
were seen united in Hermes. Whoever had Hermes
for a friend and was thoughtful with his gifts, he was

of use for all affairs of life. The crafty Odysseus had
to thank the god on this account. He told the swine-
herd Eumaios that he was well suited to offer his
services to the suitors, "for," continued he, "lightly
might I do good service among them, even all that they
would. For lo! I will tell thee, and do thou mark
and listen. By the favour of Hermes, the messenger,
who gives grace and glory to all men's work, no mortal
may vie with me in the business of a serving-man,
in piling well a fire, in cleaving dry faggots, and in
carving and roasting flesh and in pouring of wine,
those offices wherein meaner men serve their betters." [1]

Activity of the mind, however, shows itself in speech
and in shrewd ideas. In the presence of Hermes all
mortal speech was hushed; and if in a party there was
all of a sudden silence, people would say, "Hermes
has come in." Thus Hermes came to be looked on
generally as the patron of every form of intellectual
work. Every unexpected discovery was a gift of
Hermes, but also each enquiry, explanation, and interpretation was an "art of Hermes." How, then, could
the aspiring boy and youth fail to look to him? Even
children's sport was a work of Hermes, and when the
boy became a young man he dedicated to Hermes ball,
top, knuckle-bones, and whatever else he had been
wont to use in play.

It was not, indeed, every thought and aspiration
that had a noble aim. But cunning was the affair of
Hermes. In the *Iliad* the gods require of Hermes to
steal the corpse of Hektor, and it was Hermes who
had actually instructed the grandfather of Odysseus in

[1] Homer, *Odyssey*, xv., 317-24, Butcher and Lang's translation.

thieving and perjury. Therefore Hermes became also the god of thieves. Traders, too, were his special favourites, when they aimed at opening sources of gain in every possible way. In the oldest times, when trade consisted in barter, this was closely connected with the endeavour to outwit men. For the value of that which was given in exchange might often be quite uncertain and doubtful. Hermes, as dispenser of wealth in general, must have been much in esteem among the mercantile community in their efforts after riches. Even till our own day the wand of Hermes has continued to be the token of the merchant. Originally it was only the switch with which the herdsman-god kept the grazing herds together, but soon a mysterious power was ascribed to the wand with which the conductor of the dead guided them into the lower world. The switch consisted properly of three sprigs, of which one served as a handle, while the others were united in a knot. In the eyes of the Greeks this form of the wand assumed a wonderful importance: they called it the "herald's wand" (*kerykeion*) of Hermes; quite inaccurately, for heralds, when performing their duties, held in their hands simply a long straight staff. When, however, painters and sculptors wished to represent the wand of Hermes, they made out of the branching switch a wand encircled by snakes, and often gave it two wings, to indicate the swiftness of the "wandering" god. The wand has retained this form even to our own day.

(B) MERCURIUS.

The nations of Italy had no god who, like Hermes, had become, from a powerful lord of nations, a dis-

penser of fruitfulness, conductor of the dead, and model
for youths. They learned, however, to recognise the
Greek Hermes through their intercourse with the
commercial Greek colonists of Southern Italy, among
whom the protector of travellers and traders had
naturally a position of special honour. Since, moreover,
they had a trade-god, Mercurius,[1] they soon transferred
to him all that the Greeks knew of their Hermes. In
the year 495 B.C., for the first time, a temple was
dedicated to him in Rome, and gradually the Roman
poets also sang of him as the Greek Hermes.

Horace addressed praises to him in a famous ode[2]
as—

> " Who the wild ways of early man did'st shape,
> Skilful, with speech, and with the practice, too,
> Of glorious wrestling ; "

also as the messenger of the king of the gods, the
inventor of the lyre, and the cunning thief. In another
ode Horace calls himself, in his quality of poet, a " man
of Mercurius ; " and so too the god at the battle of
Philippi wrapped him in thick mist and bore him
through the foe.

When Cæsar came to Gaul he found there a native
god whom he felt obliged to recognise as the Roman
Mercurius, for, says he, he was the inventor of all arts,
the god of the way and of journeys, the dispenser of
riches and protector of trade. Just so, at a later time,
the Romans denoted as " Mercurius " the Teutonic god
Wodan, the wanderer, the master of all magic and
astute guider of human thoughts. The special propagator, however, of the worship of Mercurius was, no

---

[1] From *mercari*=to trade.   [2] I., 10, 2-4.

doubt, the trader who marched in the rear of the victorious hosts of Rome to buy up booty, or make money by the sale of his own wares. Hence it happens that at the present day we find numerous bronze statuettes of Mercury in almost every place where a Roman army was quartered. These little figures are rarely without the large purse; they are frequently

FIG. 16.—MERCURIUS, THE GOD OF TRADE, WITH FORTUNA.
A Pompeian wall-painting.

distinguished by the horn filled with treasures and gifts of the earth, or the cock was placed beside them, to suggest the god as active from early dawn and ever intent on gain. Figure 16 shows us how this Roman Mercurius, with full purse, flies over the world, and leaves behind him Fortuna, the goddess of good luck, with horn of plenty, rudder, and globe. Wealth guides like a rudder the mind of man, but the rolling ball points to the instability of fortune.

CHAPTER VI.

DEMETER (GAIA)—CERES (TELLUS).

(A) DEMETER (GAIA).

1. GAIA; DEMETER, THE WRATHFUL MOTHER EARTH.

WE do not know whether the Greeks ever worshipped
Gaia, *i.e.*, the Earth, specially under that name. Earth
was indeed called to witness at times on occasion
of a solemn oath, for since the dead rest in her
bosom, it was believed that she avenged perjury by
death; but Mother Earth does not appear actively in
Grecian legend, and was almost entirely supplanted
through the belief in the goddess Demeter. Generally
the distinction is this : Gaia is not arable land, whereas
Demeter is that portion of the earth that may be
cultivated by the plough. Artists at times represented
Gaia rising, with the upper portion of her body out of
the earth, when, for instance, she raises lamentation
for the fall of her wild sons the giants (see Fig. 17),
whom Zeus, for their presumption, overwhelmed with
lightning (see p. 19). Or she appears at full length
lying down, as a symbol of the mainland. Then,
however, artists put in her hand a horn filled with
fruits, so that she could be recognised as the fruit-

giving earth.   But of her nature and action poets told
the people nothing.

All the more richly had the myths decked out the
goddess Demeter.   With her name an ancient stock of
the Grecian nation had indicated Mother Earth.   She is
at once the mother of all mankind, and into her bosom

Fig. 17.—GAIA.

From the frieze of the Altar of Zeus at Pergamon, now in Berlin.

man returns again after death.   On this account the
dead in Attica were called " Demetreioi," *i.e.*, children
of Demeter, for they lay in their mother's lap.

Full of blessings was the rule of Demeter, for it was
she that bade the fruits grow and ripen ; if, however,
the earth produced nothing, then was Demeter sad,
spoke and ate nothing, smiled not, stayed far away

from the other gods, and even lost her former beauty, so that no one could recognise her again.

Wondrous was the tale that people had to tell of this wrathful goddess. Perhaps she mourned her lost husband, but his name had been forgotten. Perhaps it was Iasion, of whom Homer tells that he dwelt on the thrice-ploughed plains of Crete ; for a thrice-ploughed field produces luxuriant fruit, and where would Mother Earth have sooner sojourned than where the crops came to fullest maturity ? So a city of Thessaly, Pyrasos (*i.e.*, Wheat-town), is called by Homer " the holy place of Demeter." That Iasion was, however, struck by Zeus with lightning, and then the cheerful time of Mother Earth was past and gone, and the mournful time of her sorrow began. Later the belief was that she was seeking her lost daughter,—the meaning of this will be seen later,—but it was not this that in earlier days was supposed to be the cause of her sorrow. Let us hear, however, what the poets tell us as to this.

Nine days Demeter wandered through the country without tasting nectar and ambrosia, or bathing. With two torches in her hands she rushed during the night over the earth, to look for her lost daughter. No god, no mortal, no bird, could make known the track of the vanished one. Then, on the tenth day, the moon-goddess Hekate met her, who had just come forth with her torch from the dark cave. Now both goddesses hastened together to Helios the sun-god, who sees everything that passes between heaven and earth. He could tell the mother that, in accordance with the will of Zeus, her daughter had gone

down into the realms of the dead. Then most painful
anger seized the goddess. She forthwith turned her
back on the assembly of the gods, went among
mortals, and changed her form to that of an old
woman, so that no one could recognise her. At
length she came to Eleusis in Attica, where a pious
king held sway. There she seated herself beneath
the shade of an olive tree at a spring, and waited till
the king's daughters came to draw water and spoke to
her, when she pretended she had been carried off
from Crete over the sea by pirates, but had escaped
while they were preparing their food, and was seeking
a shelter. Then the maidens asked her to come to the
house of their parents, and to undertake the charge of
the youngest child, Demophon.

Demeter consented and followed them; but as she,
deeply veiled and in her long dark robe of mourning,
stepped over the threshold of the king's palace, her
head touched the top, and she filled the doorway with
divine brilliancy, so that the king's wife, who sat in
the hall with her infant at her breast, rose from her
seat to make place for her. Yet Demeter did not take
the place of honour, but remained sorrowfully with
downcast eyes on an ordinary seat, till the waiting
maid, through her droll jests, at last compelled her to
laugh. The red wine, indeed, that the queen offered
her in welcome, she declined, but bade them prepare
for her a mixture of barley and water. Then
she undertook the care of the king's little son
Demophon.

She fed him, however, with no earthly food, but gave
him ambrosia by day, breathed on him with her divine

breath, and held him at night in the fire as a firebrand, in order to burn out of him all that was mortal. So the boy, who was growing up like a flower, to the joy of his parents, would have become immortal, had not the queen once surprised the goddess at her work and uttered a loud cry. Then Demeter, taking the child from the hearth, laid it on the earth ; let herself be seen in her true form by the queen, who was trembling with anxiety ; and bade her build a temple at Eleusis, and worship her henceforth with solemn rites. And so it was done.

Demeter's grief was not yet assuaged. In her anger she would let no grain spring up, and she made the year unfruitful. Zeus sent Iris and all the gods to her as messengers to propitiate her, but Demeter insisted that she would not guide her footsteps towards Olympos before she had seen her daughter Persephone once more. Now Hermes, the messenger of the gods, was obliged to go down into the realms of Hades, king of the dead, and bid him let Persephone go free again to the light of day above. Gladly she sprang on the chariot drawn by milk-white steeds that bore her to the upper world ; but the reunion of mother and daughter could not last for ever. For Persephone's husband had given her in the realms of the dead a seed of a pomegranate to eat, and so she was bound to him. Therefore Zeus decided that Persephone should dwell a third of the year, when the earth lay torpid and unfruitful, deep down beside her husband, but two-thirds with her mother, when it was spring and the summer came. Thus Demeter was propitiated, and allowed the corn to spring up once more.

2. DEMETER, THE FOUNDER OF AGRICULTURE, AND TRIPTOLEMOS.

Who fails to see that by the death of Demeter's daughter the fading and withering of plants is meant ; and by her return to the upper world the fresh sprouting of the germs from the dark bosom of the earth ? As mother and daughter, so earth and plants are closely connected, and therefore especially in Attica Demeter and Persephone were, for the most part, worshipped together : they were called briefly " the two goddesses," and Persephone also simply Kore, *i.e.*, girl or daughter.

If Kore and Demeter were united, then the earth had clothed herself in green, and fresh food could be relied on both for man and beast. Important above all else, however, was the blessing of corn, and therefore Demeter was glorified as the dispenser of corn. She was specially the founder of agriculture. Agriculture, however, brings prosperity and riches in its train, and so the name of Pluto, or Riches, was given to the son of Demeter, or of Kore, for both worked together for the re-awakening of the fields. To Demeter men prayed before sowing, to her they dedicated the gifts of harvest, and to her were sacred all objects and animals that belonged to agriculture,—the seed, the sheaf, the poppy, the fruit-basket, the plough with the ox that drew it, and the turtle-dove that built her nest when spring began ; but no less the crane, for when he made his appearance it was known that the rainy season was at an end, and the farmer's work began. But the most acceptable sacrifice that could be offered to her was the pig, which was, at the same time, highly esteemed as food by the farmer.

The people of Eleusis, however, had a story to tell

FIG. 18.—DEMETER, TRIPTOLEMOS, AND KORE.
Relief from Eleusis, now at Athens.

of an old king of their country, Triptolemos, whom Demeter had first initiated in the arts of ploughing and sowing. For the plain of Eleusis was almost the only district of Attica in which corn was grown, and therefore it was believed that the knowledge of agriculture had been thence disseminated. Of this the inhabitants of Attica were no little proud ; for with the spread of agriculture civilization also had been spread among men. Even in later historical times the Athenians ranked themselves above the Spartans, in that a king of their country had introduced agriculture, and civilization also, among foreigners. And in this matter people recognised such wisdom in Triptolemos that the poets made him the judge of the dead in the Lower World. Indeed, there were three laws of Triptolemos quoted in Attica : to honour parents, to torment no domestic animal, and to offer to the gods sacrifice without shedding of blood.

As, however, Triptolemos was regarded as the favourite of Demeter, the result was that he was often confounded with the boy Demophon, whom the goddess had brought up in the house of the king of Eleusis (see p. 90), and was himself represented as a boy. So we see him on a beautiful piece of sculpture (Fig. 18) found at Eleusis ; between mother and daughter stands Triptolemos. Demeter hands to him the first seed-corn, which the boy receives modestly ; and Kore, holding in her hand a torch, with which she lighted up the darkness in which she so long sojourned, places a wreath on his head. Still later, indeed, it was fancied that Demeter rode over the earth in a car drawn by serpents, to bring corn to man, for the serpent is the mystic creature that is sacred to all gods. Or people believed that her favourite Triptolemos relieved Demeter of this task. Thus we see him on a vase-painting

(Fig. 19), borne through the air by a serpent-car, and strewing over the earth the golden seed-corn from his righth and raised on high.

FIG. 19.—TRIPTOLEMOS.
From a Greek vase in the Vatican Museum, Rome.

3. DEMETER, THE GODDESS OF CIVILIZATION, AND THE ELEUSINIAN MYSTERIES.

The earliest real civilization of mankind begins with agriculture. When a man tills the land he no longer roams homeless through the forests ; he makes him a permanent habitation, and founds for himself and his wife the comforts of a home. Therefore Demeter was worshipped under the title Thesmophoros, as the founder of the obligations and laws of marriage. It was to her that the Athenian maidens prayed for husbands ; and every year at the end of October, when the seed had been sown, all respectable matrons and virgins celebrated, in honour of Demeter and her daughter, the festival of the Thesmophoria, from which men were excluded. Hence it was the custom in Attica that the priestess of Demeter should consecrate marriages, and should impress on newly-married couples Demeter's precepts. The priestess only acted for the goddess herself under whose protection the nuptial tie was contracted. But before the wedding procession, in which the bridegroom conducted home the bride, the bride's mother went with two torches which she had kindled at Demeter's altar.

The case was much the same when the league of the so-called *Amphiktyones,* one of the most ancient associations of Grecian tribes for the purpose of good order and peaceful intercourse, assembled in the temple of Demeter at Thermopylæ. This took place yearly after the sowing of the corn. In other places, also, Demeter was worshipped as guardian of corporate bodies and national assemblies. At the Olympic games the priestess of Demeter occupied a place of honour ; and in Athens the judges or jurymen, when entering on their office, took an oath in the name of Zeus, Athena, and Demeter.

Rhea Kybele also, the mother of the gods introduced

among the Greeks from Asia, was considered as a
guardian of cities and communities; but there still

remained an
important dis-
tinction be-
tween the two
goddesses.
Rhea Kybele
was wor-
shipped in
Asiatic fashion
with noisy
cymbals and
shrill pipes;
she was, at
the same time,
the mother
of the beasts,
and goddess
of the wild
nature of the
mountains. To
the gentle De-
meter, on the
other hand,
peaceful spots
and well-tilled
fields were
sacred. Peace-
ful and simple,

FIG. 20.—DEMETER.

Statue in the Vatican Museum, Rome.

earnest and gentle, thus was it that the Greeks represented Demeter, who as a queen, indeed, with her sceptre

(see Fig. 20) holds her place among the gods, and passes
for a sister of the king of the gods, of equal birth; but,
as the bundle of ears of corn in her hand proves, is
intent only on the well-being of man, to whom she has
brought the noblest food, and with it morality and
order.

Some, too, perceived in the belief in Demeter a still
greater blessing for mortals than the spread of agriculture and the institution of marriage could assure
them. This was the mysterious doctrines which the
priests of Demeter imparted at Eleusis. We do not,
indeed, know with sufficient certainty in what these
doctrines consisted, for in this service of Demeter the
people were initiated in solemn and secret fashion,
whence these initiations were denominated "mysteria,"
and the initiated, or "mystai," had to bind themselves
to a strict silence about all they had seen and heard.
Sacred symbols and pledges for the favour of Demeter
were then exhibited to them; they had themselves to
undergo the trials of the sorrowing Demeter, and through
darkness that inspired terror were brought at last to
light.

For in the estimation of the heathen the consoling
power of the Eleusinian mysteries lay precisely in
this, that darkness was followed by light, death by
life. Persephone, believed to have been dead, was
on her mother's breast, returned again; and so the
Roman Cicero, who had been initiated in the Eleusinian
mysteries, called them "the beginnings" of a better
and nobler life. Now it was known that death was
not simply an annihilation, if one only believed in the
protecting grace of Demeter, and did not give way to

doubt, like that queen of Eleusis who, through curiosity, was foolish enough to lose the gift of immortality for her son. Thus Antigone felt able to look death in the face; for she knew that righteousness ruled with the judges of the dead, and apportioned according to merit reward and punishment.

At a later time there was united to the belief in the resurrection of Kore also the belief in the death and resurrection of a god of spring, called sometimes Dionysos, sometimes Iakchos. For "Iakche" was the cry of joy of those initiated in the Eleusinian mysteries, when, at the great autumn festival, in long procession, they made their pilgrimage by the Sacred Way from Athens to Eleusis, and brought the image of Dionysos Iakchos to the temple of the two Eleusinian goddesses.

The resurrection of Kore, like that of this Dionysos, who also was considered a son of Demeter, betokened the re-awakening of nature after her winter sleep, and that might be also, for men of devout feeling, the surest pledge of a re-awakening after the night of death.

(B) CERES (TELLUS).

I. THE EARTH-GODDESS TELLUS.

In the case of the earth-goddess Tellus worshipped in Italy, we meet with almost exactly the same characteristics as the Greek assigned to Demeter, his goddess of earth and arable land. Beside Tellus there stood a male being, Tellumo, whose functions were pretty much the same as hers. As the goddess of the earth Tellus was at once the revered dispenser of corn and the holy mother of the dead, to whose lap they returned. It was, therefore, the same idea as when in Attica the name " Demetreioi " was applied to those sleeping in death. Had one neglected to pay the last honours to the dead, it was necessary at least to sacrifice a pig to Tellus in order to ensure her favour ; and one could hardly count on a good harvest without this sacrifice. For man was of earth, and Mother Earth had therefore a claim on him after death. But the pig must have been as acceptable to Earth as to the farmer.

As was Mother Earth so was Tellus called to witness, together with Zeus, on the occasion of taking oaths ; she alone was the unchangeable one amidst the varied changefulness of nature and human affairs alike. When an earthquake took place in the midst of a battle, the Consul P. Sempronius vowed a temple to Tellus ; for if Earth quits her accustomed state of rest, then there is an end of the security of man's existence.

2. Ceres, a Goddess of the Plebeians ; her Festivals.

It appears that the goddess Tellus bore also the name of Ceres, equivalent to "mother." This name eventually gained the ascendency, and when the Greek goddess Demeter came to be known, people ascribed to Tellus or Ceres everything that they heard of Demeter. This was not difficult, for the two were like enough. Nay, the Romans did not hesitate to recognise in their Ceres the guardian of marriage, and not only the goddess of corn crops. Accordingly they decreed that in the case of divorce for insufficient reasons one-half of the husband's means should be assigned to the wife, and the other to the temple of Ceres; and besides this the husband had to propitiate by a sacrifice the spirits of the dead beneath the earth, the *manes*. Ceres, in the meantime, gained among the Romans a special importance, and this had to do with the time at which a service akin to that of the Greek Demeter was introduced in her honour. It happened after the expulsion of the kings that the Dictator Aulus Postumius, to avert the danger of a famine, consulted the sacred "Sibylline" books, and received the direction to introduce the worship of Demeter, Dionysos, and Kore. To these three deities then, under the names of Ceres, Liber, and Libera, the dictator vowed their first temple in Rome in the year 496 B.C. It was called "Ædes Cereris," *i.e.*, the house of Ceres, and in its building Greek architecture for the first time took the place of the Etruscan style that prevailed in Rome. Of Greek origin also must have been the priestess of Ceres, generally sent from Naples, who, however, received the Roman franchise as soon as she entered on her office. Since the secession of the Plebs had taken place shortly before this, and it was seen to be necessary, in order to avoid greater troubles, to provide for a quicker supply of corn, the new sanctuary of the corn-goddess Ceres was regarded as a special sanctuary of the Plebeians. The Tribunes of the Plebs appointed to protect the Plebeians kept in the temple of Ceres the laws approved by them; the property of those who had sacrilegiously attacked the inviolability of the Tribunes was allotted to the temple of Ceres; and the Plebeian assistants of the Tribunes are said by some to have derived their name "Ædiles" from the *Ædes*, or house of Ceres. Their special function was to watch over the corn-market and the importation of bread-stuffs, in order to prevent possible famine or scarcity.

Finally there was established, probably again in pursuance of the directions of the Sibylline Books, a special spring-festival in honour of Ceres, celebrated in April. This was called the "*Cerealia*," and here also it was the duty of the ædiles to exhibit the games which were connected with the festival. After a solemn procession, the games were commenced with a horse-race, and then followed a fox-hunt. Wisps of dry stuff were fastened to the tails of foxes and set on fire. The foxes were then hunted through the circus, and it was believed that in this way the cornfields could be protected from blight, which, like a fox, runs through the ears. Great gaiety distinguished the *Cerealia;* it was a genuine festival for the people, and while a little earlier, at the *Megalesia*, celebrated in honour of the mother of the gods (*Magna mater*), the distinguished Patricians had entertained themselves with great feasting, the Plebeians were wont to invite themselves to the feast of Ceres, and during the games to throw about nuts and little presents.

Moreover, the distinguished men among the Romans did not forget Eleusis and its mysteries. Whoever had the means required for it determined on a journey thither. For on the holy ground of Eleusis the Roman also believed new hope and comfort for life were to be found. Therefore the attempt of the Emperor Claudius to transplant the mysteries from Eleusis to Rome was unsuccessful.

CHAPTER VII.

APOLLON—APOLLO.

(A) APOLLON.[1]

1. Apollo the God of Light and Spring, and Apollo the Dragon-slayer.

Apollo was the dispenser of light ; the bright gleam of day, the light, too, of night, were alike his work. Each day on which for the first time the moon shone forth once more was sacred to him ; then, too, in house and home everything had to be bright and clean in honour of the new light. " Quick, ye maids ! " cries Eurykleia, the housekeeper of Odysseus. " Come hither ; let some of you go busily and sweep the hall, and sprinkle it, and on the fair-fashioned seats throw purple coverlets ; and others with sponges wipe all the tables clean, and cleanse the mixing bowls and well-wrought double beakers ; and others again go for water to the well, and return with it right speedily. For the wooers will not long be out of the hall, but will return very early, for it is a feast-day, yea for all the people." [2]

This was new moon, a festival of Apollo. The

---

[1] This is the Greek form of the god's name ; we, however, generally use the Latin form *Apollo.*

[2] *Odyssey*, xx., 149—156, Butcher and Lang's translation.

power of Apollo was noticed as soon as people stepped out of the house; for the houses of the Greeks were dark, and provided only with small openings for windows. In the street, however, it was bright enough, and here stood before the doors small round pillars to remind them of the Light-god Apollo.

But the light of day proceeds from the sun, and in very early times Apollo must have been also god of the sun. In later times this belief faded away, when the god Helios was made the driver of the chariot of the sun. Beneficent, above all, to mankind was the light of the sun, when, after gloomy days of rain and winter, it shed its beams once more on earth with fresh power, when it was springtime and the herdsman drove his herd into the open air. As the Greeks were still concerned chiefly with agriculture and raising cattle, it was necessary that Apollo should have more importance as a protector of herds. The legend tells how he himself pastured the herds for King Laomedon of Troy; and when he looked after the horses for King Admetos of Thessaly, they throve so splendidly that Eumelos, the king's son, could boast the finest steeds among the combatants before the walls of Troy. It was to the god of the sun also that herds of oxen were ascribed (*cf.* p. 70), and the theft of oxen of which Hermes was guilty was committed on Apollo's herds. Another god of the herdsman was Aristaios, at once seer and physician, "For whom" (sings the poet Vergil)[1]—

"Thrice a hundred snow-white steers graze in Cea's luxuriant brakes;"

and this Aristaios, too, was deemed Apollo's son.

[1] *Georgics*, i., 14, 15.

Both, however, father and son alike, loved well to sport with nymphs of meadow and mountain as they tended their flocks. This characteristic of Apollo was, indeed, gradually forgotten as the Greeks ceased to be simple herdsmen and husbandmen.

Remembered, however, and much celebrated, was Apollo's victory over the powers of darkness, or, as it was called, his fight with the dragon or huge serpent. For under the form of such a monster did the Greeks, like the ancient Teutons, conceive of the destructive powers of death and darkness. Pytho was the name of the serpent that had its lair in the ravine of Delphi. On Apollo's subduing the monster with his arrows he himself obtained the title Pythoktonos, or Dragon-slayer, and the memory of this victory was celebrated by a representation of the contest and by musical performances at the festivals that recurred every four years at Delphi.

2. Apollo the Destroyer, and Apollo's Retirement.

These festivals were celebrated at Delphi till Christian times, for how could the heart of man fail to be filled with joy at the thought that light and warmth had got the better of winter ? But the sun's glowing heat may, indeed, breathe forth sudden destruction, and the destructive force is especially perceptible in the lands of the South, where the scorching glow of midsummer covers the earth with an arid grey, and breeds deadly pestilences which sweep men away and spare not even youth in its bloom. We have seen, indeed, how, in early days, the same destructive frenzy was ascribed to

Zeus the Wolf-god on Mount Lykaios (p. 4), but Apollo
also cut off as a ravening wolf the blooming life, and in
token thereof there stood before his temple at Delphi
the image of his sacred wolf. The Greeks themselves
did not exactly know why the wolf was sacred to
Apollo, and thought he, as guardian of the herds, was
a slayer of wolves. This, however, was not the real
state of the case. The wolf was rather an image of
the destroying god. Of similar import were also his
arrows which flew from his bow like lightning, and the
golden sword that he brandished. And so the poets
call him the " Far-striker," for the death that Apollo
sends draws nigh suddenly out of unknown distance.
But the more unexpectedly and suddenly such a death
falls on men, the more he spares man the pains of long
death-agony, and the corpse remains free from the
repulsive traces of slow-wasting diseases.

So sank down gently and suddenly smitten the
youthful beauty of the heroes Patroklos and Achilles,
both struck by arrows which mortals, indeed, had dis-
charged, but Apollo had guided on their course; and
before the corpse of her son Hektor, Hekabe cries in
lamentation :—

" But now all dewy and fresh thou liest in our halls,
like one on whom Apollo, lord of the silver bow, hath
descended and slain him with his gentle darts." [1]

Dreadful and terrible did Apollo's nature appear
when he aimed his shafts, not at one individual, but
at whole hosts of men and also beasts. Thus Homer
depicts for us the god when, to avenge his priest

---

[1] *Iliad*, xxiv., 757-59, translated by Lang, Leaf, and Myers.

wronged by Agamemnon, he sends pestilence amid the
ranks of the Greeks :—

"So spake he in prayer, and Phœbus Apollo heard
him, and came down from the peaks of Olympus wroth
at heart, bearing on his shoulders his bow and covered
quiver.   And the arrows clanged upon his shoulders
in his wrath, as the god moved ; and he descended like
to night.   Then he sate him aloof from the ships, and
let an arrow fly ; and there was heard a dread clanging
of the silver bow.   First did he assail the mules and
fleet dogs, but afterward, aiming at the men his
piercing dart, he smote ; and the pyres of the dead
burnt continually in multitude." [1]

Most painful, however, is it for man to observe this
death-dealing power on the bodies of youth that has
the greatest claim on life, and therefore Apollo also
was held to be specially a destroyer of male youth,
that he most loves to snatch away in the midst of their
strength and activity and from their vigorous sports.
Thus pitilessly laid he low the sons of Niobe at play,
and with his arrows struck the steersman of Menelaos
on his voyage.   But in Spartan Amyklai a festival
of mourning was held in honour of Apollo, to com-
memorate his having slain his fair darling Hyakinthos
with a .quoit hurled on high and falling from the clouds.
And who at this tale of the quoit would not be ready
to think of the sun, that from amid the clouds above
casts down his deadly heat, and cuts off from man
and beast that which might nourish life ?   Apollo
then is esteemed the exterminator of locusts and of

---

[1] *Iliad.*, i., 43-52.

mice, and the warriors before the walls of Troy pray often to Apollo the Mouse-slayer (*Smintheus*).

Swift death, however, overtakes men most on the field of battle, and so it happened that from the fatal sun-god arose the idea of Apollo as a god of battle. Courageously does he fight amidst the combatants before Troy, and strikes fear into the foe by the shaking of the ægis, even as does Zeus (*cf.* p. 6). After the battle, therefore, the tenth of the spoil was dedicated to Apollo, and of him men thought as they began the fray. "*Paian*" was the name given to the solemn battle-chant imploring victory and defence against disaster, a chant sung in honour of Apollo. Not till this was done was the real war-cry raised. On this account the god had the surname Paieon, and a paian could be sung in any case of peril. For that god who has power to send death and pestilence can also ward them off.

When in the year 279 before Christ the wild Gallic hordes advanced against the god's Delphian sanctuary, Apollo himself hastened up to help and protect his temple ; it was again as when before Troy he shook the ægis, and threw down walls as "a boy does the sand on the seashore," so violently did a storm break forth, and stones roll down on the Gauls from the mountains, so that they fled thence in dismay ; so full of wrath, and at the same time so beautiful, seems the face of the avenging god in one of his most famous images, that which is called "the Apollo Belvedere," of which Pl. III. gives a representation. The destructive force, however, of the Light-god lasted only for a part of the year, and when the glowing heat of the sun faded, the

III. APOLLO.

In the Belvedere of the Vatican Museum, Rome.

power of Apollo passed also away. Now Apollo himself was become liable to death, which the myth expresses as if Apollo were become a serf of the god of death, whose herds he is obliged to keep. We heard before how he pastured the horses of King Admetos of Thessaly (see p. 104), and how for King Laomedon of Troy he "pastured the lumbering oxen through the woody vales of Ida with many a peak," while the god Poseidon, equally reduced to slavery (see p. 46), helped Laomedon to build the walls of Troy. The latter, however, cheated the gods of their stipulated reward, so that to punish him Apollo sent a pestilence, Poseidon a sea-monster, from which Herakles set the land free. But Laomedon and Admetos are only appellations of the god of death, for the name of the first means "Ruler of the people," and that of the second "Unconquerable." Apollo's serving them means therefore the annihilation of light during the winter season.

Other myths expressed this again otherwise. So it was said at Delphi that during the winter the god was absent; and, indeed, it was believed he had gone to Lykia, where the god had many temples, for example at Patara. Besides, the name Lykia reminded the Greeks of the word "Light," and on this account this retreat was very suitably contrived for the god who had migrated.

Or it was said that Apollo had gone to the pious men who dwell beyond the North Wind. They were called the Hyperboreans, whose country was always light and warm, where everything was brilliant, and the wondrous griffins, half bird, half beast of prey, were

established guardians of the glittering gold. Here
Apollo was honoured throughout the whole winter
with sport and dance, and at Delphi, meanwhile,
Apollo's loved brother presided over the sanctuary.
But as soon as spring came Apollo returned to Delphi,
borne through the air by a snow-white swan. For
there was always his favourite abode in Greece.

3. APOLLO'S BIRTH AND THE SANCTUARY OF DELPHI.

But if nature were waked afresh, then Apollo, too,
was born anew, and an ancient hymn full of inspiration
has thus represented the story of his birth. Out of
night and darkness the light of day struggles forth.
So Apollo was a son of Leto (Latona), *i.e.*, of darkness.
And at the same time as he a twin-sister, Artemis, first
saw the light. Many a pang, hunger, and thirst had
Leto, mother of the two, to suffer. In Lykia, when she
wanted to quench her thirst at a pool, she was hindered
by rough peasants, and these were in punishment for
this turned into frogs. It was in the island of Delos
that the ill-fated one first found rest. Delos, therefore,
was held to be the birthplace of Apollo, for Delos
means really the light; and the god was called henceforth Phoibos Apollo, or the bright Apollo. Originally Delos was a constantly-moving island, floating
hither and thither in the sea; but now, when beneath
a palm-tree on Mount Kynthos,[1] Apollo saw the light
of day, then together with universal nature the unfruitful rocky isle of Delos shone forth in golden brilliancy,

---

[1] On this account Apollo is often in poetry called the "Cynthian."

and four pillars sprung up as its firm support. So told
the poet Pindar; and Theognis sang,—

> "Great Delos was all filled with ambrosial fragrance; and
> the mighty earth smiled, and glad were the depths of the
> grey sea." [1]

From that time forth the island of Delos was deemed
holy, and had to be kept free from everything impure;
no dog might set foot on the island; and when in the
fifth year of the Peloponnesian War the plague, which
Apollo had sent, came to an end, the Athenians again,
as on a previous occasion, expressed their gratitude to
Apollo; they had all the remains of the dead removed
from Delos and carried across to the small neighbouring
island of Rhenaia: this was for the future the burying-
place for Delos.

Scarcely, however, had the newborn god beheld the
island and tasted ambrosia when he sprang up and
cried, "Sacred to me be the lyre, sacred the bow;
but to man I make known the certain will of Zeus."

Noble to look on was the youthful god, alike terrible
and beautiful. The gods trembled when he strode
through the hall of Zeus, and leaped from their seats
when he drew nigh to them and bent his mighty bow.
Leto alone remained seated beside Zeus, who delights
in the lightning; she took from her son the bow,
closed the quiver, hung it up, and led Apollo to a seat,
where his father Zeus welcomed him with the golden
cup of nectar. Not till then did the other gods seat
themselves; but Leto rejoiced in her princely son, and
Zeus too recognised him as his favourite son among
the gods.

[1] *Gnomai*, 8-10.

Now Apollo had become an Olympian god among the rest ; nay, his power soon appeared greater than that of any god. This came about because Delphi, situated in the midst of Greece, was the chief centre of his worship, and from this place was spread abroad— on account of the oracle here established—the belief in Apollo, and his influence throughout Greece ; nay, not only throughout Greece, but also throughout the islands great and small, and as far as Asia Minor and Italy. But how close was the union, even in the oldest times, between Delphi and Crete, is shown by the following story :—

Once on a time Apollo was meditating as to what men could best serve him in the rocky island, perform his sacrifices, and make known his precepts ; then he caught sight of a swift-sailing vessel on the sea. In this vessel were several sturdy men of Crete, who as traders were voyaging with their goods to Pylos. Phoibos Apollo went forth to meet them, and sprang on board their ship in the form of a great dolphin. Hardly a moment, however, had the mighty monster lain there when the ship began to tremble and the timbers to creak, so that the anxious crew let the vessel have free course. So they were carried round the point of the Peloponnesos, and guided—such was Apollo's will —into the haven of Krisa at the foot of Parnassos. On the heights of the mountain stood the sanctuary of the god. Scarcely, however, had the vessel touched the shore when out sprang Apollo from the ship like a flashing star, so that the sparks flew and the brightness rose to heaven. He glided into his sanctuary on the mountain and filled all Krisa with brightness, so that all the maidens and women who saw it cried aloud with joy. Thereon the god leapt down again, swift as thought, to the ship, but now in the guise of a blooming youth with waving locks ; he told the sailors to be of good cheer, and bade them go ashore, for he was Apollo, and they should here rule his rich temple ; and as he had once as a dolphin (*Delphin*) guided them over the misty sea, so must they raise here on the shore an altar to Apollo Delphinios. So did they ; and when they had sacrificed to him and to the other gods, and had taken their food, they followed Apollo, who, with the *kithara*—thus was his stringed instrument called—in his hand, led them on up the mountain to Pytho, the spot where he had slain the dragon. Meanwhile he chanted the Paian, as the Cretans were wont to chant. But when the first among them, full of anxiety, asked the god on what they were to live in his temple, Apollo smiled and replied, "In your right hands shall ye ever hold sacrificial knives, to slay sheep, and rich gifts shall the tribes of men bring to my temple forthwith."

In truth the men had no need to be anxious on this score ; for from all nations and all lands flowed gifts to Apollo's venerated shrine at Delphi. The dragon's grave was become the place of an oracle. But the altar in the temple at Delphi was soon considered the central point of the Greek world, the "common hearth of Hellas." When after the battle of Plataiai all Grecian sanctuaries seemed violated and defiled, then, by order of the priestess of Delphi, every sacrificial fire had to be quenched, and taken pure and fresh from Apollo's altar at Delphi.

4. Apollo, God of Prophecy, and Apollo, God of Expiation.

That the worship of Apollo at Delphi obtained this importance in the eyes of the Greeks resulted chiefly from the fact that Delphi was the seat of an oracle in the earliest ages. Stupefying vapours, which rose out of a cleft in the rock, and threw into convulsions all who approached them, seemed the clearest proof of divine presence. The oracle was certainly known before the worship of Apollo had spread; now, however, the god himself took possession of the oracle and gave it new glory.

Together with a hemispherical stone covered with woollen fillets, the so-called grave of the dragon, there stood over that fissure in the earth a tripod with a cauldron. In the cauldron lay the dragon's teeth, and his hide was wound round the feet of the tripod. It was certainly believed that the dragon's carcase had something to do with the vapours which caused inspiration; for the serpent was in general esteemed as a creature connected with prophecy, and was sacred to Apollo, as it is often represented with him by sculptors. At this tripod, then, Apollo had established himself to declare to mankind the future, or, in other words, the will of his father Zeus. In place of Apollo, however, at a later period, a grey-haired virgin of Pytho, selected by the god and called the " Pythia," mounted this seat at stated times. When she was stupefied by the vapour, and had fallen into convulsions through the god's power that seemed to prevail over her, she uttered strange sounds. These were turned into verses by the priests, and imparted to those who had come to question the god.

The priests, of course, often had it in their power to frame the answer as they chose; and when their aim was such that the result was good and consistent with morality, and so long as they were not stained by bribery, they established a real blessing. Their god Apollo stood for the essence of all wisdom; whatever he said was believed. By him were the ordinances of Lykourgos examined and found good; to him turned every individual Greek at the beginning of every important enterprise, and so did a state before a war and before sending forth colonies. The highest piece of wisdom of Greek antiquity, displayed in the saying "Know thyself," stood at the entrance of the splendid temple of Apollo at Delphi.

For the rest, the belief in prophecies was of remote antiquity, but all prophets and prophetesses were cast into the shade by Apollo, for it was said that the god had breathed into them his inspired knowledge. So was Kassandra, Priam's daughter, endowed by him with the gifts of prophecy,—with the condition, indeed, that no one should believe her; and her brother Helenos received the power of prophecy with the limitation of predicting only misfortune to his countrymen. Also diviners and priests, as Kalchas and Teiresias, are in the service of Apollo; especially so were grey-haired virgins, like the Pythia herself, persons called Sibyls, whom the god had to choose for the purpose of announcing his wisdom. So there were besides the Delphian a whole series of famous oracles of Apollo, especially in Asia Minor, as at Erythrai, at

Lykian Patara, at Thymbra in the Troad, and in the sanctuary of Branchidai near Miletos. The Greeks brought, indeed, to Italy, into their colonies, the respect paid to their prophetesses, and among these colonies the Sibyl of Cumæ, near Naples, a servant of Apollo, gained the highest importance with regard to the Romans and their whole religion. What, however, gained this importance for the oracle of Apollo was the moral influence proceeding therefrom over Greece. Men gradually ceased to fear Apollo as the destroyer and the sender of the plague, and began to praise him rather as the averter of evil. For he who sends evil can also recall it, and whoever gives courage for battle can also bestow the victory. Therefore Apollo was recognised also as the father of Asklepios, god of healing.

Higher, however, than freedom from bodily harm is the deliverance from moral harm, for without a quiet conscience all freedom of external life is of no avail. Therefore Apollo was a god of expiation. And what could have been of higher importance to man than deliverance from guilt? In Athens there stood an ancient shrine of Apollo Delphinios called the Delphinion, and this spot served for the purification of those stained with crime.

If, however, Apollo wished to make atonement for penitent sinners, he had himself to be the prototype of all penitents; for it is only one purified through repentance and self-abasement that can purify others from sins and faults. Therefore the poets sang how Apollo through the slaying of the dragon had brought upon himself a blood-guiltiness for which expiation

must be made. Of his own free will he retired from
Delphi to serve King Admetos for the space of eight
years ; so long originally was the time between two
Delphic festivals, a so-called "great year," which was
later shortened to four years. In token of expiation
Apollo was purified in the lovely vale of Tempe by
means of the bay-tree that is a native of those parts,
for to this aromatic shrub a purifying power was
ascribed. But the slender bay with its bright leaves
Apollo, who had conquered himself, brought as a
conqueror to Delphi, and thenceforward was the bay-
wreath, in place of the earlier oak-wreath, the sign of a
fortunate result, and remained always closely associated
with the worship of Apollo. With branches of bay
suppliants approached him ; bay was the decoration of
the poets who gained the prize, and still at the present
day the bay serves the artist, as laurel the victor in
battle, for a token of honour achieved. Poets, however,
at a later time devised the story of Apollo's love for
the nymph Daphne,—for Daphne is the name of the
bay-tree,—who was pursued by him, and, to escape the
god's love, was changed into a bay-tree.

So none but the god thus purified and absolved, who
now is regarded himself as founder of pious expiatory
usage, and frees men from their guilt, may occupy the
seat of oracle and mount the tripod standing over the
fissure in the earth. Now mercy prevails over justice,
and milder manners thrust aside the old rigid vengeance for blood. Thus Apollo gave the ill-fated King
Oidipous the means of escaping the curse that clung to
him ; and even on Orestes, slayer of his mother as he
was, the god exercised the fair right of mercy ; and if

he could not procure for him recognition among his fellow-mortals,—for this only the regular verdict of the Areopagus at Athens could effect,—yet he can give rest to his conscience tortured by the Erinyes, goddesses of vengeance, since he allows him to enjoy the means of expiation connected with his cult. These rites of expiation usually consisted in the person to be expiated being sprinkled with the blood of an impure animal,— generally a sucking pig,—and then washed with pure consecrated water. Now consecrating powers were possessed in an especial degree by the water of the spring Kastalia, which flowed not far from Delphi. On this account all pilgrims to the Delphian temple washed themselves with the water of this fountain, and found in the outer court of the sanctuary artistic basins set up for this purpose. In part they were rich gifts of the Lydian monarch Crœsus. Of Apollo, however, the model of these pilgrims, the poet Horace sings that he too—

" With Castalia's limpid dew washes his flowing locks." [1]

The special expiation, however, followed in the interior of the temple close to the holy tripod, over the dragon's grave, the so-called *omphalos*, or central point of the world.

5. Apollo and the Muses.

Whoever, then, would have his conscience free from guilt, and whoever in his need and misery would seek advice, such as these resorted to Apollo at Delphi. For he was the wisest god. It was his lips that

[1] *Odes*, iii., 4, 61 and 62.

imparted the will of Zeus, and with him were truth and wisdom to be found. But the wisest god must also be the god of poets, who above all were skilled to recount the deeds of the past, and to implant the germs of good precepts in their hearers' hearts. So happened it that Apollo gained the leadership of the Muses' choir and the surname Musagetes, or leader of the Muses. The Muses were, no doubt, originally goddesses of springs to which was ascribed a power of inspiration. It seems that the Thracians were the nation most given to the worship of the Muses. They brought their beliefs to Central Greece, and now shrines arose in honour of the Muses in the range of Helikon in Bœotia and on Parnassos in Phokis. Thus the Muses became also in a more obvious sense neighbours of the Delphian Apollo. Originally they had no fixed names, and their number was not known. It was not till a later time, when man's intellect developed the most varied spheres of activity, and poets too no longer simply recounted the deeds of heroes and ancestral glories, that there arose the belief in a fixed number of Muses, of whom one bestows on mortals these gifts, another those. Their father was called Zeus, their mother Mnemosyne, or Memory: for the knowledge of the facts and thoughts of the past seemed the greatest treasure of the human mind. There were nine Muses, distinguished as follows : Kleio was the muse of history, Kalliope of epic poetry, Melpomene of tragedy and elegy, Thaleia of comedy, Terpsichore, " she that de-lights in the circle-dance," the muse of the chorus with voice and step, Erato of the love-song, Polyhymnia muse of the grave stringed instruments, Euterpe of the flute, and Ourania, or "the heavenly one," muse of the order of the heavens, the science of the stars and their courses, whence she is often represented with a celestial globe in her hand.

To all gifts of the Muses, however, it was Apollo that lent inspiration, and therefore he is inseparable from the choir of the nine maidens, whose dance and song he accompanied with the refined notes of his kithara. For the simple lyre with its slight sound, as produced by the strings stretched over the back, formed by a tortoise, was rather the instrument with which Hermes made merry, Hermes the cheerful friend of the herdsman; while the kithara was a skilfully-formed instrument with wooden sounding-board and long strings, whose responsive tones could express even exalted feelings. The kithara or harp is then Apollo's special instrument, and artists loved to picture him busied with this, when, with head thrown back in enthusiasm, he marches on as the singer in long flowing robe with many a fold (see Fig. 21). But to mark the god still more clearly as the victorious singer, one arm of his kithara is adorned with the figure of the Satyr Marsyas, who chose to contend with Apollo, and who, as a punishment, was hung up and put to death.

As, however, Apollo finally became the god of poets, so it happened also that the tripod from which he at Delphi announced the will of Zeus became the sign of victory gained in a poetic contest, so closely was the art of the seer connected in men's minds with that of the poet. At Athens, the *choregos*, who with his exhibition of a tragedy had gained a victory over his competitors received the privilege of erecting a tripod

FIG. 21.—APOLLO WITH THE KITHARA.

in commemoration thereof. This sign sufficed to indicate that Apollo had supported his efforts and brought them to success.

(B) APOLLO.

I. THE SIBYLLINE BOOKS AND THE INTRODUCTION OF THE CULT OF APOLLO AT ROME.

"In the days of King Tarquinius Superbus there came to the king a strange old woman who was known to no one. She brought with her nine books, which contained, according to her account, divine oracles, and she explained that she meant to offer them for sale. Tarquinius enquired the price, and the woman demanded an excessively high one. The king laughed, because he supposed the woman from extreme age had become childish. Thereupon she places a small brazier just in front of him, burns three of the books, and again asks the king whether he will buy the remaining six at the same price. Tarquinius only finds more cause for mirth in this, and exclaims aloud that the old woman must without doubt be not quite right in her mind. Thereupon the woman once more throws three of the remaining books into the fire, and quite quietly asks again the same question, whether he will not now buy at the same price the last three books that are left. Now the demeanour of Tarquinius became more serious, his spirit more thoughtful. He clearly feels that behind such calm and confidence something of importance must be hidden, and directs the full price to be paid her for the remaining books which she had demanded for the whole number. Further, it is generally admitted that the woman was never seen again after she had left Tarquinius." [1]

Such is a Roman author's account of the origin of the so-called Sibylline Books, which became most important for the religion of the Romans. For it was through these in the main that the worship of the Greek Apollo was first introduced into Rome, since the Romans had no god whose functions were at all parallel to those of Apollo. These books, however, were called Sibylline because their contents came from the Sibyls (see p. 115), those prophetic women who were in the service of Apollo. Possibly these books had their origin in Asia Minor. But the sacred writings which are said to have been laid before King Tarquinius probably came from Cumæ, in Southern Italy. There, according to legend, lived a famous Sibyl in a cavern, and there also stood a temple of the Greek Apollo. It was to leaves of trees that the famous grey-haired virgin of Cumæ entrusted her mysterious characters:

> " What she commits to leaves, in order laid,
> Before the cavern's entrance are display'd :
> Unmov'd they lie ; but if a blast of wind
> Without, or vapours issue from behind,
> The leaves are borne aloft in liquid air,
> And she resumes no more her museful care ;
> Nor gathers from the rocks her scattered verse,
> Nor sets in order what the winds disperse." [2]

It was left to the sagacity of intelligent men to fathom the import of the oracle, and therefore the Romans instituted a special board of fifteen men, who were commissioned to pick out from these Sibylline

---

[1] A. Gellius, *Noct. Attic.*, i., 19.

[2] Vergil, *Æneid*, iii., 445-51, Dryden's translation.

sayings all ordinances that were required for religious purposes. Most important, however, was it to make sure whether the introduction of a still unknown god was not enjoined by the Sibylline oracles, as in the case of Apollo.

When in the year B.C. 432 a great pestilence and an earthquake had terrified men's minds, the Sibyl's utterances pointed to Apollo of the Greeks, the warder off of pestilence and the dispenser of health. To Apollo Medicus, that is, to the god of health, was dedicated in B.C. 429 his first temple in Rome. But the people, unacquainted with Greek, made out of his name at first Apello or Aperta,[1] which was about equivalent to the god who drives away evil or discloses the future. For the Romans considered that the chief characteristic of Apollo lay in the revelation of previously unknown means of curing the sick.

2. The New Cult, the New Sibylline Books, and Apollo Palatinus.

This new power of Apollo had soon to stand a new test. When fresh misfortune visited the commonwealth, Apollo ordered the establishment of a general day of humiliation and prayer for the whole people. Whereas Patricians and Plebeians had hitherto had separate religious rites, sacrifice was not on this holy day offered to the images of the gods in their individual temples, but they were carried into the streets, where cushions were spread for them and small altars erected. Now the crowd, decked out in holiday garb, surged through

---

[1] There seems to have been a supposed connection with *apellere* (to drive away), or *aperire* (to open).

the streets of the city; and when they had offered sacrifice and prayer before the images of the various deities, the festival concluded with a cheerful meal at home. Through this public celebration, however, the feeling of unity throughout the nation was strengthened to the advantage of their common country, and this again was due to the influence of Apollo the dispenser of health.

When in B.C. 212 the foreign enemy threatened the Roman commonwealth with destruction, and the bold Hannibal had already forced his way into Campania, it was again determined, in accordance with the directions contained in the books of the ancient seer Marcius, to establish the " Games of Apollo," and to celebrate this festival in the *Circus Maximus*. The spectators had to appear wreathed with bay, for it had been learned from the Greeks that the bay-tree had a purifying virtue (p. 117), and Apollo above everything demanded purity of his votaries if his aid was required by them.

Now, however, on the occasion of a great fire in the Capitoline temple, in which the Sibylline Books were kept, the books themselves perished, and it was necessary to devise a substitute for them. There was actually found a similar collection of oracular utterances to take their place, but this conceived more nobly of Apollo than the older collection. Whereas in earlier times he had been treated specially as the helper and rescuer in distress, there was now hoped for from him a complete revolution in circumstances. Sad indeed, to say the least of it, were often the feelings of the ancient world in the last century before the birth of Christ. All men were yearning for peace, the better-disposed among them were yearning also for a purer morality, and almost universal was the hope of a new era, in which at length justice and righteousness should rule supreme. This new era, according to the indications of the new Sibylline Books, was to be initiated through the agency of Apollo. For he was a god of light, he was the sun, and the purity of mankind must interest him more than anything else. This yearning of the whole world after peace rose, however, to its highest point when, after the crushing blows with which the Roman magnates strove for empire, the wise rule of Augustus at length brought the longed-for peace. Now the new era of Apollo seemed really to dawn. An additional circumstance was, that through the Sibylline Books the legend of the Trojan Æneas, of his flight to Italy and his sovereignty, was spread abroad ; and it was exactly the successors of Æneas who were the reputed ancestors of the Julian family, and consequently of the Emperor Augustus. That family must, therefore, have been specially favoured by heaven, and selected for the highest things ; nay, the Emperor Augustus himself was not disinclined to give out that he was a son of Apollo. The god had been his most faithful counsellor and guardian. The battle of Actium, in which he defeated his most dangerous opponent, was fought under the eyes of the god, and in front of his temple built on the lofty shore ; and with this he had laid the foundation of his power, for thus sings the poet Vergil :—

> " This seen, Apollo, from his Actian height,
> Pours down his arrows, at whose wingèd flight

> The trembling Indians and Egyptians yield,
> And soft Sabæans quit the wat'ry field." [1]

It was then only a duty of gratitude if Augustus erected to his protector at Actium a lordly temple, and instituted the "Actian games" in commemoration of the glorious victory. It was his wish, however, also in Rome to be as near as possible to the protection of Apollo. He therefore founded in the neighbourhood of his palace on the Palatine the noblest shrine that the god as yet had possessed in Rome, adorned with the finest works of art. Between sister and mother stood the image of Apollo, as sculptured by the Greek Skopas, in flowing robe with left hand touching the strings of the kithara (see Fig. 21). The temple on the Palatine was henceforth the depository of the Sibylline Books. In B.C. 17 Augustus celebrated in honour of Apollo, with incredible splendour, the *Ludi Sæculares*, which had been celebrated only four times before. It was on this occasion that Horace composed his famous "*Carmen Sæculare*," sung on the third day of the festival by thrice nine boys and as many maidens, in the temple of the Palatine Apollo. This celebration of a new age was continued as late as the fourth century of the Christian era, and it was not till A.D. 400 that the Sibylline Books were committed to the flames by Stilicho. So long did the worship of Apollo hold its ground against Christianity even in Rome itself.

----

[1] *Æneid*, viii., 704-6, Dryden's translation.

CHAPTER VIII.

ARTEMIS—DIANA.

(A) ARTEMIS.

1. Artemis, the Arcadian Goddess of Fertility.

In the same rugged mountainous region of Arcadia where the primeval worship of the "Wolf-god" Zeus on Mount Lykaios was longest maintained (see p. 3) the goddess Artemis also, the giver of fruits, the nurturer of men and beasts, the dispenser of the moonlight, seems first to have been worshipped. With awe the Arcadians looked up to this goddess, for she called Arkas, the ancestor of all Arcadians, her son. And as Zeus could change into a wolf, so Artemis could change into a she-bear. The Greeks of a later age, indeed, declined to recognise such rude ideas; they now ascribed to Kallisto, priestess of Artemis, what originally pertained to Artemis herself, and related that Kallisto, because she had loved the Lykaian Zeus, had been changed through Hera's jealousy into a bear, and had been shot dead by Artemis. Kallisto, however, meaning "the most beautiful," was only an appellation of the moon-goddess Artemis herself. The moon also was believed to dispense nutriment, and, above all, through the dew of night, to nurture herbs, and indeed every living thing. Artemis, however, not only in Arcadia, but also throughout the whole Peloponnese, was considered as the fosterer of herds, and especially of goats, which perhaps formed the sole wealth of the Arcadian herdsman. Artemis Agrotera, that is " Artemis of the field," was the title given to this goddess by the Greeks ; and the Spartans retained, even to the latest times, the custom of offering before battle a goat to " Artemis of the field." Oxen, also, were dedicated to her, and Artemis was often actually called Tauropolos, or " goddess of oxen."

As, however, the Arcadian race long remained without any nobler civilization, so too their worship of the native goddess was savage and terrible. And as in the case of the Lykaian Zeus, so also to this Artemis human beings were offered in sacrifice. At a later time, indeed, the imagination of the Greeks transferred this practice to a distant clime. They told of the mythic northern land Tauris that whoever was cast upon its shores was sacrificed by the natives to the Tauric Artemis. And the priestess Iphigeneia, who served her in her temple in Tauris, had once been offered to the goddess in the harbour of Aulis, because her father Agamemnon had offended Artemis. Some years afterwards Orestes, Iphigeneia's brother, carried away the image of the goddess, and brought it to Brauron, in Attica. Here, too, were the rites of the Brauronian Artemis performed in all their severity. At length, however, the milder views of the Greek race (especially through the direction of Apollo) altogether opposed such barbarous sacrifices, and changed them to more humane arrangements. At Brauron no maidens were any longer sacrificed to Artemis, but as a substitute for such sacrifice the young maidens remained till marriage in her temple. Yet the custom was retained of calling these maidens "she-bears," as the goddess, too, had shown herself in the form of a bear.

Sparta also possessed an ancient stiff image of this severe goddess, called Orthia, *i.e.*, "the Erect." To her, too, were youths in their prime sacrificed; but the lawgiver Lykourgos got rid of such barbarity, and from his time it was deemed sufficient every year at the altar of Artemis to scourge a number of boys till the blood flowed.

A nation that lived entirely on the products of the earth had to stand in special dread of the wrath of the goddess, who was a guardian of agriculture and a dispenser of the blessings of harvest. When King Oineus of Kalydon (his name may be rendered "man of wine") began to undervalue the gifts of the field, and neglected to bear Artemis in mind at the harvest-sacrifice, the goddess sent into his land a gigantic wild-boar, who trampled under foot and destroyed everything.

2. Artemis, Goddess of the Waters ; the Nymphs and the Ephesian Artemis.

When, however, deities of other Greek tribes had gradually gained a high esteem in the belief of the nation, when Demeter in particular was invoked as goddess of the blessings of the field and the fruits of the earth, the old belief in Artemis, the dispenser of the fruits of the field, subsided. There remained to her, however, the power which is displayed in the waters of springs and lakes, and which contributes so much to the growth and increase of plants and trees. Thus the marshes, the meadows watered by springs, the rivers and lakes, were always sacred to Artemis. Therefore she was called Artemis of the pools or of the rivers. When Xenophon, in the retreat of the Ten Thousand Greeks, the auxiliaries of the unfortunate Persian prince Cyrus, came upon a lake in Asia Minor with clear warm water, he thought he perceived a sanctuary of Artemis. As, however, brooks and rivers were sacred to Artemis, there was in Elis a story even of a love of the river-god Alpheios for Artemis, or for one of her friends among the nymphs, Arethousa. A prey to ardent desire, Alpheios pursued her, even beneath the sea, till Arethousa reappeared on the small island of Ortygia at Syracuse, and there Alpheios was united with her. In commemoration of this myth, the people of Syracuse represented on their coins the head of Artemis or Arethousa with a wreath of reeds (see Fig. 22 [1]), and often surrounded by fishes and shells. The whole island of Ortygia, however, was sacred to Artemis, and, according to some, was even to be considered as her birthplace.

FIG. 22.
HEAD FROM A COIN
OF SYRACUSE.

This Artemis, whose power was displayed in marshes, had for her dearest playmates and companions the nymphs of the fields, who lived their own happy life

---

[1] This may be Persephone with a wreath of corn-leaves (see Head, *Coins of the Ancients*, p. 51). Arethousa, however, often appears on the coinage of Syracuse.

beside plashing fountains and luxuriant meads.   Men
called them Naïades or water-maidens, and loved to
imagine them spinning and weaving, and so busily
employed.   Thus the messenger of the gods, Hermes
(see p. 74), found the nymph Kalypso working at the
loom, in a luxuriantly-embowered grotto, on her island
watered by four streams.   The grotto of the nymphs
indicates the retirement so essential to them.   For
Nature's laboratory must not be profaned by human
eye.   The mortal may, indeed, behold the external
beauty of such grottoes of the nymphs, but he is not
permitted to penetrate their inmost recesses.   An abode
of the nymphs in Ithake is thus pictured for us :—

"Now at the harbour's head is a long-leaved olive
tree, and hard by is a pleasant cave and shadowy,
sacred to the nymphs that are called the Naiads.   And
therein are mixing bowls and jars of stone ; and there,
moreover, do bees live.   And there are great looms
of stone, whereon the nymphs weave raiment of purple
stain, a marvel to behold ; and therein are waters well-
ing evermore.   Two gates are there to the cave : the
one set toward the North Wind, whereby men may go
down ; but the portals toward the South pertain rather
to the gods, whereby men may not enter : it is the way
of the immortals." [1]

Artemis loves to join these nymphs as they dance in
their ring on the high mountains.   So Homer compares
Nausikaa, dancing on amidst her playmates, to Artemis,
as he says,—

"And even as Artemis, the archer, moveth down the
mountain, either along the ridges of lofty Taygetus or

[1] *Odyssey*, xiii., 102-12, Butcher and Lang's translation.

Erymanthus, taking her pastime in the chase of boars and swift deer, and with her the wild wood-nymphs disport them, the daughters of Zeus, lord of the ægis; and Leto is glad at heart, while high over all she rears her head and brows, and easily may she be known,—but all are fair; even so the girl unwed outshone her maiden company."[1]

As, however, these nymphs, who in the stillness of nature create and promote growth, were ever ready to bring up and rear children of the gods (see p. 71), Artemis also was considered as the fosterer of youth. As she herself is distinguished among all deities for beauty and elegance, so she bestows beautiful growth especially on maidens. Therefore it is with Artemis that Homer compares Penelope or Helene, the fairest of women.

Maidens and youths were under her special guardianship. The Brauronian Artemis, for instance, received from maidens dedicated to her (the so-called she-bears, see p. 130), on their marriage, the girdle as a pledge of purity; in the same way in Delos the boys, on becoming young men, gave a lock of hair as a sacrifice to Artemis; and the women of Troizen offered a lock, too, before the wedding-day, to the chaste favourite of Artemis, the hunter Hippolytos.

In Asia also a great goddess was worshipped, who was considered the creator of animals, especially wild ones. Consequently she was usually represented holding by the forepaws a lion, stag, or panther. At Ephesos this goddess of nature and of the wild beasts was especially renowned. When the Greeks

---

[1] *Odyssey*, vi., 102-9, Butcher and Lang's translation.

became acquainted with this deity they accordingly gave her the name of Artemis. For example, the Greeks who, under the command of Xenophon, came through Ephesos in their retreat from Asia, honoured her with oblations just as their native Artemis. Xenophon himself describes [1] how he commissioned a curator of the temple, whose name was Megabyzos, to make an offering to the goddess if he fell in the expedition he was about to make with Agesilaos against the Thebans. Later on, when he had long since reached home, that temple curator met him at Olympia, and paid him the money back. But Xenophon purchased with it an estate in Elis, comprising fertile arable land, pasture, and forest; built thereon a temple to Artemis; and erected an image of cypress wood, an exact copy of the Ephesian Artemis. Whoever enjoyed the use of the land had to offer the tenth of the produce to the goddess; but on the feast-day those who attended enjoyed the game and the meat, together with the products of field and tree. All these were gifts of Artemis; and woe to him who deprived her of her due!

3. Artemis, Goddess of the Chase; the Amazons.

This goddess of free Nature, who with her shouting nymphs hurries noisily over hill and dale, was averse to love and all womanish toying. Woe to the man who ventured to approach her! Aktaion, who surprised Artemis in the grotto when she and her nymphs were cooling themselves with water and bathing, was changed by her into a stag, and torn to pieces by his own hounds.

---

[1] *Anabasis*, v., 3, 6-13.

"Chaste and holy" calls Homer the form of Artemis, and just as she herself was so had her priestesses to be. Iphigeneia, who presided over her worship in distant Tauris (see p. 129), rejected the advances of King Thoas; and the huntress Atalante, who seems a reflection of Artemis, pierces with her arrows the Centaurs who lie in wait for her, forces her suitors, like the Teutonic Brunnhilda, to a contest in running, and kills each that is defeated by her. Atalante, however, was probably originally another name for Artemis herself; it is said of her that in infancy she was suckled by a bear—hence her savage tastes.

So, then, Artemis has become a deity of the chase. Manly amusement pleased her above all, and only too gladly did the "arrow-pouring" Artemis pursue into the loneliness of mountain and forest the wild creatures that already belonged to her as goddess of nature. With loud hunter's cry she follows over the ranges of Taÿgetos or Erymanthos the fleeing deer and boars, and she loves to teach the hunter the art to strike his game. So he, too, dedicates to her the firstfruits of his chase, heads and feet of boars and stags, and hangs them in her honour on trees or on her temple. From hunting the stag she got her name " Elaphebolos," or "Stag-striker," whence also the month of Artemis at Athens got its name.

The Greeks, however, have not been the only people to represent warlike ability in a maiden. Races dwelling to the north of Greece also had tales to tell of such masculine virgins, who found pleasure in the chase and war alone. These were the tribe of Amazons. When the Greeks came to hear of them, they made them into companions of Artemis and fellow-hunters. And the similarity between her and the Amazons was indeed great enough. Homer calls the whole race of Amazons "hostile to men," for they were wholly engaged in bloody wars. They formed a state, composed solely of females, where in later days lay the kingdom of Pontos on the south coast of the Black Sea, and were not allowed to live in cities, but scattered about. Hence they made their onslaught on the states of Asia Minor and Greece; for they lived in unceasing hostility against the members of well-ordered communities. They had already been at war with King Priam of Troy, and near Troy was a hill pointed out as the tomb of the swift Amazon Myrine. The Amazons were said, indeed, to have made an inroad as far as Attika, where, in the market-place of Athens, they had a fight with King Theseus, in which their queen fell. But, among other heroes of the myth, it was specially Herakles who undertook an expedition against the land of the Amazons, in order to fetch the girdle of their queen Hippolyte; and he killed her on this occasion. When, however, we read in Homer that the hero Bellerophon, riding in the air on his horse Pegasos, warred against the Amazons in Asia, then one is tempted to believe that in the earliest times men conceived of these Amazons also as riding through the air like Valkyries, the Battle-maidens of the Teuton. Artists, in fact, represented the Amazons sometimes on foot, sometimes on horseback. Peculiar, however, and differing from Greek ideas as to dress, were the close-fitting trousers of dappled skins, such as the peoples of the North wore, and the Phrygian leather cap. Their weapons were, for

the most part, the light crescent-shaped shield called
" Pelta," the javelin, an axe with a spike, or the double-
axe, the Scythian bow, and the quiver hanging on the
left side. With all this war-
like equipment, however, the
Amazons, like Artemis, are
distinguished by great beauty.
Achilles was moved by the
beauty of Penthesileia, the Amazon wounded by him to death,
as she sank dying in his arms.
But artists, in order to express
this beauty still more clearly,
often represented Amazons, not
in battle, but in an attitude of
repose, as wearied with fierce
warfare. Thus the renowned
sculptor Polykleitos made a
statue of an Amazon for the
sanctuary of Artemis at Ephesos; faint and weary the
Amazon lays one arm above
her head, and only the spur on
the left foot suggests still the
warlike maiden (see Fig. 23).
That sanctuary at Ephesos
was fabled to have been
founded by Amazons, and
they were said to have per-

FIG. 23.—AMAZON RESTING.
Old Museum, Berlin.

formed the first choral dance in honour of Artemis;
so closely united did the Greeks think Artemis and
the Amazons. Therefore Hippolytos, the favourite of

Artemis, was the reputed son of the queen of the
Amazons, Antiope, and of Theseus; and when artists
represented Artemis they often equipped her, like the
Amazons, with hunting-boots and short, tucked-up
frock.

4. ARTEMIS, APOLLO'S SISTER, AND THE GODDESS OF THE MOON.

The huntress Artemis, however, had also a kindly
look. "When," says an ancient hymn, "Artemis has
gladdened herself with the chase, she loosens her bow-
string, and goes to the great temple of her loved brother
Apollo, in rich Delphi, and prepares to lead the circling
dance of the Muses and the Graces; but they raise
their divine voices and praise Leto, in that she could
claim as her children such a noble pair."[1]

In fact the goddess, in the glow of youth, beauty,
and health, appeared a female counterpart of Apollo,
"the Helper," and might well be accounted his sister.
So Artemis and Apollo were looked upon as children
of one mother, Leto (see p. 110); and, as with almost
all other children of deities, Zeus was declared to be
their father. On Ortygia, the island near Syracuse,
under which name some, indeed, understood the island
Delos, Artemis first saw the light, and the brightness
that filled the earth on the birth of Apollo (see p. 110)
beamed also on his sister. Henceforth Apollo, Artemis,
and Leto were united, and in the temple of Apollo at
Delphi his sister and his mother also had a place.
Apparently Apollo and Artemis were worshipped

---

[1] *Homeric Hymn* [to Artemis], xxvi., 11-20.

together in several temples. Both fought before Troy
on the side of the Trojans, both had a sanctuary in
common on the citadel of Troy, and the wounded
Aineias was handed over by his rescuer, Apollo, god of
healing, to Artemis and Leto to be cured.

This Artemis, however, the sister of the Light-god
Apollo, not only externally took part in these honours,
but special attributes of Apollo were transferred to
Artemis. As he is not only the healing god, but the
arrow that flies from his silver bow also gives a stroke
of death, so death-bringing power was seen in the bow
and arrows of Artemis ; and thus Artemis became a
goddess of death that snatches people away. Just as
Apollo gently and swiftly lays low the young men with
his darts that strike from afar, so Artemis slays the
women and maidens; and Penelope wished that the
divine maiden Artemis would send her a gentle death.
Also the bride abandoned by Theseus, Ariadne, the
daughter of King Minos of Crete, fell by the hand of
Artemis ; and so again her arrows slew the daughters
of the proud Niobe, because she had boastfully glorified herself against Leto on account of the number of
her children.

Finally, however, Artemis became still more similar
to her brother Apollo in this, that she was regarded as
ruler of the moonlight, as in the case of Apollo men
thought of the distributer of the light of day. For
the worship of a special moon-goddess appears to have
been early abandoned in Greece, and whatever was
known of such a being was later ascribed to Artemis,
or other females of heroic legend, as Helene or Io.
Since Apollo was the pure god of light, Artemis also

became the pure chaste virgin of the moonlight. Now artists often placed in her hand the torch as well as the bow and arrows, and made her step forward in long robe, not in her short hunting-dress (see Fig. 24).

Such a moon-goddess Artemis, with the appellation Mounychia, was, for example, worshipped on the small peninsula of Peiraieus, attached to the mainland of Attica. Probably she had her name from the place Mounychia that was there. In her honour were established races with torches, and during the full moon cakes garnished with lights were offered to her. Since, however, the great harbour of Athens also was situated on this peninsula, and a

FIG. 24.—ARTEMIS.
Statue in the Vatican Museum, Rome.

lively traffic of foreigners resulted in settlements of aliens, it happened that the Thracians who dwelt here brought with them also Bendis, their deity of hunting and the moon; and this deity was soon amalgamated with the Grecian Artemis. This Artemis Bendis was honoured with torch-races on horseback.

Lastly, Artemis has had to allow herself to be blended with another deity essentially foreign, who was glorified as queen of the three kingdoms of Earth, Air, and Water. In air she ruled as goddess of the moon, and as such the Greeks

FIG. 25.—HEKATE.
Marble Group in the Museum of the Capitol, Rome.

called her by the old name of the moon-goddess Hekate, or the distant one. Since this moon-goddess was thought to be accompanied by dogs, it was not out of the way to interchange her with the hunting-goddess Artemis, who was equally accompanied by dogs; besides, the name Hekate reminded people of Apollo Hekatebolos (the "Far-striker"). When, however, it was wished to explain the three figures of such a representation of Hekate as is seen in Fig. 25, one of them was called the Moon-goddess Hekate or Selene ("Moon"), another Artemis, and the third the mistress of the lower world, Persephone. The power of the moon, however, appears at all times enigmatic and mysterious; and especially as the season of night is that of magic apparitions and of spectres, people understood by Artemis Hekate, the goddess of all sinister enchantment. The Romans, who at a later time became acquainted with this goddess, are said to have called her on this account *Trivia*, or goddess of the three cross-roads, because such a spot, above all others, was haunted by the midnight spectre.

(B) DIANA.

1. DIANA, THE GODDESS OF THE GROVE, AND PROTECTRESS OF THE PLEBEIANS.

Exactly as the Greeks in the earliest times had honoured in their Artemis the fosterer of budding nature and of beasts, but also the dispenser of the moonlight, so an ancient stock of the Italian people worshipped a goddess of nature, of the verdant grove, the well-watered valleys, but also of beasts and men. This goddess was named Diana, consequently almost exactly as the spouse of Zeus of Dodona, Dione. Men loved to fancy her as sojourning in the lonely forest; and in groves, too, were found her oldest sanctuaries. One of these stood on the cool slope of Algidus, not far from the later Tusculum, where distinguished Romans were fain to seek refreshment during the sultry season of the year; another near the noble mountain tarn of Nemi[1] that was styled "Diana's mirror," some three miles from Aricia, on the Alban Mount. From this sanctuary Diana derived her surname *Nemorensis* ("Diana of the grove"). Close to Rome, too, on the Aventine, was a most ancient temple of this goddess of the grove. For the Aventine also originally, before it was incorporated with the city of Rome, was quite clothed with forest. It is even asserted that the archaic image of Diana that stood here was fashioned closely on the model of the Ephesian Artemis; like her, then, Diana must have been worshipped as giver of fertility and guardian of wild beasts. But because she, as a nurturing Earth-goddess, gave increase and growth to all, cows were offered her in sacrifice. A very ancient pair of cow's horns was hung up in the vestibule of the later temple on the Aventine, and this gave rise to the following statement.

Once upon a time a Sabine was desirous of sacrificing to Diana on the Aventine the finest cow of his herd, since seers had assured him that if he performed this sacrifice he would become ruler of the state. But the crafty priest at Rome pointed out to the honest Sabine that he should first cleanse his hands for this sacrifice with water from the Tiber. While, then, the man went off to wash, the Roman offered the beast as a sacrifice to Diana.

[1] Connected with *nemus* = grove.

In fact, the Romans had the superiority over the Sabines, and that was what was to be pointed out through this story. When, however, one race conquers another, it puts the deities of the conquered also in a position of inferiority. And this was the case with Diana. She remained the principal goddess of the subordinate inhabitants of the state, the Plebeians, and, indeed, of the slaves, and might, in all probability, meet with no great regard among the nobility. In very early times, however, she must have been looked upon with the utmost awe. Those were the times when it was still sought to conciliate and win over the mighty goddess of the grove by human sacrifice. From those times comes also the tale of her love for Virbius, god of the grove and the chase. Virbius dies, indeed, when the leaves of the forest wither ; but the love of Diana, the goddess of life and light, raises him again from death, so that he can serve her again as priest. Hence originates the usage that a priest of Diana of Aricia (and he, too, was called *Rex Nemorensis*, or king of the grove) was always a runaway slave. This man had, as token of challenge, to break off a bough from the grove of Diana, and fight to the death with the "king of the grove." This was a substitute for human sacrifice offered to the goddess. The victor on each occasion retained or succeeded to the sovereignty of the grove, and exercised the priestly office till the like fate of a challenge to combat met him.

Scarcely had the Greeks become acquainted with this idea, when they believed they had found again the darling of Greek Artemis, the chaste huntsman Hippo-ytos. But Hippolytos had lost his life through the treachery of his frail stepmother, Phaidra. She had falsely accused him to her husband Theseus, who had implored his father, the sea-god Poseidon (see p. 49), to punish his son. Thereupon the god sent a sea-monster out of the waves, as Hippolytos was driving along the shore, and his horses, terrified at it, became restive, and destroyed him. To this tale the poets added that Asklepios, god of healing, had brought Hippolytos to life again, and that he was carried to Aricia to the nymph Egeria, nurtured and tended, and, under the name of Virbius, appointed priest of Diana. The Romans were actually weak enough to feel flattered by this Greek invention. They believed that Virbius was the same as Hippolytos, and the poet Vergil even has to tell of a son of Virbius and the nymph Aricia, who followed King Turnus to the field against Aeneas :—

> "The son of fam'd Hippolytus was there,
> Fam'd as his sire, and as his mother fair;
> Whom in Egerian groves Aricia bore,
> And nurs'd his youth along the marshy shore,
> Where great Diana's peaceful altars flame
> In fruitful fields; and Virbius was his name.
>
> *   *   *   *   *   *
>
> " But Trivia kept in sacred shades, alone,
> Her care, Hippolytus, to fate unknown,
> And call'd him Virbius in th' Egerian grove;
> Where then he liv'd obscure, but safe from Jove.
> For this, from Trivia's temple and her wood,
> Are coursers driven, who shed their master's blood,
> Affrighted by the monsters of the flood;
> His son, the second Virbius, yet retain'd
> His father's art, and warrior steeds he rein'd." [1]

In fact, there was a law that horses might not enter

---

[1] *Æneid*, vii., 761-64, 774-82, Dryden's translation.

the grove of Diana of Aricia. The reason, however, for this was, no doubt, that horses were favourite animals with those of knightly rank, while the service of Diana had to be a prerogative of the Plebeians. At Rome especially was Diana regarded as the protecting deity of the Plebeians. The sanctuary on the Aventine formed, at an earlier period, the central point at which the old Latin League assembled, before Rome exercised the sole supremacy. The temple, too, was held to be a building of the popular King Servius Tullius, whose mother, indeed, had been a slave. When, therefore, the old Latin League was dissolved, and the Aventine came into the possession of the state, that district was divided among the Plebeians. After this both Plebeians and slaves celebrated the foundation festival of the temple with special delight. All fugitive slaves were under the protection of Diana, and were called *cervi*, or "stags," for the beasts of the forest were also under her protection.

2. DIANA, THE SISTER OF APOLLO, AND PROTECTRESS OF THE ROMAN STATE.

When, in the year 399 before Christ, a place was found for the Greek Apollo among the Roman national deities, the cult of his divine sister Artemis also was introduced, and she received the appellation of Diana. Now was Diana honoured in the same fashion as Apollo; was provided in B.C. 179 with a new temple in Rome, built in Grecian style; and at public functions, whether of humiliation or thanksgiving, her image, just like that of Apollo, was publicly exhibited on a cushioned sofa (see p. 124). Whatever was known of the Greek Artemis was recounted of Diana; nay, the Greeks themselves were never tired of discovering similarities between the two. For example, since they were aware that origi-nally human beings were sacrificed in the worship of Diana of Aricia, they recalled to mind the equally bloody worship of the Tauric Artemis (see p. 129), and said that Orestes had brought her ancient image from Tauris by way of Rhe-gion to Aricia. Nay, the Romans enter-tained a decided belief that they possessed the bones of Orestes at Aricia, and at a later time had them dug up and buried in the Roman Forum. For it was thought that in the bones of Orestes they possessed a

Fig. 26.—DIANA OF GABII.
In the Glyptothek, Munich.

pledge for the protection of the Roman state at the hands of Diana.

When, therefore, the commencement of a new age

was celebrated in honour of Apollo with especial pomp, Diana, also, was remembered, and the poet Horace, in his famous ode composed for the festival [1] (see p. 127), could pray that, together with Phœbus Apollo, "Diana, ruler of the woods, bright ornament of heaven," might no less guard with her power the Roman state, and, above all, take under her protection the newborn infant, that a new generation might grow up as a blessing to the fatherland. For newborn children were believed to be under the protection of Diana, just as much as the beasts of the forest; and this power over the life of nature was preserved to the Roman Diana, whatever trouble the poets might take to keep it in the background through the myths of the Greek Artemis, and the confusion with the Moon-goddess Luna, or the goddess of enchantment Hekate, or Trivia (see p. 142).

Also in a statue of Diana from Gabii, in Latium (Fig. 26),—a statue, indeed, of a somewhat late period, —we see the goddess represented as holding with her right hand the fore-feet of a fawn that has sought refuge beside her, and with her left a bow. The belt supporting her quiver is ornamented with a hunting-scene, and her head-dress with roe-bucks, between which stand candelabra, as an indication that the guardian of the forest also, as moon-goddess, sends the light of the night.

---

[1] *Carmen Sæculare*, 1 and 2.

CHAPTER IX.

HEPHAISTOS—VOLCANUS.

(A) HEPHAISTOS.

1. Hephaistos, God of Fire; Hephaistos Cast Forth from Olympos; his Forges and Metal-work; his Return to Olympos.

THE characteristic features of Hephaistos as deity of fire are clearly traced in the *Iliad*, and little in the way of myth was left to be added by later writers. Hence we may infer the great antiquity of his worship; and it should be remarked that the personality of the fire-god of the Romans (and indeed of other Aryan races) presents no essential difference.

Of all the gods of the Hellenic Pantheon, Hephaistos, however, remained most intimately connected with the element of which he was originally the type, and this, too, in the language of ordinary life as well as in poetry.

Hephaistos was son of Hera; his father, according to Homer, being Zeus. Interfering in a family quarrel on behalf of his mother, whom Zeus had suspended from Olympos by a golden chain, he was hurled from heaven, and fell on the island of Lemnos. Hence the lameness which was his permanent characteristic, though in Homer we find him lame from his birth. This fall illustrates his connection with the lightning that descends from heaven. In Lemnos he established forges. It was, however, in Olympos, according to Homeric tradition, that he made impenetrable armour for heroes, as for Achilles ; constructed mechanical prodigies, as golden handmaids endowed with speech ; and the gold and silver dogs that guarded the palace of Alkinoos. We see him beside his anvil when Thetis, who had befriended him in misfortune, comes to beg new armour for Achilles :—

"He said, and from the anvil rose, limping, a huge bulk, but under him his slender legs moved nimbly. The bellows he set away from the fire, and gathered all his gear wherewith he worked into a silver chest ; and with a sponge he wiped his face and hands, and sturdy neck and shaggy breast, and did on his doublet, and took a stout staff, and went forth limping ; but there were handmaidens of gold that moved to help their lord, the semblance of living maids. In them is understanding at their hearts, in them are voice and strength, and they have skill of the immortal gods."[1]

Graphic indeed is this description of the workman-god, but how different from the lithe beauty of an Apollo or a Hermes !

Later poets represented Hephaistos as forging beneath Ætna the thunderbolts of Zeus, with the help of the Kyklopes, each of whom had a single eye placed in the middle of his forehead.

These Kyklopes did not confine their attention to metallurgy, for they were said to have built the walls of Tiryns, as well as other structures composed of

---

[1] *Iliad*, xviii., 410-20, translated by Lang, Leaf, and Myers.

huge irregular blocks of stone, and belonging to the unknown past.

According to one legend it was Hera who, disgusted with her son's deformity, threw him out of heaven. It was in revenge for this that he sent her the present of the magic throne (see p. 34) ; and in order to extricate

Fig. 27.—Return of Hephaistos to Olympos
Vase-painting, Munich.

her from its clutches, its inventor had to be recalled to Olympos. This was effected by Dionysos, who conveyed him on a mule, as depicted on the François vase ; or by help of one of his Satyrs, as in Fig. 27.

2. Relation of Hephaistos to other Deities.

In an age of continual warfare the armourer held an important position ; the few works of art in metal, too, that had survived the Dorian immigration were attributed by their unskilled admirers to the hand of Hephaistos; both gods and men were equally dependent on his cunning hand.

At the opening of the *Iliad* we find him re-established in friendly relations with both his parents; and when a serious rupture between them seems imminent, he steps in and with a few sensible words restores harmony :—

"Then Hephaistos, the famed craftsman, began to make harangue among them, to do kindness to his dear mother, white-armed Hera : 'Verily this will be a sorry matter, neither any more endurable, if ye twain thus fight for mortals' sakes, and bring wrangling among the gods ; neither will there any more be joy of the goodly feast, seeing that evil triumpheth. So I give counsel to my mother, though herself is wise, to do kindness to our dear father Zeus, that our father upbraid us not again and cast the banquet in confusion. What if the Olympian, the lord of lightning, will to dash us from our seats ! for he is strongest far. Nay, approach thou him with gentle words, then will the Olympian forthwith be gracious unto us.' So speaking he rose up and set in his dear mother's hand the double cup, and spake to her : 'Be of good courage, mother mine, and endure, though thou art vexed, lest I behold thee, that art so dear, chastised before mine eyes, and then shall I not be able for all my sorrow to save thee ; for the Olympian is a hard foe to face.' "[1]

Hobbling about he pours out nectar for the assembled gods, and puts all in a good humour by that

[1] *Iliad*, i., 571-89, translated by Lang, Leaf, and Myers.

comic vein that underlies the whole conception of this
somewhat undignified Olympian. Such usefulness and
popularity secured him the hand of Aphrodite, but
not the heart; and he
learned by bitter ex-
perience the dangers
of marrying a great
lady. His relations
to Athena and Erich-
thonios will be de-
scribed in the next
chapter. In common
with her he was hon-
oured as the represen-
tative of the highest
m e c h a n i c a l s k i l l.
Athens was the home
of the arts, and in no
other city did Heph-
aistos meet with such
honour. He had a
place close to Athena
on the eastern frieze
of the Parthenon, and
no god was more
popular among the
craftsmen of the lower
town. It seems, how-
ever, that a time

FIG. 28.—HEPHAISTOS AS ARTISAN.
Bronze statuette, London.

came when the more aristocratic Athenians grew a
little ashamed of the plebeian smoke-begrimed deity,
and we do not find him often represented in works of

art. When he does occur he is generally bearded, dressed in short garment and leather cap, and armed with pincers or other implements of his trade (see Fig. 28), with which he fought the giants. As an exception he appears as a comely youth free from all deformity on the kylix from Nola, formerly in the Bale collection, now in the Third Vase Room at the British Museum.

3. HEPHAISTOS AND PANDORA; PROMETHEUS; EPIMETHEUS.

The subject of this kylix is Pandora (*i.e.*, "the all-gifted one"), or, as she is here called, Ainesidora, created by Athena and Hephaistos. She was the first woman, and was designed by Zeus to bring misfortune on Prometheus, who had stolen fire from heaven to animate figures of clay. While she received beauty from Aphrodite, and similar gifts from other deities, Zeus gave her a box to present to her husband. Mistrusting the gods, Prometheus (Forethought) declined to receive Pandora, and sent her to his brother Epimetheus (Afterthought), who married her, and opened the box, from which flew out all sorts of evils and diseases, Hope alone remaining at the bottom.

Prometheus, however, did not escape scot-free, for Zeus commanded Hephaistos to fasten him on the Caucasus, where an eagle continually gnawed his liver, till Herakles shot the bird and set Prometheus free.

At Athens Prometheus was the object of special honour ; for him the torch-race was celebrated as for

Hephaistos; and he was regarded, like Athena and Hephaistos, as a pioneer in civilization and one of the greatest benefactors of mankind. As connected with the Titans he was hostile to the Olympian gods, and especially Zeus, who pursued him with vindictive cruelty, a cruelty met by disdainful scorn. Prometheus was the Irreconcilable of classical mythology. He may have been the fire-god of a subject race.

4. THE KABEIROI.

Closely connected, too, with Lemnos were the Kabeiroi, who also had sanctuaries in Samothrace and elsewhere. Recent discoveries in the neighbourhood of Thebes have shown that they were father and son (Pais). Their worship, though widespread and existing in an undercurrent till the latest times, has left comparatively little trace in literature or art. They seem to have been spirits of subterranean fire, and to have been connected with Dionysos as well as with Hephaistos. The friendly relations of the god of the grape with Hephaistos and his crew are illustrated by the excellent wine produced by volcanic soil; and Lemnos, as befits a seat of the fire-god's worship, bears the strongest traces of volcanic action.

(B) VOLCANUS OR VULCANUS.

VOLCANUS, GOD OF FIRE.

To a people at once so practical and so warlike as the Romans, a deity who could secure for them both well-tempered weapons and well-baked pottery must always have been a personage of the highest importance. It has already been remarked (p. 149) that his worship was of such antiquity as to be practically the same throughout the various branches of the Aryan stock. As in the case of the Greek Hephaistos, the connection of the god with the element over which he presided was so close that the one often stands for the other. Thus Horace uses "*dilapso Volcano*" to express the idea of *fire* falling out.

Besides his beneficial powers, Volcanus was responsible for the terrible conflagrations that too often spread through the ill-built streets of Rome, and on this account there was need to propitiate him. At the *Volcanalia*, a festival celebrated on August 23rd, fish were thrown into the fire, as a substitute for the human sacrifices originally offered to the god.

CHAPTER X.

ATHENA—MINERVA.

(A) ATHENA.

1. Birth of Athena.

Second in interest to none of the Olympian circle is Athena, she who inspired alike Homeric song and Attic art. Of all deities she is most Hellenic, and has least to do with the East.

There was an ancient legend that Zeus had devoured his wife Metis, fearing her offspring would be greater than himself. In due time, however, he called in the aid of Prometheus (or, as others told, Hephaistos), and when his head was struck with an axe Athena leapt forth already armed.

Thus sprung in full panoply from the brain of Zeus, she knew no mother's care, and well might lack the more tender feelings distinctive of the gentler sex. Free, too, was she from a woman's frailties, and the softer passions of the female heart. Even the cold severity of Artemis might melt before the beauty of Endymion, but from Athena's keen grey eye no love glance ever stole. A few favoured heroes, indeed, were nerved to their toilsome tasks by her stern counsel and encouragement. She stands beside Perseus as he strikes off the Gorgon's head ;[1] the black-figured vases show her as the ever-present supporter of Herakles in his labours.   In Theseus she shows a like interest.   It is Athena that prepares the sail for the Argo.[2]   In the *Iliad* she seizes Achilles by the hair to check his mad onslaught on Agamemnon ; in the *Odyssey* she secures to its hero Odysseus a return to his native land, and supports his son Telemachos against the overweening suitors.   Nay, a whole race, as the Ionians, and, above all, the men of Athens, her namesake, may be the object of her watchful care.   As her attributes we find on the coins of Athens the owl, bird of wisdom, and her own olive branch.   Her sacred serpent wreathed its coils beside her statue in the Parthenon ; and on the great frieze from Pergamon it takes an active part against the enemy of its mistress.

2. Athena as a Warlike Goddess ; Athena as a Goddess of Storm.

The goddess of wisdom, however, was merged in the deity of battle.   She was, above all, warlike, and wore the ægis as daughter of the all-powerful sire (Fig. 29). With ægis, helmet, shield, and spear she stood imaged by Pheidias in bronze on the rock of the Acropolis, the Promachos to be seen afar of friend and foe.   Thus did Athena arm herself when she went forth to fight, and urged on the hero Diomede to battle against the god of war himself.

"And Athena, daughter of ægis-bearing Zeus, cast

---

[1] As on the metope from Selinous.
[2] As on the terra-cotta frieze in the British Museum.

down at her father's threshold her woven vesture, many-coloured, that herself had wrought and her hands had fashioned, and put on her the tunic of Zeus the

cloud-gatherer, and arrayed her in her armour for dolorous battle. About her shoulders cast she the tasselled ægis terrible, whereon is Panic as a crown all round about, and Strife is therein, and Valour, and horrible Onslaught withal, and therein is the dreadful monster's Gorgon head, dreadful and grim, portent of ægis-bearing Zeus. Upon her head set she the two-crested golden helm with fourfold plate, bedecked with[1] menat-arms of a hundred cities. Upon the flaming chariot set she her foot, and grasped her heavy spear, great and stout, wherewith she vanquisheth the ranks of men, even of heroes with whom she of the awful sire is wroth."[2]

FIG. 29.—ATHENA.

Statue in the Louvre, Paris.

The birth of Athena from the brain of Zeus has been explained as a reference to

[1] Others render this "*fitting*," *i.e.*, large enough for a hundred men.
[2] *Iliad*, v., 733-47, translated by Lang, Leaf, and Myers.

the lightning bursting from the thunder-cloud; and Roscher[1] compares her with the Teutonic Valkyre, as originally a goddess of the storm-cloud and the lightning that springs from it.

Thus Homer says with regard to Diomedes, "She kindled on his helmet and his shield unresting fire, like to a star of summer that most brightly shines after bathing in Ocean."[2] This idea of the lightning may account for the epithet Glaukopis, or "goddess of the gleaming eye," often applied to Athena.

The place of her birth was supposed by some to be the river Triton; hence the epithet Tritogeneia, or Tritogenes, as in the twenty-seventh Homeric hymn.

As a war-goddess Athena was distinguished from the savage, half-civilized Ares, who had more of the Thracian about him than of the Greek. She was credited with the invention of the trumpet and of the flute, both martial instruments. She, too, introduced the war-horse with the chariot. She taught Erechtheus to harness his team; and it was by her that Pegasos was bridled for Bellerophon. Hence she was with good reason surnamed Hippia.

The ship-of-war, too, was said to have originated in the Argo designed by Athena; and it was Athena that taught Epeios to frame the wooden horse at Troy.

3. Athena in Relation to Hephaistos and Erichthonios.

Besides this brilliant conception of a virgin goddess (*Parthenos*), the warlike supporter of heroes, there

---

[1] *Lexikon*, p. 675.   [2] *Iliad*, v., 4-6. The Dog-star (Seirios) is meant.

lingered here and there old traditions of an Athena wedded to Hephaistos and presiding over industrial arts. There was such a cult at Athens in connection with the temple of Hephaistos (probably the so-called "Theseion"[1]) that stood on the hill called Kolonos Agoraios. Here, according to Pausanias (i., 14, 6), was an image of Athena beside that of the god, a union which that writer connects with the account of the birth of Erichthonios. This legend is given by Apollodoros, who relates that Hephaistos, deserted by his wife Aphrodite, vainly desired Athena to replace her.[2] These tales may have pleased the older Athenians, as the descendants of Erichthonios and Hephaistos ;[3] but the aristocratic worshippers on the Acropolis would not hear of such a helpmate for their virgin goddess. Their views as to Erichthonios are thus formulated in the *Ion* of Euripides (vv. 269, 270), no respecter of orthodox tradition :—

" Did Athena indeed raise him up from earth ? "

"Yes, into her virgin arms ; she was not his mother."

Such is the scene depicted in the Athenian terra-cotta *emblema*, of the fifth century, at Berlin, where the figure of Athena receiving Erichthonios from Gaia is balanced by that of Kekrops, with his right forefinger raised towards his lip in token of silence. In the days of Pausanias, Hephaistos and Gaia were said to be the parents of Erichthonios.

---

[1] See Miss Harrison's *Mythology and Monuments of Athens*, pp. 113-20.

[2] A terra-cotta pinax from Athens (No. 2,759), in the Berlin Antiquarium, has been thought to refer to this.

[3] *Cf.* Æschylus, *Eumenides*, 13.

4. Worship of Athena beyond Attica.

Lover of Athens as she was, Athena was not without honour beyond the Ionian borders. At Sparta
she was housed in a temple decorated with bronze,
and is thus mentioned with Apollo of Amyklai and
the Tyndaridai in the closing lines of the *Lysistrata*.
In both pediments of the great temple in Aigina she
presided over the triumphs of heroes belonging to
the Achæan stock. At Tegea her temple was rebuilt
and adorned by Skopas, a marble temple among
the most famous in the Peloponnesos.[1] At Corinth
she shared the homage of a cosmopolitan commercial
centre with Poseidon, a god of foreign extraction.
This partnership, however, was commemorated on the
Acropolis of Athens itself both in the Erechtheion
and the western pediment of the Parthenon. At
Pergamon the cult of Athena was especially prominent,
but this was natural in the capital of a dynasty eager
to connect itself with the glories of Athens.

Here she held a place parallel to that of Zeus
himself on the great frieze that surrounded the platform
supporting his altar.

5. Athena with the Giants, and the Gorgon Medusa.

In the struggle between gods and giants (see p. 19),
which formed the subject of this frieze, Athena took a

---

[1] *Pausanias*, viii., 45, 5. The statement of Pausanias that it was
the largest in the Peloponnesos is not true. See Murray, *History of
Greek Sculpture*, p. 290.

leading part, a subject embroidered by the maidens of
Athens on the *peplos*, or shawl, presented to her every
year at the *Panathenaia*. She is depicted on countless
black-figured vases as piercing with her spear a
prostrate or falling giant, usually identified as Pallas
or as Enkelados, who, when Sicily was cast upon him,
still breathed fire through Ætna. On the Pergamene
frieze she grasps by the hair a youthful giant, while
Nike hastes to place on her brow the victor's wreath.
At other times Nike is merged in
the greater goddess, and appears
merely a special phase of Athena
herself.

FIG. 30.—HEAD OF
ATHENA PARTHENOS.
From a gem of
Aspasios, at Vienna.

The idea of the Gorgon is closely
associated with Athena in her warlike capacity, and as protectress of
Athens (Polias and Promachos).
Athena by her presence encourages
Perseus to slay Medusa, and wears
the Gorgon's head in the centre of
her ægis. Nay, a gem from Cyprus
in the British Museum shows her
not only equipped with the Gorgon's
head as a helmet, but wearing the
monster's wings, of the archaic
rounded shape, as the Muses are said to have crowned
themselves with feathers plucked from their defeated
rivals, the Sirens. Considering the common tie of
intellectual pre-eminence, it is strange that Athena
should not till Roman times have appeared on works
of art united with Apollo and the Muses.

The ægis, though in Homer the special possession

of Zeus (see p. 7), is in art almost always seen on Athena. Originally a skin mantle with a fringe of writhing snakes, it is represented later as a breastplate with the Gorgon's head in the centre (see Pl. IV. and Figs. 29 and 30). When contending with Enkelados, Athena wears the ægis on her left arm as a shield.

6. ATHENA AS PATRONESS OF ATHENS AND ATTICA.

As the champion of Athens the goddess wore helmet and shield, while the ægis and its Gorgon's head clothed her breast, and her right hand brandished a mighty spear. Thus fully armed she is depicted on the vases which, filled with oil from the sacred olive trees, formed the prizes at the Panathenaic festival. So, too, we see her in archaic statuettes of bronze, and so she appeared in those still earlier wooden statues (*xoana*),—objects of special devotion, as fallen from heaven itself and wrought by no ordinary hand. *Palladia* is the name given to such images of the spear-brandishing Pallas Athena; and on their preservation depended, as men thought, the safety of the cities that possessed them. Thus the fall of Troy soon followed on the stealing of its Palladion by the Greek heroes Diomedes and Odysseus.

The chryselephantine (*i.e.*, gold and ivory) statue of Athena Parthenos by Pheidias, though fully armed, had the shield resting on the ground; and on a festive occasion, as at the Panathenaia, the goddess might well lay aside her helmet. So we see her on the east frieze of the Parthenon bareheaded, and with the ægis crumpled up upon her knee.

IV. ATHENA.

Marble Bust at Glienicke, near Potsdam.

In still milder mood Athena appears as the protector of the produce of the earth, typified by Erichthonios, whom she entrusted to the three daughters of King Kekrops, Aglauros, Herse, and Pandrosos, names connected with the dew that nourishes the seedlings. Hidden in a basket, as the seed is hidden in the earth, Erichthonios was left to these maidens, with strict injunctions that they should not examine what was entrusted to their care. Pandrosos obeyed; the others gave way to curiosity, and beheld, not only a child, but a serpent. Seized with frenzy, they cast themselves headlong from the Acropolis.

7. Athena and the Olive; Athena, Goddess of Wisdom and of the Arts.

Most suited to the soil of Attica was the olive; hence the especial care of her tutelary goddess. The *moriai*, or sacred olive trees, that yielded the oil for Panathenaic prizes (see p. 164), were offshoots of the ancient stock enshrined within the Erechtheion, originally the abode of Erechtheus, one of Attica's earliest mythic rulers, but shared by his patroness Athena, surnamed Polias, as guardian of the city (*polis*). The olive, nursling of the husbandman when free from war's alarms, became the symbol of peace; peaceful, too, was Athena Ergane when presiding over works of woman's skill. Not weaving and embroidery alone, however, were objects of her care. It was she who lent a helping hand to heroes when engaged in some intricate work, or to those who, like Odysseus, excelled in the higher arts of deliberation, counsel, and debate.

(B) MINERVA.

A Thunder-wielding Deity of Ancient Italy; the Roman Minerva, Goddess of Arts.

The name Minerva or Menerva is, as Preller re-marks,[1] to be traced to the stem of *mens* (mind), and suggests the ideas of divine intelligence, thought, and inventive power. It appears on Etruscan mirrors as Menrfa, or in similar forms. The Etruscan Menrfa, sometimes represented with wings, wielded the thunder-bolt, and as a warlike deity resembled the Athena of the Greeks, though not credited with the stern asceticism of that virgin goddess.

Among the Romans Minerva, like Juno, shared the temple of the Capitoline Jove. Besides the Capitol, other hills were selected for the site of her sanctuaries, as the Aventine and the Cœlian. This choice of high places for her worship points to the original connection of this thunder-goddess with the wilder forces of nature, amid peaks wrapped in cloud and storm.

Her great festival was the *Quinquatrus* or *Quin-quatria*, celebrated in March. Less important was the festival celebrated in June (*Quinquatrus Minores*), which was specially connected with the *tibicines*, or players on the flute. These artists were of more importance than might at first sight be supposed. At Rome every sacrifice (to say nothing of games and funerals) was accompanied by the sound of the flute, and without flute-players the superstitious Roman would have been in a pitiable condition. Once only,

---

[1] *Römische Mythologie*, 2nd ed., p. 258.

in 312 B.C., was an attempt made to check their excessive power. The innovating censor Appius Claudius Cæcus deprived them of their annual feast in the Capitol. The whole flute-playing fraternity, however, forthwith seceded to Tibur. A strike of flute-players involved a stoppage of sacrifices, and attempts at conciliation failed. Stratagem was resorted to ; a great feast was given to the recalcitrant performers, and when thoroughly intoxicated they were carried back to Rome in waggons. Carousing, as usual, was followed by repentance, and they consented to resume their functions on condition that their former privileges should be restored to them.

The flute was a warlike instrument, as was the *tuba* or trumpet, from which another of Minerva's festivals, the *Tubilustrium*, derived its title.

In the Rome of the Empire, however, her associations were more pacific. On the ruins of the temple in the Forum Transitorium, built at Rome by her votary Domitian, but completed by his successor Nerva, are still to be seen remains of the sculpture that portrayed at once Minerva's patronage of woman's work and her vengeance on Arachne, whose overweening folly had brought her into disastrous rivalry with the goddess. For Arachne having challenged Minerva to a trial of skill in weaving, the goddess struck her with a shuttle. Arachne hung herself, and was changed by Minerva into a spider.

The most sacred image of Minerva was the Palladium said to have been brought by Æneas in his flight from Troy. There was an ancient family at Rome, the Nautii, who claimed to have carried it from

Lavinium to Rome. Their ancestor Nautes, so ran the tale, had received it for Æneas from Diomed himself. It was kept, with other sacred objects on which Rome's safety hung, within the temple of Vesta, far removed from vulgar gaze. When this building was destroyed by fire, the holy image was borne off to a place of safety by L. Metellus, then Pontifex Maximus, or head of the Roman religion. He lost his eyesight in the effort, but was rewarded with the highest distinctions the Senate could bestow.

CHAPTER XI.

ARES—MARS.

(A) ARES.

ARES, GOD OF BATTLE.

OF the few children of Zeus who could claim Hera as their mother, the most important was Ares, god of battle, originally, like his fellow-Olympians, a nature-god. To this latter character, however, we find but scanty allusion in literature. Violence and great size are frequent characteristics of these vague nature-powers; and size is attributed to the Homeric Ares when he covers a couple of acres in his fall. Violent enough, and more than enough, was he to remind the Homeric student of the fierce northern blasts that started from his Thracian home. In sculpture we do not often come across an Ares of the old bearded type, as we do in the case of Hermes and other gods. Representations of Ares, indeed, of any kind, are by no means common. It might have been supposed that among a people so warlike as the Greeks the god of war would have been a universal favourite. Yet this was far from being the case. From Homer downwards, and not only through later philosophic or humanitarian innovations, the name of Ares was

169

associated with reprobation, not unmingled with contempt. There were two reasons for this. In the first place, he was a barbarian of Thracian origin, and to be a foreigner was a serious disqualification in Hellenic estimation. Aphrodite, indeed, and Poseidon came from beyond sea, but they came from the civilized settlements of the East and South; and even they, too, had occasionally to yield precedence to divinities of older Hellenic standing. Again, opposition was at first offered to the introduction of the novel cult of Dionysos; but the gifts of the wine-god would soon render him (like the goddess of love) universally acceptable, to say nothing of the strong support he received from the drama.

With Ares, on the other hand, there were no such pleasant associations; and he never became, so to say, domesticated among the Greeks. Sophokles speaks of him as the neighbour of the inhospitable Salmy-dessos, a place on the Euxine, near enough to the Bosporos to be the scene of many a wreck of a good ship bound for Greece. The pirates and professional wreckers of these Thracian coasts were only too well known to the Grecian sailor, and the Athenians were not unwilling to make game of a Thracian deity, such as he who talks bad Greek in the *Birds* of Aristophanes.

In the second place, Ares was utterly eclipsed by the martial prowess of Athena, the most blue-blooded of Hellenic deities. To such an extent is this carried, that we actually have him driven wounded and howling from a contest with Diomede and with his imperious sister, " who most is wont to bring him to grievous pains ; "[1] his mother Hera fully acquiescing. " Next Diomedes of the loud war-cry attacked with spear of bronze ; and Pallas Athene drave it home against Ares' nethermost belly, where his taslets were girt about him. There smote he him and wounded him, rending through his fair skin, and plucked forth the spear again. Then brazen Ares bellowed loud as nine thousand .warriors or ten thousand cry in battle as they join in strife and fray."[2] Hastening to Zeus he complains of Athena, how she urged on the son of Tydeus to wound first Aphrodite, then Ares himself ; adding, " Howbeit my swift feet bare me away ; else had I long endured anguish there amid the grisly heaps of dead, or else had lived strengthless from the smitings of the spear."[3]

Not much sympathy was to be got from Zeus :—

" Nay, thou renegade, sit not by me and whine. Most hateful to me art thou of all gods that dwell in Olympus ; thou ever lovest strife and wars and battles. Truly thy mother's spirit is intolerably unyielding, even Hera's ; her can I scarce rule with words. Therefore I deem that by her prompting thou art in this plight. Yet will I no longer endure to see thee in anguish ; mine offspring art thou, and to me thy mother bare thee. But wert thou born of any other god unto this violence, long ere this hadst thou been lower than the sons of heaven."[4]

This superiority of Athena was a superiority both

[1] *Iliad*, v., 766.
[2] *Ib.*, 855-61, translated by Lang, Leaf, and Myers.
[3] *Ib.*, 885-87.
[4] *Ib.*, 889-98.

mental and bodily. She takes Ares by the hand, and he submits quietly to be led from the battle. Again, he smites his thighs in his anger, and prepares to avenge his son in defiance of the will of Zeus.

"Thereby would a greater and more implacable wrath and anger have been caused between Zeus and the Immortals, had not Athene, in terror for the sake of all the gods, leaped out through the doorway, and left the throne whereon she sat, and taken from Ares' head the helmet, and the shield from his shoulders, and drawn the spear of bronze from his stalwart hand, and set it apart; and then with words she rebuked the impetuous Ares : 'Mad that thou art, and distraught of wit—this is thy bane! Verily thou hast ears and hearest not, and perished have thine understanding and thine awe. Hearest thou not what she saith, the white-armed goddess Hera, that even now is come from Olympian Zeus? Dost thou wish both thyself to fill up the measure of mischief and so return to Olympos ruefully, of necessity, and for all the other gods to sow the seed of a great wrong? For straightway will he leave the high-hearted Trojans and the Achaians, and to us will he come to make tumult in Olympos : and he will clutch us each in turn, the blameless with the guilty. Wherefore now again I bid thee to abate thine anger for thy son; for already many a man stronger than he, and more hardy of his hands, has fallen, or yet will fall; and a hard thing it is to save the lineage and offspring of all men.' So spake she, and made impetuous Ares sit down on his throne." [1]

[1] *Iliad.*, xv., 121-42.

Athena's physical superiority is equally pronounced when attacked by Ares, boasting that he will take revenge for the treatment he had received from her and Diomed.

"Thus saying, he smote on the dread tasselled ægis that not even the lightning of Zeus can overcome— thereon smote blood-stained Ares with his long spear. But she, giving back, grasped with stout hand a stone that lay upon the plain, black, rugged, huge, which men of old time set to be the landmark of a field; this hurled she, and smote impetuous Ares on the neck, and unstrung his limbs. Seven roods he covered in his fall, and soiled his hair with dust, and his armour rang upon him. And Pallas Athene laughed, and spake to him winged words exultingly: ' Fool, not even yet hast thou learnt how far better than thou I claim to be, that thus thou matchest thy might with mine.' "[1]

So Aphrodite led him away "groaning continually, for scarce gathered he his spirits back to him."

Nor was it from Athena alone that Ares experienced humiliation. Dione consoling her daughter Aphrodite says, "So suffered Ares, when Otos and stalwart Ephialtes, sons of Aloeus, bound him in a strong prison-house; yea, in a vessel of bronze lay he bound thirteen months. There might Ares, insatiate of battle, have perished, but that the step-mother of Aloeus' sons, fair Eeriboia, gave tidings to Hermes, and he stole away Ares, already pining; for the grievous prison-house was wearing him out."[2]

These Aloadai grew every year a cubit in breadth

---

[1] *Iliad.*, xxi., 400-411.   [2] *Ib.*, v., 385-91.

and a fathom in height; fortunately they were killed at an early age, when they were meditating piling Ossa on Olympos and Pelion on Ossa, in order to scale the heights of heaven.

Ares is thus addressed by Athena :—

"Ares, Ares, pest to mortals, thou slaughter-stained stormer of cities!"

If a pest to mortals, he was not always much more in favour with his immortal kinsfolk. When he wished to avenge on Herakles the death of his offspring Kyknos, Zeus had to separate his two sons by hurling his thunderbolt between them. Again, the ancients accounted for the name of the Athenian hill Areopagus by reference to the legend that Ares was put upon his trial there by Poseidon for the murder of Halirrhothios, son of the latter.

On the François vase his constant persecutor, Athena, looks down on him as he crouches in abject posture, and seems to be twitting him on the ill success of an attempt to secure by force the return of Hephaistos to Olympos (see p. 151). A humiliation of a less painful character is seen in the subjection of Ares to Aphrodite. Love has in all ages been the weak point of the warrior ; and this in the case of Ares exposed him to the derision of the other gods. The sculptor of the Ludovisi Ares has placed by his side a sportive Eros (Fig. 31).

It is only fair to state that a Homeric hymn represents Ares in a more favourable light. Still, as a rule, while his brother-Olympians took pleasure in the festivities and peaceful joys of mortals, Ares alone sat impatient of idleness, nursing his knee as

on the Parthenon frieze, an attitude similar to that
of the Ludovisi statue, and employed for Hektor in
the Shades by the great painter Polygnotos.

On the same eastern frieze of the Parthenon, Athena,
as a many-sided person, has laid aside her armour,

FIG. 31.—ARES WITH THE GOD OF LOVE.
Statue in the Ludovisi collection, Rome.

and sits quietly enjoying the scene, while Ares, devoid
of such versatility and intellectual resources, naturally
feels himself out of his element. At Thebes alone
of Greek cities was he really at home ; Harmonia, wife
of Kadmos, who founded Thebes, was his daughter.
Thebes seems to have been connected with Thrace.

His companions were Enyo, a war-goddess, Eris (Strife), Deimos (Dread), and Phobos (Terror), the last two being his sons.

(B) MARS.

1. Mars, a God of Nature; the Salii.

If the glory of Ares among the Greeks was intercepted by the warlike genius of Athena, the more peaceful conception of Minerva left the field clear for Mars, the Roman god of battle. His reputed union with Rhea Silvia had laid the foundation of the Julian race, and gave in due course to Rome the warlike glory of a Cæsar, the imperial power of an Augustus.

The first month of the old Roman year derived its name from Mars; and indications are not wanting that he was at an early period regarded as god of nature in general. Hence his association with the wolf and the woodpecker; hence he is invoked in the hymn of the Arval brethren.

His festival was celebrated on the first of March and several successive days by the twelve Salii, his priests, who had charge of the *ancilia*, or sacred shields, one of which had fallen from heaven, while the other eleven had been made exactly like it, to lessen the danger of its being stolen, for the safety of Rome depended on its preservation. These Salii traversed the city with dance and song, their exertions being rewarded by a banquet of proverbial luxury.

2. Mars, God of War.

It is, however, as god of war that we chiefly hear of Mars in historical times. His sacred spear was preserved in the Regia at Rome with the twelve *ancilia*. When he went forth to battle he was accompanied by Bellona, goddess of war, his sister, or, as some said, his wife. His ancient sanctuary stood in the plain that bore his name, the *Campus Martius*, the parade-ground of ancient Rome, now covered by the modern city.

"Father" Mars was no mere bloodthirsty brawler like the Greek Ares, but the patron saint, as it were, of the Roman people, and the father of Rome's founder, Romulus.

The poets of the Augustan and later ages, following the Greeks, made Venus the wife of Mars. Nor was this devoid of political meaning, for as Mars, through Romulus, was the founder of the Roman state, so Venus, through her son Æneas, was the ancestor of Cæsar and the emperors of the Julian house. The statues of both deities stood in the splendid temple of Mars Ultor, which commemorated the vengeance of Augustus on the murderers of his great uncle and adoptive father.

CHAPTER XII.

APHRODITE—VENUS.

(A) APHRODITE.

I. Aphrodite, the Goddess of Awakening Nature; Adonis.

Every Semitic tribe, save the Hebrews, had its goddess of the moon, exercising power at once over human fertility and (through the dew) over the fertility of plants.   Such was—

> " Astarte, Queen of Heaven, with crescent horns;
> To whose bright image nightly by the moon
> Sidonian virgins paid their vows and songs." [1]

Such, too, was Istar of Chaldæa and Assyria.   So Babylon had her Mylitta, Askalon her Derketo.   This moon-goddess, indeed, as such found little favour among the Greeks, who had other moon-goddesses of their own; but in her derived function as inspirer of love she made good her footing, under the name of Aphrodite, throughout the Hellenic world.   She had to discard, however, much of the coarser sensualism of the East, though retaining traces of Oriental rites at Corinth and other centres of Phœnician trade.

In Bœotia the chief deities worshipped in the earliest

---

[1] Milton, *Paradise Lost*, book i.

times were Ares and Aphrodite. It was they who had power of life and death, and ruled nature and man. At their bidding flowers and trees withered, and it was they who summoned them forth afresh from the earth in spring. When, then, the Greeks met the trading nation of the Phœnicians, they found in the principal goddess of that nation a being closely resembling their own Aphrodite. She had the title of "the Heavenly," for from heaven she ruled over the whole universe; and so the Greeks gave the title of Ourania, or "Heavenly," to their own Aphrodite. Soon Aphrodite stepped into the place of Astarte, and wherever Phœnicians had carried the worship of their goddess there arose temples of Aphrodite. Conspicuous among all were the islands of Kypros and Kythera, after which Aphrodite was called "the Cyprian" or "the goddess of Kythera." On this account the latter island is called in the Homeric poems "the most sacred." From Paphos in Kypros she bears the title "Paphia," for it was Paphos—

> "Where garlands, ever green and ever fair,
> With vows are offer'd, and with solemn prayer;
> A hundred altars in her temple smoke." [1]

But not only in the larger Greek islands, but in almost every place where there are traces of Phœnician settlements, we find the cult of the heavenly Aphrodite spread abroad,—on the coasts of the Peloponnesos and in Corinth; in Sicily on Mount Eryx and in Segesta.

This "Heavenly Aphrodite" displayed her power, above all, in the awakening of the spring. As the light renews its youth in the spring raised up out of

[1] Vergil, *Æneid*, i., 416, 417, translated by Dryden.

the sea, so Aphrodite emerges from the waves. Therefore the Greeks called her also "the Foam-born."
Flowers and plants budded as soon as Aphrodite
stepped forth from the sea on to the shore, and gentle
zephyrs formed her escort. The Horai, goddesses of
the seasons, put costly robes upon her, for now the
earth too decked herself out with flowers, and beneath
the moonbeams Aphrodite led the dance of Nymphs
and of the Graces. Hence at Athens Aphrodite was
worshipped in the gardens, for she is the creator of
the flowers.

With the beginning of spring, however, ships begin
to voyage anew. There is movement on the sea;
dolphins and swans—both on that account sacred to
Aphrodite—give life to the waters; and the light of
the goddess, the morning- and evening-star, becomes a
welcome sign to the seafarers to guide their course.
Hence Aphrodite was regarded as goddess of the sea
and guardian of seamen. Travellers were commended
to the favour of the Cyprian queen, and so her temples
oft stood on the cliffs, whence there was a distant view
far over the sea.

But the fair season of the year must pass away, and
then pain and sorrow take possession of Aphrodite's
breast. The legend tells how she lost her fair darling
Adonis. This was a youth fair as the spring, and
vigorous and healthy as a hunter. Over mead and
mountain roamed the goddess with him; she would
not let him go from her side, and he was quite left to
her protection. But he was too bold, and would not
listen to Aphrodite's warnings. As he was hunting,
a wild boar wounded him on the knee, and wounded

V. APHRODITE.
Head of the Statue from Melos, Paris.

him to death. Too late did the goddess haste through
the forest bushes : she could not save her darling. A
thorn tore her foot, and the blood-drops forthwith dyed
the white rose its blood-red hue. Then Aphrodite gave
herself up to lamentation shrill and wild. She would
not leave the lifeless corpse ; nay, she went down into
the realms of the dead to win him back again, till Zeus
at length decreed that Adonis should spend the unfruitful season of the year in the realm of shadows, the
other in the world above in Aphrodite's arms. Mortals,
however, in the sultry summer held their feast of
Adonis in remembrance of his death and the swift-
fading season of spring. In earthen jars were raised
quick-growing little trees, that were hung with cakes,
like Christmas-trees. But the little trees soon withered,
and with chanting of mournful ditties they were, in
a few short days, cast away into the waters.

2. Aphrodite, the Goddess of Love and Beauty.

The goddess of awakening spring is goddess also
of beauty and of love. In spring the impulse of love
is roused also in bird and beast : each and all are
swayed by Aphrodite. When the goddess approached
her favourite Anchises, who was tending his herds on
Ida's pastures, lions, wolves, panthers, and tigers followed
her like tame animals. Since, however, it is beauty
above all that subdues the heart of man, Aphrodite is
also the goddess of beauty. She herself is adorned
with all charms, and is styled " the golden Aphrodite "
and " the sweetly smiling " (see Pl. V.). Wondrous fair
are her snowy arms, her flashing eyes ; fair, too, her

majestic neck and her costly head-dress. Above everything, however, is a girdle, of glittering gold, that with
mystic spell covers all charms. It was for this girdle
that Hera begged when she, once on a time, thought to
beguile her spouse, for " Therein are love, and desire, and
loving converse, that steals the wits even of the wise."[1]

The poets compare a beautiful woman with Aphrodite or Artemis, and Paris had plainly declared that
Aphrodite was more beautiful than Hera and Athena.
In reward for this the goddess blessed him with Helen,
the most beautiful woman on earth. To this goddess
of beauty and love everything beautiful, soft, small, and
pretty was sacred : among animals, the dove, the hare,
and the rabbit, the swan and the sparrow ; among
flowers, above all the rose and the myrtle. The
Charites (Graces), goddesses of charm, are her regular
attendants. There were three of them : Euphrosyne,
Aglaia, and Thaleia ; or Cheerfulness, Brightness, and
Bloom. It was these who, when Aphrodite was risen
from the sea, decked her out with golden ornaments
and conducted her to Olympos. For now Aphrodite
too belonged to the Olympian gods, and was called
daughter of Zeus and Dione, who was worshipped with
Zeus at Dodona (see p. 11). Hephaistos was called her
husband because he was the maker of beautiful works
of art, and so the goddess of beauty had to be constantly at his side. Others, to whom the union of the
goddess of love with the industrious god of the smithy
seemed startling, made, on the other hand, the warlike
Ares her husband, for it was thought that the power of
love could conquer even the rough man of war.

[1] *Iliad*, xiv., 216, 217, translated by Lang, Leaf, and Myers.

Otherwise, indeed, Aphrodite was unfriendly to men's serious and difficult work. The effeminate Paris was her favourite among the men of Troy. Him she assisted in battle, when she broke the strap of the helmet with which Menelaos was seeking to drag him away, and it was on account of Paris that she took the side of the Trojans. When her son Aineias was wounded by Diomedes, she threw her white arms around him, and strove to draw him out from the turmoil of battle; but having her hand slightly scratched by Diomedes, she hastened weeping from the scene of warfare, and let Aineias fall instead of rescuing him. Iris bore her swooning to Olympos, and there she sank on the bosom of her mother Dione, who with gentle words sought to console her. While, however, Hera and Athena made merry over her weakness, Zeus, smiling on her, spoke soothingly thus :—

"Not unto thee, my child, are given the works of war; but follow thou after the loving tasks of wedlock, and to all these things shall fleet Ares and Athene look." [1]

It is in the house that the power of love ought to show itself. Therefore artists have at times set beside Aphrodite's figure a tortoise, emblem of retiring domesticity. Thus, in motherly fashion, Aphrodite interested herself in the daughters of Pandareos :—

"Their father and their mother the gods had slain, and the maidens were left orphans in the halls, and fair Aphrodite cherished them with curds and sweet honey and delicious wine." [2]

But as a general rule the Greeks had no great idea

---

[1] *Iliad*, v., 428-30, translated by Lang, Leaf, and Myers.

[2] Homer, *Odyssey*, xx., 67-9, Butcher and Lang's translation.

of the joy of a quiet domesticity, and so they saw in their goddess of love rather the tyranny of passion which observes no limits, and destroys the happiness of man. Love between gods and mortals resulted, for the most part, in disaster; and the greater the bliss of love is, the more difficult is it often for the mortal to sustain. Anchises was thus a favourite of Aphrodite. But he could not sustain his good fortune, and imparted the secret to others. Thereupon Zeus struck him with lightning and lamed him. Still worse, however, does the power of love appear between mortals if they pay no heed to morality and law. The love of Paris and Helen resulted in discord and tears, battles and nameless misery of whole nations; for love may lead to frenzy. Nay, not even in the lower world did Dido forget that her loved Aineias had deserted her. With words of affection he strove to address the unhappy one, but she gazed sadly and wildly, with downcast eye,—

> "And what he says, and swears, regards no more
> Than the deaf rocks, when the loud billows roar." [1]

Thus can passion harden the heart of man, and passion also is the work of Aphrodite.

(B) VENUS.

VENUS OF MOUNT ERYX, AND VENUS THE GUARDIAN OF THE ROMAN COMMONWEALTH.

The Phœnicians, that race of traders and seamen, had spread abroad as far as Sicily the worship of their great goddess Astarte, whom the Greeks called Aphro-

---

[1] Vergil, *Æneid*, vi., 470, 471, Dryden's translation.

dite. Here she was specially worshipped on the beautiful Mount Eryx, conspicuous from afar. Here were kept for her those flocks of sacred doves that every year left the island for eight days and flew to Africa; but on the ninth day came back, led by Aphrodite in the form of a red dove. Then came the spring once more, and the goddess took possession of her temple.

When the Romans, in their first great war against the Carthaginians, possessed themselves of Mount Eryx (B.C. 249), and employed as a watch-tower the rich temple that had been built there, it became evident that the goddess wished well to them. Therefore the Roman soldiers who returned home from the war took the worship of the goddess with them from Mount Eryx to Italy. In Italy a goddess of spring called Venus had long been an object of worship. She was the guardian of the gardens and of the vine-dressers, who twice a year celebrated a festival in her honour. Since the Greek goddess Aphrodite was a protector of gardens, people soon became accustomed to regard the Roman Venus also as goddess of love, and so the spring- and love-goddess of Mount Eryx was called the Erycinian Venus. It was not long before an opportunity was presented of introducing her worship in the interest of the whole Roman state. After the disastrous battle at Lake Trasimenus in the Second Punic War, it was believed that the wrath of Mars, the god of war, could be appeased only if an altar were built for him and his wife Venus,—on occasion of a public festival of atonement and thanksgiving (see p. 124), —and their images set out on a sofa for adoration. For through acquaintance with the Greeks the Romans had learned that Ares was the husband of Aphrodite, and so Mars, too, had been made husband of Venus. Two years later the first temple to this Venus of Mount Eryx was dedicated on the Capitol, and thereupon Venus became a guardian of the whole Roman state.

The worship of Venus became, however, more important in proportion as the Romans were more proud of being recognised as descendants of the Trojan Æneas ; for he was styled by the Greek poets a son of the goddess of love. Now the Roman poets could sing how Æneas in his wandering to Italy had founded that sanctuary for Venus on Mount Eryx, and indeed in honour of his half-brother Eryx, who had been killed by Herakles in a boxing-match, and buried on that mountain. Meanwhile the number of sanctuaries of Venus in Rome had much increased. One of these was dedicated to Venus Verticordia, or the turner of hearts, for it was believed that Venus not only implanted in the human heart the glow of love, but could turn this also to morality. The great potentates of the Roman republic, Sulla, Pompeius, and Cæsar, thinking to stand in special favour with the goddess who protected the state, all built temples to her. The first, whose good fortune seemed extraordinary, gave her the title of Venus Felix, *i.e.*, the luck-bringing Venus.

Pompeius, proud of his successes in the field, built a temple in honour of Venus Victrix, or the Bestower of Victory, raised up on the highest steps of the first theatre made of stone, a building he had himself erected ; Cæsar represented her under the name of Genetrix, as ancestress of his family, which was supposed to originate with Iulus, son of Æneas. At a special crisis in his fortunes, the night before the battle of Pharsalia, he vowed to this ancestress of his a new and magnificent temple; and he dedicated it with splendid games soon after he had gained the victory. His great nephew, afterwards the Emperor Augustus, erected the image of Venus near to that of Mars the Avenger (see p. 177), and poets thenceforth loved to glorify a goddess of peace in the spouse of Mars, the god of war; for only through war and peace had Rome become great. So had the poet Lucretius sung of Venus at an earlier date :—

"For thou alone canst bless mankind with calm peace, seeing that Mavors, lord of battle, controls the savage works of war, Mavors who often flings himself into thy lap quite vanquished by the never-healing wound of love." [1]

Lastly, the Emperor Hadrian united the statues of Venus and Rome in a grand double temple, the plan of which he had himself designed.

[1] Lucretius, *De Rerum Natura*, i., 31-4, Munro's translation.

CHAPTER XIII.

EROS (AMOR) AND PSYCHE.

1. Eros, God of Love and Friendship.

As an actual deity Eros is unknown to Homer. Himeros, indeed, or " Love at first sight," does appear in the description of Aphrodite's famous girdle (see p. 182), but probably as a mere image of an abstract idea. And it must be remembered that Himeros was not quite the same as Eros. The latter term was more general, including also the third idea expressed by Pothos, the yearning after what is far away, what has been loved and lost.

With Hesiod, on the other hand, Eros is a fully-developed god, and a very important one too. His form cannot be traced on monuments earlier than the end of the sixth century, but we know that under the form of a rude stone he was worshipped at Thespiai in a remote age.

In this little hill-town of Thespiai, in Bœotia, there was worshipped in very early times a god of love, who created the world anew in spring-time, and filled the hearts of men with gentle emotions. So ancient was this worship, that no image of the god had been made in human form; as pledge of his presence a rough, unworked stone sufficed. The power of this god, who was called Eros, or Love, was so important for the whole race of his worshippers, that he was honoured with festivals recurring every five years, with processions and with martial games such as elsewhere fall to the lot only of the highest deities of a tribe, as, for instance, Zeus at Olympia or Apollo at Delphi. And the same worship was enjoyed by Eros, also, in the city of Parion on the Hellespont.

The inhabitants of Thespiai could never glorify their god Eros enough. On his protection depended the prosperity of the whole state ; for without friendship between men there was no companionship in arms, and companionship in arms was for the contending ranks of combatants the safest pledge of unwearying courage, and so of victory. The inhabitants of Thespiai were, however, rightly renowned among the Greeks as the men who showed the liveliest feeling of honour in warfare, and when at Thermopylæ the courageous king of Sparta, Leonidas, despising death, strove to hold at bay the hostile masses of the Persians with his little band of Spartans, there were of all the Greeks only seven hundred men of Thespiai who stood their ground beside him, and with him died a hero's death. The god Eros, then, was a god who through friendship led on to bravery. Therefore his statue stood in the gymnasia, or recreation grounds of the youth, and in Elis were to be seen close together in the gymnasion the statues of Eros and Anteros, that is to say, Love and Return-Love, who contended over the palm of victory. The Spartans and Cretans therefore offered sacrifice to Eros before the beginning of battle, and " the Sacred Band " of the

Thebans, that gathered such noble laurels on the
battlefields of Greece, consisted only of such com-
panions-in-arms, united by the closest friendship. On
the island of Samos, too, Eros was conceived of as a
guide to courage, and was honoured with the brilliant
"Feast of Freedom." But, after all, the most brilliant and glorious of the Eros festivals were those at
Thespiai, and here the flower of the youth distinguished itself, not only in sport and dance, but, above
all, in warlike contests. Hence it naturally resulted
that Eros was represented as armed with bow and
arrows, and in the earlier time sculptors gave him the
form of a powerful youth, quite capable of bearing
sword and spear in fighting the enemies of his native
land.

The Greeks of later times, indeed, did not come up
to their forefathers in courage and warlike feeling, and
so it was gradually forgotten that Eros was also a god
of war. The poets were apt to glorify the power of
friendship rather than honour and renown. Achilles
renounced all honour of warfare when Agamemnon had
wronged him ; for his friend Patroklos was by his side.
As soon, however, as his friend had fallen, boundless
grief awoke in his soul. To avenge his friend he
forgot all defiance and enmity against Agamemnon,
king of men, and threw himself, regardless of life, into
the thickest of the fray. But the myths contain also
other models of friendship whose names have become
proverbial, as Orestes and Pylades. Orestes slew his
own mother at the instigation of his friend Pylades,
and the latter followed his friend, whom the goddesses
of vengeance were torturing with the pangs of con-

science, far over sea to Tauris, because he thought it
inhuman to abandon this friend in distress. Even in
historical times the Athenians extolled with almost
as much enthusiasm the friendship of Harmodios and
Aristogeiton, whom they supposed to have freed the
state from despotism ; and their praises were sung
when the wine-cup united men and youths at the
banquet.

2. Eros, the Universal Conqueror and Consoler in Death.

The less warlike the times became, the more readily
was it forgotten that Eros inspired the youth for battle.
People thought almost only of Eros the god of love
and tenderness, and so artists changed his powerful
form to one that was delicate and youthful. Now he
had wings given him which could bear him quicker to
the loved one ; and bow and arrows were regarded
as his weapons, with which he unexpectedly wounds
the hearts of lovers. In Thespiai, also, the old belief
in the efficaciousness of Eros must have been given up,
for we know that it was for this city the great sculptor
Praxiteles made a famous statue of Eros, which represented the god in most tender youthful beauty. This
statue was considered as the object most worth seeing
in the city. Perhaps Fig. 32 gives some idea, at least,
of a part of that work ; though some take this figure
for a genius of death.

Finally, the youth whose heart is filled with yearning,
and who loves to surrender himself to tender reverie, is
turned into a teasing child that indulges in sport and

trifling, and all sorts of whimsical freaks. For the omnipotence of love appeared quite unlimited, and stood forth still clearer when it was seen how so small a boy subdued through love the most powerful hero. For this child no personage was too venerable, no deed too difficult ; he overcame every obstacle, and every one had to submit to him. Even Zeus, the king of the gods, had to bow to the power of love ; and in this view sang

the poet Hesiod that Eros was the oldest of all the gods; nay, as old as Earth herself, and the wild elements of Chaos, that through his power were first united. Yet this thought expressed only the omnipotence of love, and Eros was usually regarded much more as the youngest child of the gods, and Aphrodite, the goddess of love, was named as his mother.

FIG. 32.—EROS.

From a statue in the Vatican, Rome.

As, however, love arises in every place where human beings meet one another, people were no longer contented with one god of love, but made from one a whole swarm of Erotes, or Love-gods. If now painters represented a lady's chamber, they peopled it generally with these little fluttering forms of children, who adorn the ladies, or help them with their dress. So utterly without limit or end does love press on in the intercourse of mankind, that many painters made the love-gods like little birds in whole flocks peep out of their nests; or they shut them up like doves in a cage, from which the seller lifted them by the wings, and offered them to the lover for purchase.

These little love-gods were concerned with all events and occurrences with which the idea of love was connected. A love-god standing between an affianced pair,

Fig. 33.—Eros as God of Death.
Statue in the Royal Museum at Turin.

with high-raised torch, the sign of burning love, was styled Hymenaios, the god of marriage. If, however, the love-god lay with smouldering torch on the loved one's grave, or if he had laid aside his bow to sleep, then was he the consoler in death. For the torch threatened to go out, as the life seemed to die away, and the arrow of the bow could wound no more; but

Eros was only sleeping, and it was known that he would wake again (see Fig. 33). Therefore the Romans were especially fond of representing on their sarco phagi two love-gods,—one with lowered and expiring torch, the other with torch raised on high and blazing. In this consolatory picture men hoped to possess an indication that the life and the vanished love of the loved one would come back, and that there would be a meeting once more after death.

3. EROS AND PSYCHE.

Since the power of the love-god prevailed over the whole soul of man, it was thought that Eros fell in love with the soul. But the soul was *Psyche.* She too suffers under the devouring torments of love, but the feeling of love purifies her at the same time, and gives immortality to the soul. Thus arose in later antiquity the beautiful legend of Eros and Psyche :—

Once on a time there lived a king and queen who had three daughters, of whom the youngest, whose name was Psyche, was too fair for mortal speech to tell her beauty, and people could compare her only with Aphrodite, the goddess of love herself. No longer did men go to Aphrodite's temples to gaze on her famous statues ; they offered sacrifice to Psyche instead when she passed along the streets, and twined garlands for her, and strewed her path with flowers. This worship of a mortal roused the jealousy of the goddess of love ; she called to her side her winged son Eros, who with his arrows pays no heed to the fancies and usages of men, but exercises an unlimited despotism over all, and she begged him to avenge the insult offered to her, and to give Psyche in marriage to the most pitiful fellow in the world.

Meanwhile Psyche gained no advantage through her beauty; for while her two elder sisters were wedded to princely suitors, she remained, lonesome and without a single wooer, in her father's palace. Since he saw in this a mark of divine wrath, he sought counsel of Apollo, who directed him to place the maiden, adorned as for marriage, on a lofty rock; for here no ordinary human lover would approach her, but a wild one who speeds on wings over the world, and before whom Zeus himself and the Shades below bend down in fear. With heavy heart the king returned and told his wife the sad response. There was lamentation everywhere, but the hateful decree imperiously demanded fulfilment.

A mournful bridal procession escorted Psyche to the lonely mountain range, but the hapless maiden herself prayed her attendants to hasten the march, and to lead her to meet the husband who was the ruin of the whole world. On a lofty precipice Psyche is left, when the glimmering nuptial torches are quenched in tears. The ill-fated parents henceforth sojourn in the gloomy seclusion of their palace closed for evermore; but the weeping maiden is raised on high by a gentle zephyr spreading her garments as a sail, and is carried on to the flowery sward of a delightful valley. Gradually Psyche falls asleep. As, however, she awakes refreshed she beholds before her a splendid building, a castle blazing with gold and jewels, inviting a visit. No bar, no gate checks her step, no warder is to be seen; yet while in astonishment she wanders through all the rooms, she hears the voice of an unseen being that bids her treat as her own everything she sees around her. In the banqueting hall costly wines and dainties are offered by unseen hands, sublime melody sounds forth after the feast, and amidst enchanting music Psyche sinks to sleep at night.

Then her unseen bridegroom approaches and declares her to be his bride. When morning dawned he had vanished. But for Psyche one day was like another, and the tones of her unseen husband's voice were her solace in her loneliness. Meanwhile old age had fallen on the sorrowing parents, and, hearing this, the two sisters are at times induced to visit them. Then Psyche's husband informs her of imminent ruin, and warns her never to receive her sisters, even if they should complain. This idea, however, arouses sadness in her soul: now, for the first time, she experiences the feeling of loneliness; the yearning to look once more on kith and kin becomes greater and greater every day, and through her coaxing entreaties and her tenderness she manages to induce her husband, in the end, to comply with all her wishes.

Now the two sisters approach the rocks at which the nuptial procession had once halted with the ill-fated Psyche, and with lamentations utter Psyche's name. She quickly summons the zephyr to bring her sisters into the valley, and receives them both in the midst of their lamentations. She shows them all her riches, and by so doing fills them with wicked envy. "Ought the youngest sister," say they on their return, "to have become the bride of a god?" This thought is unbearable to them, and they resolve to ruin Psyche.

Once more is she warned by her unknown husband

to betray nothing concerning him to the sisters ; again, however, Psyche finds means to quiet him.   Then the deceitful pair of sisters come again, and question Psyche as to where her husband comes from and what sort of person he is.   Without remembering that she had previously in conversation with her sisters spoken of a beautiful youth, she now, mindful of her husband's warning, describes him as an elderly grey-haired man, hoping thereby to impose upon her sisters.   They, however, are startled by the contradiction in Psyche's story, and become still more suspicious and envious. So they return the next day, and pretend that it is only sorrow for Psyche's lot that torments them.   Nay, they wish even to persuade her that perhaps her husband is a hideous dragon ; for the neighbouring peasants and hunters had seen such a monster dive into the river.   Certainly he would not much longer be fond of her, but would devour her.   Suspicion strikes root in Psyche's breast, and fills her with deep anxiety.   At last she can no longer restrain herself. As her sisters had advised her, she gets up one night secretly, and creeps with drawn dagger and lighted lamp to the couch of her slumbering spouse, to find out what he is, and to kill him.   For she believes that a horrible dragon will present himself to her view.   Yet what are her feelings when she beholds the god of love, Eros himself, lying in all his beauty before her !   Delicate wings spring from his shoulders ; and by the quiver, bow, and arrows that lay at his feet, she could recognise him well enough.   Still she is quite blinded by the divine vision.

Then she takes an arrow from the quiver ; for curiosity impels her to try whether these arrows are

really so sharp and wound so swiftly as is said.
Scarcely, however, does she touch the point, when it
pierces the trembling finger, and rosy drops of blood
fall to the ground. Thus was Psyche herself, without
suspecting it, struck by the love-god's arrow. Tenderly
she bends over to kiss him, but in doing so lets fall a
drop of oil from her lamp on to the god's right shoulder.
He wakes, and raises himself only to fly away without
saying a single word to his faithless wife. As he soars
upwards Psyche grasps his right foot, is raised with
him high into the air, and then floats gently back
to earth. But Eros calls to her from the top of a
cypress saying who he is, and adding that she must
now be punished through her husband's flight.

Now Psyche breaks forth into violent lamentation,
and tries to drown herself in the nearest stream, but
this bears her gently back to the flowery bank. So
she comes at last to the country of her perfidious
sisters, and tells them that Eros has cast her out, and
would now gladly wed one of them. The sisters hasten
in raptures to the well-known rocks, to summon once
more the zephyr; but in their excitement they do not
observe that another wind is blowing: they leap from
the precipice, and die a pitiable death.

While now Psyche hurries over the whole world to
seek her loved one, Eros is lying sick with ardent desire
for Psyche in his mother Aphrodite's house. As soon
as she has learned through a babbling sea-gull the
cause of her son's sorrow, she falls into the greatest
wrath, for Psyche is the very person whom she had
resolved originally to destroy.

Psyche, in the meantime, suffers every imaginable

torment. Nowhere does she find rest, and not even in the temples of Hera and Demeter can she obtain protection ; for they, too, stand in such awe of the infuriated goddess of love. Aphrodite, however, drives to Olympos her chariot drawn by doves, followed by sparrows and song-birds. Here she calls Hermes, the messenger of the gods, and commissions him to announce to all the world that Aphrodite wishes to get back her runaway slave Psyche, the reward being seven kisses. As a result, Psyche is brought to be a handmaid of the goddess of love. By the other servants she is maltreated, by her mistress scolded ; and she is compelled to perform the most menial services : from a great heap she has to pick out the wheat, barley, poppyseed, peas, lentils, and beans, in which, however, she is secretly helped by a swarm of ants.

Often and often, in her despair, she wishes to kill herself, but all her attempts are frustrated. She even has to go down into the world below to fetch water from the Styx, and to ask the queen of the shadowy realms for some cosmetics for her mistress. Yet, at last, the summit of her suffering is reached. Eros, filled with excessive yearning after Psyche, determines himself to intercede with Zeus for his ill-fated loved one. Thereupon Zeus calls all the gods to a meeting : Psyche is recognised as lawful spouse of Eros, and Aphrodite has to acquiesce. Psyche is summoned and endowed with immortality, and the reunion of the long-separated lovers is celebrated by a festive banquet. Thus was the soul ennobled through true love, and guided to immortality. The daughter of Eros and Psyche has received the name of " Blissfulness."

CHAPTER XIV.

HADES (PLUTO), PERSEPHONE (PROSERPINA), AND THE LOWER WORLD.

1. Hades, God of the Crops and of Death.

Deep in the bowels of the earth prevailed the power of a god who pushed forth the crops to light, and gave wealth to the farmer. This was Plouton, the distributer of wealth. But Demeter, also mother of earth, was considered the goddess of crops, and her worship appeared to the Greeks still more useful and acceptable. The friendly figure of Demeter aroused more confidence than that of the gloomy ruler of the under-world. It was this god who carried away again the blooming plants, and whose kingdom was dedicated to death. For dark is it on the foundation of the earth, and nothing can there grow and thrive.

Therefore Plouton received the name Hades, that is, the Unseeing or the Unseen, for he sojourned continually in gloom; where the sun sets must be sought the entrance to his realms; there everything lay in purple twilight, and "Erytheia," or "Redland," was a name consequently given to this kingdom. It was closed with strong gates, that no one who was once forced within might be able to escape. No mortal knew the look of this place, for to the dead alone was the country accessible. Hades watched carefully that no mortal gaze should ever penetrate to him. Utterly startled he sprang from his throne when, in the battle of the gods before Troy, Earth quaked in her fastnesses, and Poseidon threatened to tear the covering of earth from the head of Hades. And just as Hades holds his court in darkness, so does he conceal himself from men, and the legend has expressed this thus, that he put on a cap of invisibility.

Since all the dead eventually reached this invisible realm of Hades, he soon became a ruler of the dead instead of a god of wealth in grain. Death, however, is hateful to gods and men; the form of Hades was conceived of as terrible and gloomy, and his sternly gazing countenance was surrounded by locks of raven hue. Whoso would pray to him strikes with his hands upon the earth. But such prayer can be but a despairing utterance, for Hades is pitiless and invincible, and none escape the power of the death-god that lulls all to sleep. Only the hero of heroes, Herakles, undertook war with Death; in Pylos (some say at the gate of Hell itself) he struck with his arrow the god of the dead on the shoulder, and wounded him sore, but Paieon, that heals the gods, cured him. Ordinary mortals were powerless against Hades, and he was only dreaded by them. Nay, more, men had to beware of rousing his might through the mere utterance of his name, and therefore they loved not to name him. They might have called him Admetos, the Untamed, Laomedon, the Ruler of the People, Polydektes, the Receiver of Many; but all these names denoted only terrible sides of his nature; and so he was called "the Many-named" or

"the Renowned" (Klymenos). He was, in his own
kingdom, mighty as the king of the gods, as it were an
infernal Zeus, and therefore the poets made him a
brother of Zeus, and the artists often placed in his

hand, as a token of
his power, a sceptre
with two points. Per-
haps there was pre-
served therein the
remembrance of the
two-pronged fork,
with which the
ploughman broke up
the soil, when Plou-
ton was to let the
blessings of corn
spring up out of the
earth. For this rea-
son also he was often
represented with a
horn of plenty on
his arm, and with a
bushel - measure on
his head. For bushel
and horn of plenty
were tokens of the
rich harvest. Some-
times, however, art-

FIG. 34.—HADES.
Statuette in the Villa Borghese, Rome.

ists depicted him, without the blessings of fruitfulness,
simply enthroned in gloomy majesty. The three-headed
hell-hound Kerberos, wreathed round with serpents, lay
as watch-dog beside his master to keep off all comers

(Fig. 34).   Under the name of Pluto, the god of the
dead, Hades, became generally known to the Romans.
He was to them, however, somewhat of a foreigner, for
they had no god of their own whom they might have
exchanged for the Greek Hades-Plouton.

2. Persephone, the Goddess of Death, and her Journey into the Lower World.

The throne of Hades was shared by Persephone,
equally gloomy of aspect and equally dreaded.   For it
was natural the rule of Hades should be limited to the
males, and that as ruler of the womankind a female
deity should sit beside him.   As such she was called
" Despoina " (" Lady " or " Mistress "), for her power
was similar to that of her husband, save that it extended
rather to the women.   When Odysseus came to the
portal of the world below, Persephone sent up to him his
mother's shade ; and she, too, conferred on the seer
Teiresias the gift to continue the use of his prophetic
powers even in the under-world, while the rest of the
ghosts had lost all remembrance of their earthly existence.   What, however, caused the power of Persephone
to appear so awful was her control over the head of
Medusa the Gorgon, an image of benumbing Death.
It was for this reason that Odysseus left the place
of terror as quickly as possible, from dread lest Persephone might send to him also the image of Medusa, that
turned men into stone.

And yet the Greeks have understood how to give
more pleasing features to the gloomy queen of the
world beneath, and to attribute to her a fate that

made her seem to mortals far more an object of pity than of fear. This was the story of the carrying off of Persephone by Hades. For now the goddess of Death herself became, as it were, a prey of Death, and a prototype of him who falls a victim to Death. As she was plucking the narcissus, whose stupefying scent is an image of benumbing Death, she fell into Death's power ; or in the blossoming violet-fields of Sicilian Enna she was carried off by the Prince of Death. These violet-fields have the same import as the narcissus, for their scent was so stupefying that, it was said, still in later times hunting-dogs lost on them the track of game. Hardly had Persephone stretched forth her hands to the beautiful flowers, when the earth opened, and Hades emerged with his chariot drawn by coal-black steeds. He dragged the maiden to his car, struggle and cry as she might, and hurried her away from the spot. Of no avail was her cry to her father Zeus for aid. So long as she saw the earth and the starry heaven above, the sea teeming with fish and the brightness of the sun, the maiden did not yet lose all hope. But when this sight died away she died away too,—she had to enter the kingdom of death.

Yet not only did Persephone seem to the Greek worthy of compassion, but her sufferings were even a source of consolation to him. For after she had been called a daughter of the earth-mother Demeter, it was believed that the latter had a claim upon her daughter. Thus she succeeded in obtaining from Zeus the return of Persephone from the realms of the dead (see p. 91). Now men might hope that death was not to last for ever, but to lead to life again, and this thought must have been consolatory, especially for the heathen ; otherwise death appeared to him only as the end of all pleasure and joy. These hopes were in antiquity imparted to the faithful, especially by the city of Eleusis, in Attica, at the " Mysteries." From the Greeks the Romans also became acquainted with them, and thus learned about Persephone, the Greek goddess of the dead, only they altered her name to what was for them an easier word, Proserpina.

3. THE WORLD BELOW.

After death men were given back to earth. There, in deep gloom that no living eye could fathom, the earlier Greeks pictured to themselves the abode of departed spirits. But the more they depicted the life after death, the more extensive did they represent the world of the dead to be. It was a place very similar to the earth, but without beauty or comfort. Exactly where it lay no one could tell: far, far away in the distant West, where the stream of Okeanos encircled the disk of the earth, whither no seafaring folk had ever ventured. Here was it that the sun set in the mist, and Helios, the sun-god, pastured the herds of oxen belonging to the god of death. In the twilight dwelt the race of the Kimmerioi. But who could have had much to say of it ? Hardly might the eye distinguish forms. Poplars and unfruitful willows, the grove of Persephone, grew before the entrance to the world of the dead, and the ill-favoured flower of the asphodel, with its pale blossom, throve on the barren common, where the spirits of the dead flitted hither and thither. Thus far had

the bold and much-enduring Odysseus made his way,
but horror seized him when he looked on the meadow
of the dead.   Full well did he know many a one whom
he had seen above in the bloom of life, but the shades
glided onward, onward without a thought.   Not till
they had drunk of the victim's blood that Odysseus
had let flow into a trench did consciousness return to
them awhile.   Now was Odysseus recognised by his
wailing mother.   Thrice sought he to embrace her,
but the shade melted away like air between his hands.
He saw the mighty Achilles stalking like a king
among the heroes, but Achilles wore a gloomy look
and had no joy in his glory.   Sooner would he have
stayed on earth as the most despised of churls, than
still be so honoured in these realms below.   So terrible
did death seem to the heathen ; so devoid of hope did
man close his eyes for ever.

Gradually, however, even the Greeks felt that man
could not have been created simply to live and to die,
to face an existence so terrible ; and so, later on, they
imagined the abode of the dead not so monotonous as
in earlier times : terrible, indeed, for him who had
committed crime, but even enjoyable for him that had
lived a righteous life.

Death retained indeed its terrors, and none could
return from the unknown world beyond the grave.   A
monstrous hell-hound, Kerberos (see Fig. 34), lay at
the portal of the kingdom of Hades, fawning on each
that enters, but raising himself with awful fury against
him who ventures to return.   And that no escape
might be thought of, raging and pest-breathing rivers
wrapped their coils around the kingdom of the dead,

chief among them the Styx, that flowed in many a winding, but also other streams,—Pyriphlegethon, the fire-stream; Acheron, the stream of woe; and Kokytos, the river of wailing. A grimy, morose old man, Charon, ferried the dead over in his boat, and inexorably extorted from each the obolos, a small copper coin, which the survivors used to put in the dead man's mouth, that it might not be lost.

When, then, the souls had arrived in the shadowy realms, they were brought before the tribunal of justice. Here sat Rhadamanthos, and Kings Aiakos and Minos, who in their lifetime had shown themselves unimpeachable judges and powerful rulers. They adjudged to each soul the fate it deserved. The criminal was delivered over to perpetual torments. The gossiping Tantalos, who had not been able to curb his desires, and had divulged the secrets of the gods at whose table he had sat, had to stand for ever in water. But when he would moisten his parching lips the water flowed back, and if he would quiet his hunger and grasp the overhanging fruit, this, too, was swept away far above. Even the cunning deceiver Sisyphos was made to see that after death all his artful devices profited nought. He was condemned to roll up the mountain a heavy stone; yet scarce had it reached the top when down rolled the mass again. Sisyphos knew not how to escape the galling toil. Nothing had the Danaides, the daughters of Danaos, gained by the murder of their husbands; in the world below they found a still more fruitless task; they were continually drawing water in a cask, but the cask was never full, for through a hole in the bottom the water flowed away. Inexorable, then,

were the avenging spirits that tormented the criminal
after death.

Of rewards for the righteous, however, there was
no lack in the world below. In the Isles of the Blest
ruled grey-haired Kronos, and song and dance re-
sounded from the choruses of those who in life too had
been just and noble. For whatever was dear to a man
in life followed him also in death, were it weapons or
horses, were it joy in dance and feasting, or love for
music and song. There, beside the defenders of their
native land, were noble priests, pious seers, and whoever else in any way had done good to his fellow-man
and gained a fair renown. Thus poets sought, to some
extent at least, to soften the dread of the sojourn in the
lower world.

4. THE ERINYES (FURIÆ).

In the lower world, according to the belief of the
Greeks, dwelt the terrible Erinyes, or goddesses of
vengeance. They were the handmaids of Persephone,
and at her bidding inflicted punishment on trans-
gressors. But the power of the Erinyes showed itself
in the lifetime of men, and warned them to abstain from
all injustice. In particular they watched over the laws
of the family. With madness and despair did they
strike him who raised his hand against his parents, and
the Erinyes, thirsting for his blood, hunted him, as
hounds hunt game, from place to place. Thus they
pursued the matricide Orestes to the sanctuary of the
Delphian Apollo, and granted him even there no rest.
Not even the gods are secure against the goddesses
of vengeance, if they show themselves unmindful of the

reverence due to their parents. Ares roused the Erinyes of his mother Hera because he opposed her in the battle before Troy ; and even the pious Telemachos dreaded the Erinyes, if he were to thrust his mother from the house against her will.

But not only do the Erinyes watch over the laws of the family, but they check especially all that is contrary to nature and morals, as, for instance, excessive good fortune of men. Thus they would not permit the horse Xanthos to predict to his master Achilles more than Fate allowed. But because the observation of morality and of all that is right is a great blessing for mankind, the Erinyes are the guardians of oaths, and protectors of the unfortunate and of beggars. Hence in Athens the Erinyes were named " Eumenides," *i.e.*, " the Well-disposed," or " the Venerable," for the requital of wrong is full of blessing for mankind. Nay, the poets ascribed even to the Erinyes a forgiving spirit in cases where iron strictness would have been an injustice, and it was indeed consolatory for man if unintended wrongdoing might meet with pardon. The ill-fated king Oidipous had unwittingly outraged his own parents most frightfully, yet in the grove of the Eumenides at Athens even he found the rest he so eagerly sought. He ventured to enter the lower world through the grotto of the Eumenides, and they were appeased.

The Romans also were acquainted with goddesses of vengeance, or Furiæ, but poets could tell only of their rage and wrath. On the Grecian stage they had often seen these goddesses of vengeance enter, in dark robes, with tangled serpent-locks, perhaps, too, with torches in their hands ; and so the Furies appeared to them as the powers of frenzy and despair. Everything noble was hateful to the Roman Furies, and to the Fury Allecto Juno cries,—

> " 'Tis thine to ruin realms, o'erturn a state,
> Betwixt the dearest friends to raise debate,
> And kindle kindred blood to mutual hate.
> Thy hand o'er towns the fun'ral torch displays,
> And forms a thousand ills ten thousand ways." [1]

The serpents that the Furies twined round their heads, breasts, and arms are, at the same time, their weapons. When Allecto hurls her serpents on a man's breast, the poison penetrates his heart, and strikes his head with frenzy. With blows of a hissing scourge the Furies deaden the mind; and when they thrust their smoking torches against a man's breast, cold sweat breaks forth from him in streams. But because the Romans recognised in the Fury only the deity of madness, it has resulted that their poets could also call a woman who caused disaster a "Fury," as, for instance, Helen, who through her faithlessness had brought her native country to the brink of ruin.

[1] Vergil, *Æneid*, vii., 335-38, Dryden's translation.

CHAPTER XV.

DIONYSOS—BACCHUS.

(A) DIONYSOS.

1. Dionysos, the God of Awakening Nature; the Bacchic Frenzy.

Dionysos was a foreign god, coming from the East, and associated with the lion and the bull as expressing power. Not like Zeus is he to be sought on the wild mountain-tops, but in rich valleys and in moist places (for instance, the Limnai, at Athens), as representing the fertility of nature. His coming was regarded differently by different men. By some he was received with joy, by others repelled as an alien. So too there were two views of his appearance. According to one he was bearded, according to the other he was the smooth-faced youthful lover of Ariadne, with a luxuriance of beauty apt to degenerate into effeminacy. In the Homeric Pantheon he occupies no distinguished position. It is Hesiod who first recognises him as the giver of wine. Whoever would know how the oldest inhabitants of Greece conceived of the god Dionysos must not dwell on the fact of his being considered at a later time as the god of wine. For Dionysos was perhaps worshipped in Greece before men had learnt

the art of cultivating the vine. Nay, the god was
rather looked on as the powerful creator of the spring,
who in well-watered meadows and luxuriant river-
valleys calls forth the fruitfulness of earth after its long
winter sleep. During the unfruitful season of the year
Dionysos had ruled in the world of the dead, and as
a great hunter (Zagreus) had hunted men as game.
At Delphi, in the temple of Apollo, was shown to the
faithful even the grave of Dionysos, for the god was

Fig. 35.—Satyr and Mænad with the Infant Dionysos.
Terra-cotta Relief in the British Museum.

dead. When, however, spring drew nigh, nay, as soon
as the days of the winter solstice had come, then the
god woke again to life, and the hope of the new fruitful
season filled men's hearts with exultation and joy.

At Delphi, where Dionysos was in earliest times
worshipped, a remarkable festival took place about the
winter solstice. The so-called "Thyiades," or frenzied
women, who were appointed priestesses of Dionysos,
swept like a storm up the mountain heights, beneath

the glare of torches, as though maddened with joy. Their gestures were as though they were rousing to life the child Dionysos in his cradle (see Fig. 35) ; and they took to such mad acts that people believed supernatural power had fallen on them. With dishevelled hair, a fawnskin girdle round the breast, they rushed on encircled by serpents, that familiarly licked their cheeks, and in their hands they brandished the thyrsos, a cane with a crown of ivy. For as the luxuriant green leaves burst forth from the dry cane, so with the blow of the thyrsos the worshippers of Dionysos knew how to draw milk and honey from the arid earth. Thereupon wild ecstasy was wont to seize the women, so that with the wild cry " Euoi " they caught young fawns, aye, and any beasts of the forest, as they ran, tore them to pieces, and devoured the flesh raw. Thus sang the poet Euripides of these frenzied women :—

> "Some in their arms held kid, or wild-wolf's cub.
>
> *   *   *   *   *   *
>
> One took a thyrsus wand, and struck the rock,
> Leaped forth at once a dewy mist of water ;
> And one her rod plunged deep in the earth, and there
> The god sent up a fountain of bright wine.
> And all that longed for the white blameless draught,
> Light scraping with their finger-ends the soil
> Had streams of exquisite milk ; the ivy wands
> Distilled from all their tops rich store of honey." [1]

When, however, Dionysos let the water well up from the earth, then he was a friend of the nymphs (see p. 132). In fact, it was to a grotto of the nymphs on Parnassos that the train of " Mainades," or frenzied

---

[1] *Bacchæ*, 699, 704-11, Milman's translation.

women, at Delphi hastened, and it was said that the little Dionysos had been handed over to the nymphs to bring up. So the child soon became great, and displayed his mighty power in the growth of nature. But the bloom of the year sinks again, smitten by the wasting ray of the glowing sun. This was Lykourgos, that struck with an ox-goad the frenzied nymphs who had nurtured and brought up Dionysos, for the ox-goad denotes the sun's ray. Terrified, the nymphs threw down the budding thyrsos, and Dionysos in flight dived beneath the waves of the sea, where the goddess Thetis received him, and lovingly cherished and protected him in the depths of ocean till he might return again to earth. For Lykourgos had become hateful to the gods, and was punished with blindness. The wasting glow of the sun ceased, and its light was quenched. At the winter solstice all worshippers of Dionysos celebrated his rising again. Without doubt his earliest ministrants offered human sacrifices to him, for in some parts Dionysos bore the title "Omestes," or "Raw-eater," and the tearing to pieces of fawns and deer, as ascribed to the Mænads, was certainly a substitute for such a sacrifice. Even just before the battle of Marathon, two Persian prisoners were sacrificed to Dionysos. This may well have been the last instance of human sacrifice in his honour that occurred in Greece. For gradually the sacrifice of the goat had superseded that of man, and therefore the goat was considered as specially consecrated to Dionysos.

Perhaps it was the priests and worshippers of Apollo at Delphi, who at the suggestion of the Pythia put an end to that barbarity. For generally speaking, as the worship of Apollo became established at Delphi, that of Dionysos was somewhat curtailed. Now both gods had to share the great sanctuary between them; and it was said that while Apollo during the winter left Delphi, Dionysos ruled there as lord of his temple. When, therefore, the temple of Apollo, after a great fire, was built up again on a grander scale, in the front pediment Apollo was represented with Leto, Artemis, and the Muses; in that at the back, Dionysos with the Mænads. Thus he, in fact, enjoyed almost equal honour with Apollo here on Parnassos. Gradually, however, the worship of other gods as well as Dionysos began to prevail, and the result was that in no long time he ceased to be considered the chief creator of the whole life of nature. Henceforth he remained the god of wine, but the intoxicating power of wine was indeed often very much like the inspired enthusiasm which had been wont to seize on the female votaries of Dionysos, at the festival of the winter solstice.

2. The Spread of the Cult of Dionysos.

When the Greeks heard with what enthusiasm the ministers of Dionysos were filled in his worship, what miracles they performed, how they dealt with serpents and wild beasts as with tame birds and lambs, they might well think that no more powerful god was to be found than Dionysos. His worship had soon spread throughout the whole of Greece. Now it was declared that he was the son of a divine father, Zeus, and, at the same time, Dionysos was recognised as an Olympian god, who claimed worship from all Greeks. His most ancient worshippers had, indeed, named as his mother

a mortal woman, Semele, daughter of the Theban King
Kadmos, but she too obtained divine honours through
the favour of Zeus. At first she believed that her
husband was a mortal prince; but the jealous Hera
disclosed to her the secret, and enticed her to beg Zeus
to appear to her for once in true godlike form. Zeus
did appear to her as the supreme god of heaven, in
fiery brilliancy, amidst thunder and lightning. This
was too much for mortal eye, and Semele perished.
Zeus, however, rescued her son Dionysos from the
house now bursting into flames, and Semele was after
her death raised to divine honours under the name of
Thyone. A similar name was borne by the frenzied
handmaids of Dionysos; he too was often called by the
poets Thyoneus, or son of Thyone.

With irresistible force the worship of Dionysos made
its way through every land. Even those who resisted
were finally overpowered by the contagious enthusiasm
of his disciples. The daughters of Proitos, at Argos,
at first would have none of the worship of Dionysos;
but the god punished them for this with madness, so
that they fancied themselves cows, and ran lowing
over the hills. Now the god had brought them to
what they would never have come to of their own free
will. Much the same happened to the daughters of
Minyas in Bœotian Orchomenos; they too heard without believing the wondrous stories told of the new god
Dionysos by the maids, as they sat at their spinning.
Thereupon they were torn from their seats and changed
into furious birds of night, and now they too fly
whizzing over the mountain slopes, through the gloom
of night, just like the Mænads on Parnassos.

Most impressively, however, was the fate of such an unbeliever represented in the myth of King Pentheus at Thebes. From the very first his name, meaning as it does the sufferer, suggested that he was doomed to pain and torments. He considered the foreign god Dionysos as an impostor and an effeminate creature, refused to admit him to his realm of Thebes, and was specially zealous against the Mænads wandering in wild enthusiasm amid the mountain solitudes. But the despised god took terrible vengeance on him. In the first place, to show his wondrous power, he caused the palace of Pentheus to fall in ruin amidst flames. Yet this wrought no change in the heart of Pentheus ; nay, he doubted the morality of the enthusiastic women, and desired to see with his own eyes their doings in retirement. Then the god devised a terrible vengeance. He dressed Pentheus up as a woman to facilitate his design, brought him to the mountain as one of his servants, and showed him a place of concealment upon a lofty fir-tree ; hence he was secretly to observe all that went on. Then, however, the god loudly summoned the Mænads to vengeance :—

> " And as he spake, a light of holy fire
> Stood up, and blazed from earth straight up to heaven.
> Silent the air, silent the verdant grove
> Held its still leaves ; no sound of living thing.
> They, as their ears just caught the half-heard voice,
> Stood up erect, and rolled their wondering eyes.
> Again he shouted. But when Cadmus' daughters
> Heard manifest the god's awakening voice,
> Forth rushed they, fleeter than the wingèd dove,
> Their nimble feet quick coursing up and down." [1]

---

[1] Euripides, *Bacchæ*, 1082-91, Milman's translation.

With their hands they tore the fir-tree up by the roots, and flung themselves on the unhappy Pentheus, who had been dashed to the ground with the uprooted tree. His own mother Agave gave the signal for her son's murder, whom she in her madness took for a lion. She tore off one of his arms, and the other women completed the horrid work. Soon nothing but dismembered limbs was left of Pentheus, who had denied the divinity of Dionysos.

FIG. 36.—DIONYSOS, THE GOD OF WINE.
Marble bust from Ostia, in the Vatican.

As, however, the myth has depicted in a terrible example the chastisement of hostility to Dionysos, so it could announce a rich reward awaiting the worshippers of the god. Oineus, a king of Aitolia,—his name is literally Wine-man, and was probably in early times a designation of Dionysos himself,—welcomed the god hospitably in his country, and in return received the vine as a gift. In Attica, however, the same story was told of Ikarios, who entertained Dionysos as his guest, and received for this the vine, as well as the knowledge of how to tread the grapes. Ikarios wished in gratitude to impart the valuable gift to the rest of mankind; but when he came to some herdsmen they drank the wine without mixing it with water, and in excess, so they became intoxicated. Then imagining they were poisoned, they slew Ikarios and threw him into a spring. The same fate then befell him as the god himself, who when chased by Lykourgos sprang into the sea, and no doubt Ikarios, the propagator of the Dionysiac cult, is only another name for Dionysos himself. For in the watery surface, be it sea or fountain, lies the living force of the earth, which in spring-time causes plants to shoot up. Gradually, however, men came to think of Dionysos only as the rearer of the valuable vine, and thus he became entirely the god of wine, and the artists were most fond of representing the god as crowned with vine-leaves (see Fig. 36).

3. BAKCHOS, THE GOD OF WINE; DIONYSOS AND TRAGEDY; THE BLESSING OF MORTALS.

Next to corn, which of all the fruits of the earth could fill man with greater joy than the vine? On this ground the worship of Dionysos must have found ever wider diffusion, and in this sense the grey-haired seer Teiresias addresses the atheist Pentheus in a tragedy of Euripides :—

"Youth! there are two things
Man's primal need : Demeter, the boon goddess

> (Or rather will ye call her Mother Earth ?),
> With solid food maintains the race of man.
> He, on the other hand, the son of Semele,
> Found out the grape's rich juice, and taught us mortals
> That which beguiles the miserable of mankind
> Of sorrow, when they quaff the vine's rich stream.
> Sleep too, and drowsy oblivion of care,
> He gives, all-healing medicine of our woes.
> He 'mong the gods is worshipped a great god,
> Author confessed to man of such rich blessings." [1]

The knightly heroes warring before Troy call Dionysos " the joy of mortals," and praise wine as a precious drink. Daily must ships from the wine-district of Thrace and the neighbouring islands bring wine to the camp before Troy. How much greater must have been the love for Dionysos among the peasants toiling day by day in the cultivation of the land ! To them a draught of wine was a downright bringer of joy and deliverer from all burdens. Yes, indeed, Dionysos the wine-god, called Lyaios and Eleutherios ("Redeemer" and "Deliverer") was truly a god of the peasants. Therefore the tyrant Peisistratos, whose power rested chiefly on the favour of the people, introduced the worship of Dionysos at Athens, and the people believed that they had to thank Dionysos for deliverance from the oppression of the aristocracy.

Boorish and rough, too, were the jests with which the country folk amused themselves at the festivals of Dionysos. In the festive humour that the gift of the god produced, he was called " Bakchos," and this colloquial term was almost more usual than the more solemn Dionysos. The country folk gave themselves

---

[1] *Bacchæ*, 274-85, Milman's translation.

up to all imaginable pranks at these festivals of the vintage; people masqueraded and rallied their acquaintances with merry jests. The youths were fond of dressing up in goatskins, and so dancing and singing in the guise of the beast sacred to Bakchos. But the old name for the goat was Satyr, and therefore the chorus of Satyrs struck up the so-called "Tragœdia," or goat-song in honour of Dionysos. But they did not stop at this cheerful song of "the goats." A man of the deme of Ikaria (where the worship of Bakchos specially flourished), by name Thespis, first added a dramatic representation to this "goat-song." Hence Thespis was considered the inventor of the drama, and the name of "Tragedy" was still given to the drama after it passed into the hands of highly-educated Athenians. Henceforth tragedy was the most brilliant feature of the festival of Dionysos at Athens. The celebration commenced with the sacrifice of a goat, and the chorus of servants of Dionysos continued to be the distinguishing mark of Greek tragedy. Still, at a later time, the permanent troops of actors called themselves "Dionysiac artists." But people did not want to give up the old cheerful "goat-song" of the Satyrs, and therefore it was usual at least to wind up the performance of serious tragedies with the old countrified jokes of the Satyr-play.

Through tragedy Bakchos, the god of the peasants, had become also a god of the educated citizens of the towns; and in place of the enthusiasm caused by wine, he could now also fill the heart of man with nobler emotions. For in tragedy man learned to distinguish noble from ignoble deeds; his sympathy was stirred when he saw ill-fated heroes suffer, and good resolutions took root in his breast. Thus, then, it was really Bakchos who brought consolation and happiness to man, and helped him on to more noble emotions.

As, however, Bakchos helped men to forget earthly sorrows, it was believed he had power even over death. He himself had gone down to Hades, and had conducted his mortal mother Semele up to Olympos, so that she, as Thyone (see p. 216), enjoyed divine honours. And he had brought the sulky deity Hephaistos back into the circle of the gods (see p. 151). Also Bakchos took to himself the deserted Ariadne. She, a daughter of Minos, King of Crete, had, from love of the hero Theseus, given him a thread which was to lead him safely through the maze of the labyrinth, and so had rescued him from death. Then she fled with him to the island of Naxos. Here, however, Theseus abandoned her as soon as she was sunk in sleep. Ariadne awoke to frightful grief when she saw herself abandoned thus faithlessly. Then Bakchos appeared to her as a deliverer in radiant brilliancy, made her his bride, and gave her a share in his divine honours. Thus it happened that the ancients were fond of adorning coffins with the portraits of Ariadne and Bakchos. For that was to them a sign that after the greatest sorrows Bakchos led to new happiness, and a pledge that even after death a new life began. This belief in a resurrection, however, was also taught in the mysteries of Eleusis (see p. 99) through the myth of Bakchos, who after suffering death rose again ; though at Eleusis he was called Iakchos.

4. THE ASIATIC DIONYSOS AND HIS PRODIGIES.

The Greeks dwelling in Asia Minor also worshipped Bakchos as guardian of their freedom ; they were, however, all the more indebted to his protection as they had continually to be on their guard against the attacks of the King of Persia, or of savage nations of the North. Thus it was said in Ephesos that Bakchos had defended the city against the wild Amazons. He had appeared here as a hero, who marched in triumph through all cities of Asia Minor, and overthrew all that opposed him. When the conqueror of the world, Alexander the Great, began his march through Asia and penetrated to distant India, that appeared to the Greeks as a land of wonders, people thought he only followed the traces of the conquering god Dionysos. Therefore the successors of Alexander were specially fond of representing the god Dionysos as their proto-type ; and since the bull was a beast specially sacred to Dionysos, they too liked to be represented on their coins with the horns of a bull.

The Asiatic Dionysos, however, appeared not only as a hero, but he was looked upon also as lord of the whole of nature, who declared his power through prodigies of every kind. He was, on this account, worshipped in a way in which the " Great Mother " was worshipped by Phrygians, with hosts of priests and deafening noise. The dull-sounding kettledrums, mingled with the noisy cymbals and shrill pipes, belonged to the service of Dionysos, and the Greeks accordingly gave him the name Bromios, or " the noisy one." In this uproarious crowd of worshippers

marched Dionysos, dressed as an Asiatic, with the
Asiatic fillet round his brow and the Lydian " Bassara,"
a long snow-white robe, on account of which the
Greeks called him Bassareus. Around his breast he
had girded a fawnskin, like the Mænads who served
him on Parnassos, and his hair hung in long womanish
locks (see Figs. 27 and 37). At first this form of the
god appeared contemptible ; but when they heard of

FIG. 37.—DIONYSOS BASSAREUS.
Bronze bust, Naples.

his wonderful deeds, all doubt as to his divinity disappeared. So Pentheus had refused to know anything
of the god, saying,—

> " 'Tis said a stranger hath appeared among us,
> A wizard, sorcerer, from the land of Lydia,
> Beauteous with golden locks and purple cheeks,
> Eyes moist with Aphrodite's melting fire." [1]

He had, however, to his cost learnt the god's power

[1] Euripides, *Bacchæ*, 233-36, Milman's translation.

too late. The beasts of the forest were subject to Dionysos ; and as the chariot of Rhea, the Phrygian mother of the gods, was drawn by lions, so lynxes, panthers, and lions fawned on him. He gave drink to the wild panther as to a domestic animal (see Fig. 38), and the serpent was almost always by his side. Either it was carried after him in a basket, or his attendants wreathed their breasts and hands with the sacred

FIG. 38.—DIONYSOS WITH THE PANTHER.
Relief on the choragic monument of Lysikrates, Athens.

creature. His miraculous power, however, seemed all the clearer when he had changed to the form of a half-intoxicated youth, whom, judging by appearance, one would not credit with any proof of strength.

Once had Tyrrhenian pirates seized the young Dionysos as he lay half asleep with wine, and hoped to sell him at a good price. But the fetters they put on him fell off of their own accord ; and while he with his black eyes sat quietly smiling there, terror seized the steersman. They bade him look after the ship, and not trouble himself about the young fellow; but then occurred a new prodigy. A vine threw its tendrils round the sail, fragrant wine streamed around the ship, and ivy climbed high up the mast. The god himself became a lion, and the terrified sailors, changed into dolphins, sprang into the sea. His faith saved the steersman alone, who had not failed to recognise Bakchos.

But as the god appeared among the Tyrrhenian pirates, the Greeks have by preference represented his form. He is a delicate, almost girlish youth, whose head, with its wavy hair, is encircled with a wreath, and sinks dreamily towards his breast, as if heavy with wine (see Pl. VI.).

5. The Troop of Bakchos, Mænads, Satyrs, Seilenos, and Centaurs.

The Nymphs are the nurses of the infant Bakchos. If, however, the human handmaids of the god fall into triumphant excitement at his appearance, then have the Nymphs still more ground to rejoice, the Nymphs those sportive denizens of meadow, spring, and glade. For the brooks babble again, and there is life within the grove: then is their time for highest joy. So they love to swarm round the god Dionysos, and wind about him in animated dances, striking cymbals and drums. So extravagant did their ways seem to mortals, that these handmaids of the sportive Bakchos were called " Mainades " (frenzied women).

But what would be the dances of the Mænads if the

VI. DIONYSOS.

In the Museum of the Capitol, Rome.

male spirits of the fountains, the Satyrs, or " Leaping goats," took no part in them? All divinities of the fountain love music and dance, and know full well how to sing and to play. In the district of Phrygia, in Asia Minor, tales were told of a Satyr Marsyas, the god of the river of that name, who even presumed to contend with Apollo in the art of music. King Midas of Phrygia, who had to act as umpire in the contest, decided so foolishly in favour of the Satyr that his ears grew into those of an ass. Apollo, however, received the prize awarded, and is supposed to have had the skin of Marsyas flayed off, to punish his presumption. When Xenophon, in the expedition of the Ten Thousand, came through Phrygia, a skin hung up in a grotto was pointed out to him, which the Greeks regarded as the skin of Marsyas. Presumption and shamelessness were indeed distinctive marks of the cowardly and worthless Satyrs. They were a race to whose wantonness nothing was sacred, and which above everything was devoted to the pleasures of wine. In this character the Satyrs showed themselves, for the most part, in the so-called Satyric dramas (see p. 221); and in the theatre they especially vented their wantonness on the hero of the story, mimicked Theseus or Herakles, stole food and drink, swaggered shamelessly like Marsyas, but ran away like cowards when matters were to be settled. Because their behaviour, however, was so boorish and coarse, they were represented in earlier times as half beasts, with horses' legs and long tails, and also on the stage their masks were partly like beasts, with ugly snub noses, and the lower part of the face projecting. Later, indeed, the artists improved

their appearance, so that they were often recognised
only by a short little tail or somewhat pointed ears.

The Seilenoi form a special class of Satyrs. They
were also deities of fountains; and since the story ran

Fig. 39. — Seilenos and Satyrs.
Relief in the Museum at Mantua.

that Bakchos as a child was brought up by a Seilenos,
an elderly instructor of the god was made out of him.
He became too, like the Satyrs, an inseparable com-
panion of Dionysos; and because he was a great friend

to wine, he was generally to be seen in an intoxicated condition; nay, he was rarely able to stand on his own feet, and was obliged to travel either riding on a donkey or on a waggon drawn by goats, and the Satyrs had trouble enough to hold him up in the meantime (see Fig. 39).

But because this condition gave something of wildness to his appearance, the belief later spread abroad that his great learning made him neglectful of appearances. The Athenians, as is well known, maintained in mockery that Sokrates, whose features, indeed, cannot have been beautiful, looked like a Seilenos. Seilenos, however, was a wise god, for all water-gods can foretell the future. People had only to fetter him with chains of flowers, and then he prophesied; or they might pour wine into the fountain, as King Midas did; then the old toper allowed himself to be caught, and uttered oracles.

Satyrs, Seilenos, Mænads, all made up the rout of Bakchos. When the god made his triumphal progress through all countries, together with his beautiful bride Ariadne, then the Satyrs served him as cup-bearers or blew their shepherd-pipes. Then, in wild enthusiasm, they vied with the Mænads in brandishing the thyrsos, whirling round with these in the dance, or sporting with the lions and panthers which tamely accompanied the god. Whoever imagined this troop of Dionysos, as free from care it marched in noisy merriment and joy, must have seen in it an image of a life free from all earthly troubles; and thus it happened that the ancients were particularly fond of adorning their sarcophagi with Dionysos and his train. People hoped to attain after death to such an existence so free from care.

Lastly, the Centaurs also belonged to the train of Dionysos. This was the name given to a being made up of horse and man that dwelt in the wild loneliness of the mountain, and knew nothing of human morals. Probably, the Centaurs were originally spirits of wild mountain torrents, that, dragging with them rocks and trees, heeded nothing that man's hand had built or planted. Their mother was said to be Nephele, the cloud, for from the cloud spring the wild mountain torrents. Thus wild and rough did the half-bestial tribe of Centaurs show itself at the marriage of Peirithoos, King of the Lapiths, when, in their drunkenness, they sought to tear from the king his bride, and inflamed the guests to terrible conflict with them. Thus, too, the Centaur Nessos tried to carry off the wife of Herakles, when he was to take her over a river, but he was laid low by the arrows of that hero.

Two only of the Centaurs distinguished themselves by milder ways; these were Pholos and Cheiron. Pholos was called a son of Seilenos. He received Herakles in hospitable fashion; but when the latter in gratitude presented his host with a cask of wine, the other Centaurs sniffed the savour of the glorious liquor. Armed with rocks and pine-trees they came storming along, and then arose a bloody struggle till Herakles laid them low. As, however, there was among the Satyrs a wise Seilenos, so people knew of a wise Centaur, Cheiron; he was conversant with all healing virtues of plants which grow on mountains, knew how to prepare balsam, and had been the teacher of Achilles.

The more, however, the Greeks felt pleasure in the enjoyment of nature, the more human did they depict to

Fig. 40.—Centaur with Eros.
Group in the Vatican Museum, Rome.

themselves the power of the divine beings with whom the solitude of the mountains seemed to them to be

peopled. The god Bakchos knew how to tame even
the savage Centaurs. Often in pairs they drew his
chariot, and accompanied his march with the sounds of
their stringed instruments. Now the Centaurs felt pain
and joy like the children of men. Familiarly did the
female Centaurs play with their young children, and they
were delighted when the father Centaur brought home
a hare as the result of his hunting. Nay, Eros, the god
of love, who subdues the whole world, aimed also against
them his love-arrows, hurried like a bold rider on their
backs (see Fig. 40), or held their hands fettered; and
so the Centaur too was compelled to endure the torments
of ardent desire.

(B) BACCHUS, LIBER, AND LIBERA.

Just as among the Greeks the god of wine arose out
of the god of spring and growth, so from the Italian
god of crops and growth, who was called Liber, there
arose the god of the vine. When, therefore, the tribes
of Italy obtained a knowledge of the Greek god Bakchos
from the Greek colonists in Southern Italy, they believed him to be the same as their own god Liber.
Nay, the Greek name soon quite supplanted the
Italian. Throughout Italy only Bacchus was spoken
of, and the name Liber came to be used almost only by
country people. These adhered to it most at the feast
of the vintage, which they celebrated in honour of
" Father " Liber.

Liber then appeared, with Ceres, the goddess of the
crops, as the most important god for the countryman.

When, in the year 496 B.C., a failure of crops and

a famine seemed threatening, the first temple was dedicated in Rome to the Greek Bakchos under the name of Liber, and he was worshipped together with Ceres and a female deity of the vine, called Libera.   People had learned, through the doctrine of the mysteries propagated in Southern Italy, that Bakchos, who went down into the lower world, had brought home as his bride Kore, Demeter's daughter, who was down there; and so Libera was called the bride of Bacchus.   The government, indeed, in Rome forbade the worshipping of Bacchus in accordance with Greek custom, for the trooping about of the women in free nature, and the noisy style of Bacchic rites that prevailed in Greece, were not at all suited to the serious feelings of the Romans.

Accordingly, in the year 186 B.C., the celebration of the mysteries, which the Romans called Bacchanalia, was strictly forbidden, because it was feared that morality was relaxed thereby.   It was not, however, possible to prevent the continual spread of the Greek myths of Dionysos.   So it had been learned from the Greeks that Bakchos was at the same time a "Liberator" and god of the oppressed; since the Roman name Liber happened to mean also " free," and the temple of Ceres was become a special sanctuary of the Plebeians (see p. 101), the three deities, Ceres, Liber, and Libera, were regarded as guardians of the liberty of the citizens. Images of Bacchus or of his attendant Marsyas were set up in market-places, as at Rome, like the statues of Roland in Germany, and were considered as a pledge of civic freedom.   At the festival of Bacchus in March the Roman youth received, for the first time, the manly

toga, as a mark of independence.   Therefore Bacchus
became for these young men also a god of liberty.

The Romans, however, soon adopted other ideas of
the Greek Bakchos.   The fancy of Alexander's successors, to represent the triumphant Bakchos as their
emblem, found favour also with the Roman magnates,
who led their victorious legions through various lands.
Thus, for instance, Pompey, when returning, like Bacchus, from an Indian campaign, had elephants harnessed
to his car; and soon Bacchus appeared to the Romans a
second Hercules, who triumphed over all enemies, even
Death himself; before whom the hell-hound Cerberus
sneaked off whining; who guides the courses of rivers
and all nature, and brings to man deliverance from
every earthly pain.

PART II.

THE LESSER GODS.

CHAPTER XVI.

THE DIOSCURI.

1. THE DIOSCURI AS GODS OF LIGHT.

IN the Peloponnesos men worshipped a divine pair of brothers as bringers of light. They galloped along on snow-white steeds, for light breaks forth from the dark night more rapidly in the South than among us. On the same grounds the Psalmist gives to the morning wings, and sometimes the Greeks, too, imagined that this pair of brothers, powerful over light, sped along on golden pinions. To the chivalrous race, however, that occupied the Peloponnesos, the white horses seemed more appropriate to the youths of light.

These deities of light bore various names. In Messenia the two were called Idas and Lynkeus; in Lakonia, Kastor and Polydeukes; and gradually the latter were universally recognised, the former forgotten, just as the race of the Messenians was subjugated by the inhabitants of Lakonia. All deities of light, however, love the moon, and since the ancients often conceived of the moon as a maiden shining with beauty, so they also believed that the deities of light endeavoured to carry off the moon-maiden. When the moon, at first rising in the West, in its further progress gradually moves more to the East, it appeared as if it wanted to withdraw from the light of the sun ; but as a waning moon it was overtaken again by the morning sun, till it quite vanished from man's sight, and in the new month the old spectacle began again. Therefore the Messenians said that their sun-youths Idas and Lynkeus desired to pay court to two moon-maidens, the daughters of Leukippos, or "White-horse ; " Kastor and Polydeukes also sought to win them, and therefore came to a quarrel with them. Still more clearly did the Lakonians express the love of the sun-youths Kastor and Polydeukes for the moon, when they related that the youths brought back their sister Helena, who had been carried off to the distant East. For Helena is only another word for Selene, the moon, and this as it rises constantly goes further towards the East. At a later time, when this reference was no longer understood, a story was told as to how Helena was carried away by Theseus to Attica, and brought back thence by Kastor and Polydeukes ; and finally it was said she was borne away to Troy by Paris.

That these heroes of the sun were conceived of as brothers cannot be surprising to any one who reflects that every day brings a new sun, while, on the other hand, all suns seem like and related to one another as two brothers. The light, indeed, continually rises and disappears, and, scarcely born, dies again, till another day appears and takes the place of the last. Hence arose the story that the brothers Kastor and Poly-deukes could never enjoy together the light of day, but if one sojourned above the earth the other lived beneath it. As time went on, this matter also was

misunderstood, and the following narrative was recounted as a reason for the strange life and death
of the twin brothers. On account of a herd of oxen,
Kastor and Polydeukes fell into strife with Idas and
Lynkeus, and lay in wait for them under an oak.
But the all-seeing Lynkeus caught sight of the
brothers, and began the fight. Whereupon it happened
that Idas killed Kastor, and Polydeukes, Lynkeus.
Then Idas immediately hits Polydeukes with a stone,
whereupon Zeus, in his anger, kills him with his
lightning, and takes Polydeukes to himself in heaven.
Polydeukes thought life without his brother not worth
living, and consequently Zeus granted that he should
live one day, and spend the next with Kastor in the
lower world.

Others tried to account for the wonderful relation
between the two brothers by calling only one of them
the son of a mortal man, Tyndareos ; the other the
son of Zeus. But in spite of this the poets name
both brothers " sons of Tyndareos ; " both are also
equally called Dioskouroi, or sons of Zeus, for gods
of light could have only the god of heaven for a
father.

But who would be better pleased at the appearance
of the gods of light than the seafarer, who, in the
darkness of the night, had to struggle with wind
and waves ? To him, in fact, the Dioscuri were the
rescuers in time of greatest need. Often when men
had invoked them, and had slaughtered white lambs in
their honour, they came and settled as little flames or
stars on the mast-head. Consequently the Æginetans,
after the battle of Salamis, dedicated a mast with

three golden stars in the sanctuary at Delphi: it was
the thank-offering for the auspicious guidance of the
Dioscuri and their sister Helena, who was always supposed to be closely united with them. But because
the shipmen in their need most loved to turn to the
Dioscuri and their light, these were represented almost
as a regular thing with the egg-shaped felt hat which
shipmen were wont to wear. The Dioscuri are represented on the base of a candelabrum (Fig. 41), which
of itself suggested the light-bestowing deities; in the
middle the moon is thought by some to be represented
under the image of a swan, which at times swims along
as the moon does in the sea of air. The Dioscuri were
worshipped as guardians of voyagers up to Christian
times; and when the Apostle Paul made his voyage to
Italy, his ship had the sign of "the Twins," *i.e.*, the
Dioscuri.

2. The Dioscuri as Prototypes of the Greek Nobility.

In Sparta especially were the Dioscuri worshipped
from remote ages with such zeal that they were not
even named directly, but spoken of only as "the two
gods." For they belonged to each other, like two com-
panions-in-arms who die rather than abandon each
other. Consequently they became the warlike models
of the Spartan nobility; and as they stood beside the
sailor on the high seas, so during a battle on land they
frequently came galloping up on their white horses to
give a timely aid. Under their special protection, however stood the two kings of the Spartans. It was not

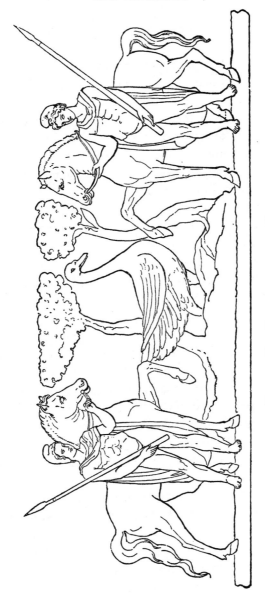

Fig. 41.—The Dioscuri with the Swan.

Relief in the Vatican Museum, Rome.

till it became a custom for only one king to take the field, and the other to stop in Sparta, that only one of the two Dioscuri could be invoked to give help in battle. The other was meantime acting as guardian of the king at home.

As aiders in battle, however, the Dioscuri were also models of bravery, and therefore they were considered as the inventors of the "Pyrrhiche," or war-dance. At a later period the poets told how Kastor was especially the rider, Polydeukes the hero of boxing, and this distinction has been generally observed.

In Attica also the Dioscuri were worshipped, and indeed under the proud title of *Anakes*, that is, "Kings." For chivalrous and distinguished was their mien. Every aristocratic virtue was ascribed to them, above all hospitality. And so not only were the Dioscuri invited in prayer as guests, but sacrificial tables were laid for them with food, and people could tell of many a noble house that had entertained the illustrious Twin Brethren in person. The families which specially prided themselves on such good fortune no doubt contributed much to the spread of the worship of the Dioscuri.

Of the power of the Twin Brethren the following story was related in antiquity :—The poet Simonides was once a guest of Skopas, a Thessalian prince. Here he delivered a panegyric on his host. Since, however, he commemorated also the Dioscuri as prototypes of hospitality, Skopas, with a disposition by no means noble, would pay the poet only half of the stipulated reward ; the other half, said he, the Dioscuri might give, who had shared the praise. Shortly after this Simonides was called out of the hall ; two youths were standing, he was told, at the door, and desired urgently to speak with him. The poet rises from his seat, goes forth, but sees no one. At that moment the banqueting-hall where Skopas sat falls with a crash, and buries him under its ruins with his companions, so that not even his corpse could be found. Thus did the Dioscuri take vengeance on a violation of proper behaviour, especially on the part of noble families.

The Dioscuri were among the Argonauts ; and the triumph of Polydeukes over Amykos is represented on the famous Ficoroni cista.

3. THE DIOSCURI AMONG THE ROMANS.

From the Greeks of Lower Italy as well as from the Etruscans settled in these parts the Romans learned to call the divine pair of twins Kastor and Polydeukes ; but the Etruscan name for the latter was Pultuke, from which the Romans formed the name Pollux. With them also Castor and Pollux were held to be the special patrons of the noble families. To them too were they youthful patterns of bravery, when on their white horses and in cloaks of purple hue they came galloping through the air to take part in the fight. So happened it in the year 496 B.C., at the battle of Lake Regillus, when the aristocracy of Rome victoriously defended the freedom of the Republic against the royal house of Tarquin that had been driven into exile :—

"Never on earthly anvil
Did such rare armour gleam ;
And never did such gallant steeds
Drink of an earthly stream."

*　　　*　　　*　　　*

> " But under those strange horsemen
>   Still thicker lay the slain ;
> And after those strange horses
>   Black Auster toiled in vain.
> Behind them Rome's long battle
>   Came rolling on the foe,
> Ensigns dancing wild above,
>   Blades all in line below." [1]

Not only did the helping hand of the Dioscuri take part in this battle, but on their snow-white steeds they appeared immediately after the fight in the Roman Forum, bearing the tidings of victory, and watered their horses at Juturna's spring, near the temple of Vesta :—

> " When they drew nigh to Vesta,
>   They vaulted down amain,
> And washed their horses in the well
>   That springs by Vesta's fane." [2]

On this spot arose one of the earliest temples in a Grecian style at Rome, the *Ædes Castoris*. In later times on the dedication-day it was an annual custom for the Roman knights to form a procession on horseback,—

> " And pass in solemn order
>   Before the sacred dome
> Where dwelt the great Twin Brethren
>   Who fought so well for Rome." [3]

But if, as with the aristocracy of Sparta and Athens, the worship of the Dioscuri in the first place concerned the families of equestrian rank, yet the Romans soon learned that the twin gods were no less the guardians of shipmen at sea :—

> " Safe comes the ship to haven,
>   Through billows and through gales,
> If once the great Twin Brethren
>   Sit shining on the sails." [4]

---

[1] Macaulay, *Lays of Ancient Rome.*   [2] *Ib.*   [3] *Ib.*   [4] *Ib.*

This explains how Horace in his beautiful ode could commend to the protection of the " Brothers of Helena" his friend Vergil when making for Athens. As they brought good fortune to the traveller and the wanderer, their statues found a place at the door of many a Roman temple.

Finally, the myth of the alternate life and death of the brothers was not without import in the minds of the Romans. Men saw in them a pledge for coming to life again after death, and were therefore fond of adorning sarcophagi with their images, as with those of the evening and the morning stars. That the Dioscuri were set as constellations in the heavens, as a sign of immortality, is a tale of a very late period. But this tale is still current, and therefore, even at the present day, two brilliant stars are still called Castor and Pollux.

CHAPTER XVII.

HERAKLES—HERCULES.

(A) HERAKLES.

HERAKLES, THE NATIONAL HERO OF THE WHOLE HELLENIC STOCK.

SCATTERED throughout this volume are many allusions to the foremost of Grecian heroes, Herakles, adored alike by Dorian and Ionian, at Athens and at Thebes, at Sparta and at Tarentum.

With Zeus as his father he ranked as a demi-god; and by sheer dogged courage, strength, and endurance he eventually won an entrance to the select circle of Olympos.

His mother Alkmene, sharing the exile of Amphitryon, had left Tiryns for Thebes; hence the Thebans claimed to share the glories of her son. When only eight months old he strangled in his cradle two serpents sent by the jealous Hera to destroy him. One of his earliest exploits was the slaughter of the lion that had its lair on the slopes of Kithairon. Thus was obtained the lion's skin, which formed henceforward his characteristic garb.

In the earlier works of art the figure of Herakles

constantly recurs. His original weapon was the bow ; afterwards we find him described as a heavy-armed warrior ; later still he is armed with the club. In almost all the mythical events preceding the Trojan War, Herakles took a leading part. After joining in the expedition of the Argonauts, he captured Troy with the aid of Telamon, Peleus, and Theseus. The last named was frequently represented by his fellow country-men, the Athenians, as the assistant or imitator of Herakles in his deeds of daring.

The adventurous spirit of Herakles led to various brawls, and occasionally to unjustifiable slaughter. One such homicide had to be expiated by servitude with Queen Omphale, who posed as hero with club and lion's skin, while the submissive athlete clumsily plied her neglected distaff.

Through the machinations of Hera, Herakles was fated to obey the behests of the craven prince Eurys-theus, who ruled Mykenai and the land of Argos. Ten—or rather twelve—dangerous enterprises were assigned to him, known as " the Labours of Hercules," and thus catalogued by Apollodoros :—

1. The slaughter of the Nemean lion.

2. The destruction of the nine-headed Hydra that infested the marsh of Lerna. This labour was dis-allowed by Eurystheus on the ground that Iolaos had given material aid by searing the Hydra's severed necks to prevent a fresh growth of heads.

3. In the third place, Herakles was ordered to bring alive to Mykenai the swift Cerynician stag, with golden horns, that was sacred to Artemis.

4. His next labour was to capture alive the wild-

boar of Erymanthos. After a serious brush with the Centaurs (see p. 230), he succeeded in catching the boar. A vase-painter has immortalized the terror of Eurystheus, who at the sight of the monster promptly retired into a large pot he had prepared for such emergencies.

5. The fifth task was to cleanse single-handed, and in one day, the stables of Augeas, which contained a vast number of oxen,—a task accomplished by diverting the courses of two rivers. As, however, Herakles had bargained with Augeas for payment, Eurystheus refused to count this as one of the ten stipulated labours.

6. The sixth was to get rid of the birds that frequented Lake Stymphalis.

7. The seventh was to bring to Eurystheus the Cretan Bull; which afterwards passed over the Isthmos to Marathon.

8. The eighth was to bring him the man-eating mares of the Thracian King Diomedes.

9. The ninth was to carry off the girdle of Hippolyte, Queen of the Amazons.

10. The tenth was to convey the oxen of Geryones from Erytheia, an island bordering on Okeanos. Geryones had a triple body. His purple cattle were herded by Eurytion, and guarded by the two-headed dog Orthros. All three were slain by Herakles, who had crossed Okeanos in a golden cup, presented to him by the sun-god Helios. The drinking-cup must have been a good-sized one, for the whole herd was ferried over in it.

The adventures with the Hydra and with Augeas not satisfying Eurystheus, two additional tasks were undertaken to complete the stipulated number of ten; viz., the obtaining of the apples from the gardens of the Hesperides, and the dragging of Kerberos from the lower to the upper world. In the course of his journey Herakles slew the great wrestler Antaios, by raising him up and crushing him in his arms, for Antaios gained strength each time he touched the ground. Bousiris, too, was killed, the King of Egypt who sacrificed strangers on the altar of Zeus. Then, after freeing Prometheus (see p. 154), Herakles secured the golden apples.

He now undertook the last of the series of twelve "Labours," and descended into the abode of Hades, rescuing Theseus on his way. After a severe struggle, he brought Kerberos to Eurystheus, and then took him back again.

The completion of the "Twelve Labours," however, was not the end of his active career. Wrestling with Death himself, he brought back to life Alkestis, wife of his friend Admetos.

The Pythia refusing to answer his inquiries, he threatened to sack the temple of Delphi; and, seizing the tripod, began a struggle with Apollo, which was ended only by Zeus hurling a thunderbolt between them. The oracle thereupon declared that as Herakles in a fit of madness had hurled Iphitos from the walls of Tiryns, he must in expiation he sold into slavery for three years. Hermes accordingly sold him to Omphale, Queen of the Lydians (see p. 247).

It was at this time that the voyage of the Argonauts took place, and the hunt of the Calydonian boar (see p. 130), in which also Herakles had a share. Then came his expedition against Laomedon, King of Troy (see p. 247), which resulted in the death of the latter.

On his return Herakles assisted the gods in defeating the giants (see p. 162), for mortal help was indispensable to them. The two most formidable, Porphyrion and Alkyoneus, were slain by him.

The gods themselves, however, were not exempt from his violence. Among others he attacked Hades, who had come to help Neleus, King of Pylos. Neleus was killed with all his sons, save Nestor; and Hades was wounded (see p. 201).

Herakles married Deianeira, discomfiting his rival Acheloos (see p. 279). Soon afterwards he entrusted his bride to the Centaur Nessos to carry her over a river. This led to a quarrel, and Nessos, mortally wounded by an arrow, told Deianeira to keep some of his blood to serve as a love-potion, if Herakles should seem likely to prove unfaithful.

The occasion soon arrived. Dreading the fascinations of Iole, one of her husband's captives, Deianeira sent him as a present a tunic steeped in the blood of Nessos, and thus infected by the Hydra's poison, in which the arrows of Herakles had been dipped. Herakles put on the garment, and forthwith the poison began to eat into his flesh. In his agony he threw himself upon a funeral pile, and as the flames rose his spirit was borne away to heaven, to live immortal as an Olympian god. Hera was now, at length, reconciled, and gave him in marriage her daughter Hebe, goddess of youth.

One of the many children of Herakles, Telephos, exposed as an infant to perish on Mount Parthenion, was saved by shepherds, and ultimately became Prince of Teuthrania, after adventures which are depicted on the smaller frieze from the great altar of Pergamon.

Herakles may, like other mythological personages, have originally represented the mighty forces of Nature; his voyaging over the Western seas seems to reflect the travels of the sun.

(B) HERCULES.

HERCULES AMONG THE ROMANS.

Fond as they were of the struggles in the Amphitheatre, the Romans could not fail to appreciate an impersonation of ideal physical force; and the name of Hercules was often on their lips. In the dialogues of the Roman dramatists one of the commonest ejaculations is *Hercule* or *Hercle*, shortened from *Ita me Hercules juvet*, "So help me Hercules!" According to Professor Key,[1] *hercle* occurs no fewer than six hundred times in Plautus alone.

The relation of the Roman Hercules to Juno was very different from that of Herakles to Hera; and probably he bore originally a different name. Gellius tells us that a Roman woman never swore by Hercules. What she did swear by was her *Juno*, a being equivalent to the *Genius* of a man (see p. 42). It has been suggested accordingly that Hercules and the *Genius* were the same person. Thus women were shut out from the sacrifice offered to Hercules on the *Ara Maxima*, while, on the other hand, men were not

[1] *Latin Dictionary.*

admitted to the ceremonies of the *Bona Dea* so nearly allied to Juno.

The Roman Emperor Commodus was so fond of the athletic hero that he had himself represented with club and lion's skin, and delighted in the title of the Roman Hercules. This title and the symbols of the god are seen on the coins of Commodus; and a gem in the British Museum (No. 1626) bears his head side by side with that of his favourite deity.

[1] See R. Peter in Roscher's *Lexikon*, p. 2258.

CHAPTER XVIII.

RHEA KYBELE—MAGNA MATER.

(A) RHEA KYBELE, THE PHRYGIAN UNIVERSAL MOTHER AND THE GREEK MOTHER OF THE GODS.

THE "Niobe" whom Sophokles apostrophises as "ever weeping in a rocky tomb," the "Niobe" carved on the precipitous cliff of Sipylos, has been claimed in recent years as an image of Rhea Kybele, or "the Mother of Sipylos." [1]

Rhea Kybele was to the Greeks originally a foreign goddess, Phrygia in Asia Minor being the chief seat of her worship. Here she was regarded with such reverence that no one ventured to substitute an image in human form for the primeval pledge of her presence— a rude, unhewn mass of stone. Kybele was considered as the mother of all living things, as the mistress of universal nature. Even wild beasts obeyed her will. Lions and panthers drew her chariot, and all trees in a state of nature were sacred to her ; above all, the pine that grows on lofty mountains, and the box-tree from which the flute was carved. For with shrill sound of pipes, dull beating of drums, and loud clash of cymbals was the Universal Mother worshipped by the Asiatics ; especially when in spring the earth

[1] *Journal of Hellenic Studies*, vols. i. (Sayce) and iii. (Ramsay).

awoke to new life. Then troops of priests, called
Korybantes, followed the sacred chariot of the goddess, and sought to express their joy by the noisy
music of cymbals, drums, and flutes; for it was said
that the goddess had then found once more her
favourite Attis.

FIG. 42.—RHEA KYBELE.
Statuette in the Vatican Museum, Rome.

When, however, the season of the blossoms had faded
away, then was Attis also, like Adonis (see p. 181),
slain by a wild-boar,—the symbol of the destructive
storms of winter,—and once more the troops of priests

marched with the image of the goddess through the land ; now, however, not merrily, but with woful cries and frantic rage against their own bodies, as the vehemently-excited peoples of Asia alone could do.

Thus the Greeks, too, became acquainted with Rhea Kybele, and through their commercial connection with Asia Minor it resulted that the worship of the Universal Mother soon found an entrance into Greece. But because the Greeks heard that Rhea was the mother of all beings, they made her mother of all gods, including Zeus. Now, as the spouse of hoary Kronos, she appeared still more worthy of veneration. She secured all the privileges of the Olympian deities, and Hermes, the messenger of the gods, became her special cup-bearer. Since, however, Rhea Kybele was worshipped as the most distinguished deity in several cities of Asia—for example, in Pessinus—she became in the eyes of the Greeks the guardian of cities. Hence the Athenians built for her in their market-place the Metroon, or " House of the Mother," and kept in it the decrees of the State. They had given her a human form not unworthy of the goddess, with long robe and veil like the goddesses Hera and Demeter ; and the only indication of an Asiatic origin was a lion couched at her feet, or the tambourine. A mural crown was often sufficient to indicate the Universal Mother Rhea Kybele as the guardian of cities (Fig. 42).

(B) THE ROMAN MAGNA MATER AND ATTIS.

The worship of the Phrygian Universal Mother reached the Romans several centuries later than it had made its way among the Greeks. Amid the disasters of the Second Punic War (205 B.C.), when men hoped from new deities the protection which the old seemed no longer to vouchsafe, the Sibylline Books advised the introduction of these foreign rites. King Attalos of Pergamon was so kind as to grant to the Roman envoys the transference of the sacred stone from Pessinus, and the Delphian Apollo concurred on condition that the best man would act as host to the image. Not without difficulty was the stone brought to Rome : at the very mouth of the Tiber the vessel ran aground, and remained there till Claudia Quinta, a lady of distinction, on whom suspicion of guilt had unjustly fallen, with a slight pull set the ship going against the current of the river, and thus made it clear to the whole people that she stood in special favour with the goddess. In Rome the highborn P. Cornelius Scipio Nasica—for him had the Senate pronounced the best man—received the image of " the Universal Mother."

A magnificent sanctuary was soon established for her on the Palatine, and the ugly stone, covered with a mask of silver, was employed as the head of a new image. Not long after the reception of the stone fortune became more favourable to the Roman arms, and in gratitude for this a yearly recurring festival was instituted, the Megalesia, at which people of distinction took their pleasure in feasting and theatrical representations. As, however, the Greeks had recognised in Rhea Kybele the mother of all the gods, so the Romans also acted after their example. It happened fortunately that the Roman god of the crops Saturnus, in whose honour the Saturnalia, a season of rejoicing common to all, was celebrated about Christmas time, who, moreover, was declared equivalent to the Grecian Kronos, had, according to Roman belief, a goddess Ops to wife. Since she too was considered a dispenser of fruits, it was possible for the Great Mother from Phrygia (or "*Magna Mater*," as the Romans said) to enter on her position.

In Imperial times the respect paid to *Magna Mater* was constantly on the increase. There was even an imitation of the Oriental mode of worship, and a reference to the commencement of spring ; and permission was given to Phrygian priests, after a day of fasting, on which people gave themselves up to mourning for the disappearance of Attis, to carry the image of the goddess through the streets of Rome with turbulent gaiety. Then the figure was bathed in the river Almo, as in the case of the Teutonic goddess Nerthus, and ragged mendicant priests, who were called Metragyrtai, collected gifts for the goddess among the people.

Finally, the worship of Magna Mater and her favourite Attis reached such a pitch of ardour that the authority of all the other gods was impaired by it. Above all, Attis was regarded as the epitome of all divine powers, and in him almost alone the Roman heathen believed he found deliverance and comfort. Possibly the heathen world was anxious not to be left behind the Christianity that was spreading wider every day, and so even the Christian rite of baptism was employed in the service of Attis. It was believed that only one who was sprinkled with the blood of a ram or bull, and dedicated acceptably to Attis and Magna Mater, was inwardly purified, and as it were born again.

For this purpose whoever was to be baptized had to get into a trench covered with planks having holes bored in them, over which the victim was killed ; its blood then ran over the person standing underneath. But since Attis himself was considered as the slain god come to life again, he was often represented by the Romans on their sepulchral monuments in his Phrygian costume, with plaited trousers, jacket, and pointed cap, as a sign that after death a new life begins again.[1]

[1] As to the death and resurrection of Attis and Adonis, see Frazer, *The Golden Bough*, vol. i.

CHAPTER XIX.

ASKLEPIOS—ÆSCULAPIUS; HYGIEIA.

(A) ASKLEPIOS AND HYGIEIA.

WHEN belief in the great gods of Olympos had begun to wane, men's thoughts turned not unnaturally to those less imposing but more practically useful ideas of comfort and advantage to mankind, that were associated with the names of deities holding a less exalted rank in the Greek Pantheon. Foremost among these second-rate Immortals was Asklepios, originally perhaps the leading deity of some less distinguished branch of the Hellenic race. For in the features of this god we may trace a certain affinity to the type of Zeus, and our magnificent bust of Asklepios from Melos [1] may stand comparison with the famous conception of the Olympian monarch that forms the frontispiece of this volume. Our representations of Asklepios belong, however, almost entirely to the fourth and later centuries, and his form would be sought in vain among the sculptures of the Parthenon. Athens, Epidauros, Kos, and Pergamon were renowned seats of his worship, and his image occurs frequently on the coins of the last-named city.

His most ancient temple, however, was at Trikka,

[1] In the Elgin Room, British Museum.

in Thessaly, from which town troops were led to
Troy by his sons Podaleirios and Machaon, the two
famous surgeons of the *Iliad*.

Thessaly was undoubtedly the cradle of the cult of

FIG. 43.—ASKLEPIOS.
From an ivory Diptychon.

Asklepios; and it is thought that he was originally
an ancient oracular deity of that part of Greece.

Asklepios was son of the Thessalian Koronis and
Apollo, and was committed as a child to the care of

the wise Centaur Cheiron, who taught him the art of medicine. Such skill did he acquire, that not content with curing the sick, he raised the dead to life. For this purpose he used the Gorgon's blood, given him by Athena. Zeus, fearing the consequences of this raising of the dead, struck Asklepios with the thunderbolt, and Apollo, in revenge, slew the Kyklopes who had forged the bolt. It was for this offence that he was condemned by Zeus to a year's servitude on earth.

Asklepios was usually (though not invariably) represented in art as bearded, and with head slightly bent. It is curious that, contrary to the usual rule, the beardless type was an archaic one, while in later times the beard was generally introduced. In his hand was a staff, round which a serpent twined (Fig. 43). The staff was the mark of a physician, and its use survived till the days of Oliver Goldsmith and the "clouded cane." The cock was sacred to Asklepios; and Sokrates, when dying, did not fail to provide for such an offering.

The votaries of Asklepios lay down to sleep in or near his temple, and during their sleep received from him oracular directions, of a more less enigmatical character, as to the treatment of their diseases. The interpretation of these dreams was the business of the priests, many of whom were probably skilled physicians.

Of the numerous retinue of Asklepios, at least two deserve passing notice. Hygieia, his daughter (some called her his wife), has come down to us as a robust maiden, generally engaged in feeding a serpent or giving it drink from a cup (Fig. 44).

Telesphoros, by some regarded as son of Asklepios, is a diminutive figure frequently appearing on the later coins of Pergamon. He is closely wrapped in a sort

FIG. 44.—HYGIEIA.
From an ivory Diptychon.

of hooded ulster, and is generally recognised as a divinity of convalescence, who completes the cure.[1]

At Epidauros a god closely resembling Telesphoros

[1] Those who care to know more of this supernatural sanitarian should refer to an interesting paper by Mr. Warwick Wroth, in *The Journal of Hellenic Studies*, vol. iii., p. 283.

was invoked under the name of Akesios. Though an averter of disease, however, Akesios does not seem to have been specially connected with the convalescent stage.

(B) ÆSCULAPIUS AT ROME.

In the mid-stream of the Tiber, as it bends towards the Capitol, lies the island of S. Bartolemmeo, the ancient *Insula Tiberina*, where " The Brothers of Charity " carry on the work of healing commenced there over two thousand years ago.

In the year 291 B.C., by direction of the Sibylline Books, an embassy was despatched to Epidauros to summon the god of healing, with a view to checking the prevailing pestilence. The embassy was successful, and the god shipped himself on board their vessel ; not in the guise of graven image, but beneath the form of the serpent sacred to himself.

Arrived in the Tiber, the serpent glided ashore on the island, where a temple of Æsculapius commemorated the event, and the spot henceforward was known by his name.

The worship of Æsculapius remained Greek in character, just as the physicians who claimed him as their patron were, for the most part, of Hellenic origin.

CHAPTER XX.

PAN—FAUNUS.

(A) PAN, THE GREEK GOD OF PASTURES AND HELPER IN BATTLE.

THE rude herdsmen of the wild, sequestered uplands of Arcadia worshipped from time immemorial Pan as guardian of the grazing flocks and herds.

These grazier folk had a peculiar conception of their deity. Since goats formed their most valuable possessions, they thought they could not honour their divine patron better than by conferring upon him the semblance of a goat. Half beast, half man, with goat's feet, with two horns, covered with hair and with ugly goat's face, thus the swift-footed god,—

"Fleeter of foot than the fleet-foot kid," [1]

raced the goats up the steepest peaks, and rested with them during the mid-day heat; then the herdsman did not venture to disturb him by any noise; not even on his "Syrinx," or shepherd's pipe, did he dare to practise, on which, otherwise, the god himself loved to play in the cool of the evening.

It was not till the time of the Persian Wars that the inhabitants of other districts of Greece began to

[1] Swinburne, *Atalanta in Calydon.*

honour the Arcadian god Pan.   When the Athenians, before the battle of Marathon, sought through the courier Pheidippides the help of the Spartans against the approaching Persians, Pan with loud shouting met the messenger on the heights of Parthenion, which separates Arcadia from Argolis.

As the runner halted in terror the god called to him, "Why do the Athenians trouble themselves so little about me, though I have already often been thoughtful for them, and am willing always to be favourable ? " And this was not mere talk, for at the battle of Marathon he filled the small army of the Athenians with such courage, and struck such terror into the Persian hosts, that the latter were glad to reach the sea and to save at least their lives.

Hence even at the present day we call a violent fear "a panic." The grateful Athenians, however, after the battle, dedicated to Pan a shrine in a grotto at the foot of their Acropolis, and instituted torch-races and sacrifices in his honour.

Henceforward the kindly Pan had ceased to be simply god of the grazing herds. Nay, the original meaning of his name was no longer understood, and it was rendered as "Universal God." But by way of explanation the poets invented the following history. Hermes, the god of the herdsmen, and a wood-nymph, daughter of Dryops, were, according to these poets, the parents of Pan. Because the child was so ugly, his mother, shocked at his appearance, had deserted him. Yet Hermes carried his dear little son to Olympos, and displayed him to the Immortals with fatherly pride. The gods were delighted with the remarkable child,

and thereupon they called him " All-god," because he
caused joy in the hearts of all.

As Hermes was a friend of the nymphs, whom he
was wont to tease and trifle with, so his son Pan also

FIG. 45.—PAN.
Greek marble statuette.

l oved to sport with the charming nymphs in forest and
in field ; and because his form, half man, half beast,
reminded people of the Satyrs, companions of Bakchos
(often goat-footed, like him), it was believed that Pan

also joined the jovial rout of Bakchos. Nay, the cheerful Greeks often associated with him a whole family of others like himself, including many a child-Pan, the so-called Paniskoi, who all vied with the Satyrs in exuberance of spirits and wantonness. Pan is distinguished from the Satyrs chiefly by his horns. In Athens alone was dignity given to the god's form. Here artists were fond of representing him with a certain shy, decorous deportment, and clad in a long cloak, like an Athenian citizen (see Fig. 45). Even thus there was always something to frighten people in this form; hence, in Christian art, features of this half-bestial god of the goatherd have been utilized in the representation of the impersonation of evil.

Plutarch [1] tells a strange story of the death of Pan, dating it with chronological accuracy in the reign of Tiberius. Off the islets named Paxoi certain voyagers heard a mysterious voice bid the steersman proclaim, " Great Pan is dead ! " The proclamation was followed by loud cries, as of sorrow and astonishment. To this Milton alludes in his *Hymn on the Nativity* :—

> "The lonely mountains o'er,
> And the resounding shore,
> A voice of weeping heard and loud lament."

(B) FAUNUS, GOD OF COUNTRY LIFE, AND OF THE LUPERCI.

There was no lack of deities of country life and free nature among the ancient inhabitants of Italy, as Pales, goddess of the herdsmen ; Vertumnus, god of gardens ; Pomona, goddess of fruits. All, however, were sur-

---

[1] *De Defectu Oraculorum*, p. 189; *cf.* p. 669 *b*.

passed in importance by the rural god Faunus. He was the kindly guardian of the country-folk generally in forest and plain, and his name itself denotes "the favourable one." It was in the forest, above all, that men thought they recognised his influence. In his honour the forest in autumn shed its leaves; and when the Italian seafarer has at last got safe to his native shore, then in his gratitude he hangs his robe on an olive-tree sacred to Faunus. To this god of the forest was ascribed, too, the power of prophecy, for in the woodland solitude each sound fills the breast with timid foreboding that a god is nigh. The grotto of Albunea, near Tibur, was in later times considered as such an oracle of Faunus. Here whatever the petitioner wished to implore declared itself to the priest of Faunus through wondrous visions and sounds. Since, however, Faunus was a prophetic deity, he could also serve as a patron of poets, and Horace, on this account, praises him in a pretty poem, because the god has protected him from a falling tree.

But as the forest and its pastures offered the best support for the grazing kine, Faunus became also the guardian of the herds; and so came it that the Romans, when they learnt of the Greek Pan, recognised him in their own Faunus. As the former, so now also Faunus had to sport with Satyrs and nymphs of the mountains, to terrify the unsuspecting wanderer, and through his appearance to chase the hostile armies in wild fearful flight. Nay, it was now believed, just as the Greeks thought of their Pan, that together with the one Faunus there were also a whole family of wanton Fauni, who spent their existence in the freedom of nature. As guardian of the flocks Faunus had the name Lupercus, *i.e.*, the god who wards off the wolf. In honour of this Faunus Lupercus a festival was celebrated twice a year— in December at the winter solstice, when after the close of the harvest the peasant's work was done and the merry dance could begin, and then in February, when winter came to an end. Most important was this February festival. Then was the time to win the favour of Faunus by special expiatory rites. The moral feelings of his worshippers did not permit of human sacrifice, but the wit of man devised other means for gaining favour in the eyes of Faunus. The fore- heads of two youths were smeared with the blood of the goats sacrificed to Faunus, and so it appeared as if the blood of the youths had flowed. When the blood had been washed off with a bit of hide dipped in pure milk, the youths had to laugh loud : this was the good omen for the propitiation of the god, who was con- tented with the sacrifice offered. Now began merry doings at Rome. Human representatives of Faunus, so-called Luperci, that is, youths whose waists were girt with a goat-skin, leaped about all over the city, playing all sorts of pranks. Their chief object was to strike with a strap of goat-skin the hands of the women who met them. Those so struck were not displeased, for the blow was supposed to promise happiness in marriage. The month in which this propitiation took place was, and still is, called Februarius,[1] or month of expiation.

The worship of Faunus seemed to the later Romans so time-honoured that he was made out to be a king

---

[1] From *februare* = expiate.

of remote antiquity, who had exercised a benign sway over the state of the Aborigines or primeval inhabitants, and had spread the knowledge of agriculture. As father of King Latinus, Faunus appeared, at the same time, the progenitor of the Latins in general, and this is the explanation of the Luperci at their festival offering to Julius Cæsar the kingly crown, which was to make him, as a second Faunus Lupercus, king of the Latin race.[1]

[1] On the animal form of Faunus and similar deities, see Frazer, *The Golden Bough*, vol. II., esp. pp. 34-7.

CHAPTER XXI.

THE INFERIOR GODS OF THE SEA AND THE RIVERS.

(A) WATER-DEITIES OF THE GREEKS.

1. THE SEA-MONSTERS ; SKYLLA AND THE SIRENS.

THE more frail the vessels of the ancients were in comparison with our own, the more terrible seemed to the sailor the dangers of the sea. How many voyaged far, far away, never to return ! The sorrowing relatives at home could not even give back the drowned man's body to the bosom of the earth, and had to content themselves with heaping up an empty grave,—called Kenotaphion,—and planting upon it an upright oar, as a sign that a seaman had perished without leaving a trace behind. Who could tell whether his bark had been driven by howling winds against the rocks and dashed in pieces, or whether a terrible sea-monster had devoured him ?

All these dangers, however, proceeded from super-human beings hostile to the seafarer. Phorkys was the name given to the father of all these sea-demons, and his wife Keto is herself called the "sea-monster." Whatever dreadful forms appeared in nature the poets called children of Phorkys and Keto. Among these the most prominent were Skylla and the Sirens. In

the distant Western sea, whither a Greek ship rarely
made her way, Skylla had her home, dwelling opposite
the whirlpool Charybdis. Usually she sojourns "in
the deep recesses of a cave, whence she thrusts out
her mouths, and drags vessels on to her rocks. At
top, a human face, a maiden with beauteous bosom;
at bottom, an enormous sea-monster—dolphins' tails
attached to a belly all of wolves' heads." [1]

Thus in Vergil's *Æneid* the seer Helenos describes
the monster, but still more terribly has Homer described Skylla, when he says she has twelve feet and
six heads; terrific baying of dogs rages round her,
and with body bent forward she snatches after fish
and seals, so that no ship can boast of passing her
by unscathed. At a later date, men believed they had
found the position of Skylla and Charybdis in the
eddies of the Straits of Messina. The feeble eddy now
observed there gives, indeed, no representation of the
description by the ancients.

Still more dangerous, however, seemed to the sailor
the island of the Sirens. Here dwelt the treacherous
maidens who, through song that infatuates the heart,
entice the sailor, in order to give him over to death.
For "whoso draws nigh them unwittingly and hears
the sound of the Sirens' voice, never doth he see wife
or babes stand by him on his return, nor have they joy
at his coming; but the Sirens enchant him with their
clear song, sitting in the meadow, and all about is a
great heap of bones of men, corrupt in death, and round
the bones the skin is wasting." [2]

---

[1] *Æneid*, iii., 424-28, Conington's translation.
[2] Homer, *Odyssey*, xii., 41-6, Butcher and Lang's translation.

The dangers of the seas did, indeed, gradually lessen in the eyes of seamen, in proportion as the vessels became stronger, and the information as to distant seas and lands more certain.

Hence, in later times, men thought of Sirens only as songstresses. Generally people could tell of three, of whom one sang to the lyre, while the other two accompanied the singing with flute and shepherd's pipe. So we often see the Siren on Greek tombstones as an image of the lament for the dead. They are beautiful maidens, whose figure ends in a bird's body. Finally, there arose the story of a contest of the Muses and Sirens. The former, of course, were victorious in the competition, and by way of punishment plucked out the feathers from the Sirens and henceforth wore them as a headdress.

2. THE GREEK SEA-GODS AS GUARDIANS OF SEAFARERS.

The more the seaman's fancy was seized and filled by the terrors of the deep, the more men desired to make sure of divine help. Nowhere more than on the lonely sea did the anxious heart of feeble man require hope and the confidence that the dangerous voyage would meet with a fortunate end. The sailor, therefore, turned to the protecting gods of the sea. Poseidon, however, was very far from being the only sea-god among the Greeks. He was only the ruler of the spirits of the sea. There were almost as many guardians of voyagers as there were Greek tribes that ventured out to sea. Of the Dioscuri we have already heard (see pp. 239, 240). Many of these sea-deities existed, indeed, only in the mouths of the poets, as Aigeus or Aigaion, properly "he of the wave." Both soon vanished from popular belief, giving way to Poseidon. Aigaion was called a son of Poseidon, and a powerful sea-giant. Thetis, the goddess of the sea, once summoned him to protect Zeus in Olympos. Aigeus, however, was distinguished by the Athenians of a later period as an ancient king of their country and father of Theseus. That he was originally much the same as Poseidon is perceived from the fact that Theseus is sometimes called Poseidon's son, and it was said of him, just as it was of Poseidon, that he had founded the Isthmian Games.

Goddesses also were invoked by seafarers to rescue them. One of the most ancient is Ino Leukothea, "the white goddess." When Odysseus was tossed hither and thither by the billows, she rose from the wave, seated herself on his raft, and gave him her girdle to save him. Then she bade him abandon the raft, swim to shore, and cast the girdle far into the sea, without looking round after it. For the ways of the sea-gods are secret, like those of the nymphs : they brook not that mortal eyes should play the spy on them. So Leukothea dived like a snow-white coot, and the dark wave closed over her.

Leukothea is the goddess of the white breaker that casts the shipwrecked ashore. But there are so many waves in the sea that no eye can grasp their number as they rise and disappear. Countless, therefore, were the Nereids, kindly sea-maidens, daughters of Nereus, the old man of the sea ; and the poets, to name a round number, speak of fifty fair-haired, silver-footed virgins.

Usually they sit together with their father, the kindly old god, deep below in the sea, in a grotto glittering as with silver ; though at times, too, the sisters rise to dance together on the waves. Fairest of the Nereids was Thetis, wedded to a mortal, Peleus, and the mother of Achilles. Great is her sympathy at all times with her son. With all the Nereids she bursts forth in common lamentation, when Achilles has lost his friend Patroklos ; and since on his friend's death his first suit of armour is carried off, she procures for him, through the art of Hephaistos, fresh splendid arms. She protects the corpse of Patroklos, keeping off the flies and dropping nectar upon it, to guard it from decay. Her sorrow for her son's suffering is all the greater, as she knows beforehand the end of his life, for all sea-deities have knowledge of the future. The old sea-god Nereus once rose from the waters when faithless Paris was bearing Helen over the sea, and disclosed to the wrong-doer the awful destiny of his native city, Troy.

Like Nereus, the sea-god Proteus was esteemed wise and knowing as to the future. As a god full of cunning he had, like all water-deities, the gift of transformation. Thetis, too, the Nereid, had taken all sorts of wondrous shapes when the mortal hero Peleus claimed her as his bride. Yet her cunning availed her not a whit. The same lot befell Proteus, who near Egypt was tending Amphitrite's flocks of seals. Menelaos in his wanderings once came across him on the island of Pharos, and through the aid of the crafty Eidothea, daughter of Proteus, succeeded in overpowering the old fellow while taking a siesta on shore in a

cool grotto. In spite of the veteran's changing himself
by turns into lion, serpent, panther, wild-boar, and
into water and a lofty tree, Menelaos managed to
bind him fast and compelled him to prophesy.

All these, however, were only inventions of the poets,
and neither Proteus nor Nereus, neither Leukothea nor
the Nereids, were worshipped in temples with sacrifice and prayer. The case was different with Glaukos
and Melikertes. The former was invoked specially in
the city of Anthedon, in Bœotia, as a god ready to help
seafarers ; and it was here said that he was once a poor
fisherman, but having eaten of a marvellous plant, he
had leapt into the sea and been changed into a god.
It was much the same with Palaimon Melikertes, the
god honoured at Corinth as the guardian of voyagers.
Of him, too, it was said that he was a son of Ino
Leukothea, and, being pursued by his father, had leapt
with his mother into the sea ; that here Poseidon had
received them, and changed both into deities of the sea.
In this way it was sought to explain why the Isthmian Games were celebrated at Corinth in honour of
Melikertes ; for it was only dead heroes that were
honoured with such athletic contests and races round
the sepulchral mound. The ancients themselves, indeed, were not quite sure whether these Games were
celebrated in honour of the god Melikertes (whose
name originated in that of the Phœnician god Melkarth)
or of Poseidon. Hence it happened that the mourning-
wreath of pine bestowed on the victor at the Games, in
remembrance of the god who had leapt into the sea,
remained sacred to Poseidon as well. For that the
pine was sacred to the latter, because its wood was

employed in shipbuilding, is an invention of a much later time.

3. RIVERS AND NYMPHS OF FOUNTAINS AMONG THE GREEKS.

Overpowering seems the might of rivers where they have made with toil a path through savage rocks, and thus laid open a passage from one district to another. Full, however, of blessings is their power where they have given earth her fruitfulness, and with their branching arms have spread the blessing over all portions of the land. Therefore the Greek did not hesitate to honour with gratitude the gods of the rivers, and to ensure their favour through victims offered in sacrifice. The poets named as father of rivers either Zeus or Okeanos, the river that surrounded the world; and when the goddess Themis in the name of Zeus summons the Olympians to council, the great river-gods and the delicate maidens of the springs also appear in the hall of Olympos. They are for mortals as powerful as Earth, Sun, nay, Zeus, god of heaven, himself, and therefore they are readily invoked with Sun, Earth, Zeus, and the infernal deities as witnesses of an oath. Almost always they appear favourable and well disposed to mortals. How welcome must have sounded the murmurs of a stream in the land of the Phæacians when, wearied to death, the much-enduring Odysseus was tossing on the sea!

But because rivers contribute to man's blessings, grant rest to the seaman, and to the country richness and growth, the youth of man when growing up is

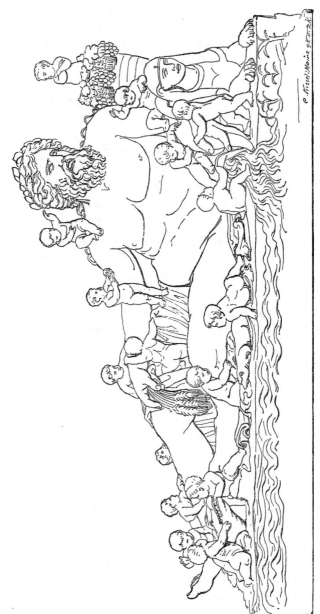

Fig. 46.—The Nile.
Vatican Museum, Rome.

consecrated to them. On attaining man's estate the youth gives to the river-god the locks of his hair, as a sign that he belongs altogether to him. Thus Peleus had vowed to Spercheios, the river of his home, that Achilles, if he returned from Troy, should offer to him his hair, as well as a sacrifice of fifty rams. The favourite victims for river-gods were bulls or horses. Like a bellowing bull the storm-swollen mountain-torrent, hurrying everything along with it, shot down into the plain, and therefore in earlier times men imagined rivers as in the form of bulls, or, at least, as provided with bull's horns. Herakles, the mighty hero who did not shun even the contest with the king of the rivers, Acheloos, broke off his horn and thereby tamed him. Now for the first time had the wild river become full of blessings for the country, and the new horn which Herakles gave Acheloos by way of amends was filled by the nymphs with flowers and fruits. The stream, become gentle, now itself caused flowers and fruits to spring forth.

After this the artists in representing river-gods were wont generally to place beside them the horn of plenty, and the place of the fierce bull's form or of the horns was taken by the form of a man stretched out at ease and crowned with sedge or leaves. Thus we see (Fig. 46) the Nile reposing that bestows on Egypt all her fruitfulness. Sixteen children sport around him : they are the sixteen cubits that the river rises in its annual flood. A Sphinx, the symbol of Egypt, serves as his support, and the children play and amuse themselves with the various creatures characteristic of the country.

Not merely mighty streams, however, but dainty

springs as well had claims on the gratitude of man;
for these too contributed to the fertility of the soil.
Especially on rocky islands might the tiniest rivulet be

FIG. 47.—NYMPH OF A FOUNTAIN.
Statue in the Vatican Museum, Rome.

welcome. Scarce had Odysseus recognised his native
land of Ithake once more and covered the ground
with kisses, when he prayed to the water-maidens,

the nymphs of the springs throughout the land, and promised to sacrifice to them goats and lambs, as in former days. So, too, the pious swineherd Eumaios apportioned from the meat at his dinner the first pieces to the nymphs and their friend Hermes, the goatherd's god. For what would become of his herds without the refreshing draught that the nymphs distribute !

The nymphs of the fountain, however, did not only distribute the refreshing moisture, but the water over which they presided possessed a mysterious potency which filled men with enthusiastic inspiration. Hence a madman was said to be " seized by the nymphs." By plashing fountain one can so well give oneself up to one's own thoughts, and so poets too were the friends of the nymphs. In almost every place where the spring leapt murmuring from the ground, there stood a little shrine of the nymphs that men loved to deck with flowers and votive gifts of every kind. And as mighty bulls were sacrificed to the great river-gods, so was the leaping kid to the more delicate nymphs. But artists have depicted the nymphs mostly as tender maiden figures, who draw water in vase or shell (Fig. 47).

In a few brief lines a clearly-defined picture of the water-deities of Greece is given in Milton's *Comus*, where the Spirit thus invokes Sabrina, the nymph of the Severn :—

> " Listen, and appear to us,
> In name of great Oceanus;
> By the earth-shaking Neptune's mace,
> And Tethys' grave majestic pace,
> By hoary Nereus' wrinkled look,
> And the Carpathian wizard's hook,[1]

---

[1] *I.e.*, the crook of Proteus ; see p. 275.

By scaly Triton's winding shell,
And old soothsaying Glaucus' spell,
By Leucothea's lovely hands,
And her son that rules the strands,
By Thetis' tinsel-slippered feet,
And the songs of sirens sweet,
By dead Parthenope's dear tomb,
And fair Ligea's golden comb,
Wherewith she sits on diamond rocks,
Sleeking her soft alluring locks;
By all the nymphs that nightly dance
Upon thy streams with wily glance,
Rise, rise, and heave thy rosy head
From thy coral-paven bed,
And bridle in thy headlong wave,
Till thou our summons answered have.
                    Listen, and save."

(B) SPRINGS AND RIVERS AMONG THE ROMANS.

The Romans were originally not a people, like the Greeks, ready to tempt with their ships the dangers of the sea; and, therefore, the belief in the helping or harmful sea-deities was not developed among them. Rivers and springs, however, were always regarded by them as sacred. Within the pure spring particularly dwelt, according to their belief, a special divine power. Whoever drank of it became filled with inspiration, his mental vision was rendered more acute and obtained a glance into the future. *Carmenæ* or *Camenæ* was the name given to these fountain-nymphs, in whom the Greeks of a later day recognised their Muses. Specially famous through her legend was Egeria, whose spring gushed forth from a pleasant grot not far from Rome. It was here that King Numa, founder of the old Roman worship, received all prophecies which he was to bestow as a blessing on the Roman people ; and the water from Egeria's fount the Vestals also drew for the rites of their special goddess.

Wherever beside the gushing water vapours rose from the ground that confused the mind and filled it with strange ideas and images, in such a spot was it believed the will of God might specially be learned. Such an oracular centre was the grotto of Albunea. When the priest had presented the offerings of those who questioned the oracle, he laid himself down in the silence of the night on the spread-out fleeces of the sacrificed sheep. As soon as he had fallen asleep, he saw forms strange and wondrous floating in air and heard voices of gods as of the dead in the lower world. But since the influence of such springs marvellously excited man's spirit, it was believed that poets enjoyed the special favour of the goddesses of springs.

All spring-water was derived from heaven, and therefore the god of heaven, Janus, was called the father of springs. But because the water was in continual movement, it was considered hazardous to cross it without further ceremony ; for thus violence is done to the freely-running power. There was need of a special knowledge, and this was possessed only by the so-called *Pontifices*, or Bridge-builders. From just such religious reason there might be no iron nail in the wooden bridge which at Rome united the two banks of the Tiber. In particular, the River Tiber appeared as a divine being, great and potent. He was lord of 'the whole bed of the river, and

possessed the power of raising to deities those who
of their own free will dedicated themselves to him.
Thus it was said that Tiberinus had been a king of
Latium, who, however, in battle had disappeared in
the stream of the Tiber, and now gave his name to
the river formerly called Albula. So, too, the Vestal
Rhea Silvia, the mother of Romulus and Remus,
was thrown into the Tiber by King Amulius, but
taken up by the river-god and proclaimed his divine
consort. In the earliest times, certainly, it was sought
to gain the favour of rivers through human sacrifices.
These gradually ceased, but their remembrance lasted
long. At Rome every year, at full moon in May,
a whole series of figures of men, made of rushes,
and called *Argei*, were thrown into the Tiber. So
ancient was this usage that no explanation could be
given at a later time. The Greeks at last told the
credulous Romans that once on a time Herakles had
come to Rome with his companions from Argos and
had left them behind there, so that through home-
sickness they had thrown themselves into the river.
But the drowning of the rush-men was only a substitute
for human sacrifice, as properly required by the god
to be propitiated ; just as when Numa once offered to
Jupiter the heads of onions instead of heads of men ;
and fish rather than men were cast into the fire in
honour of Vulcan.[1] Such respect did the Romans
display for the sacred power of the river-god.

[1] For similar instances of mock sacrifices, see Frazer, *The Golden
Bough*, vol. i., p. 252.

CHAPTER XXII.

JANUS.

Janus, the Roman God of Light and of Beginning.

No Roman deity could boast of greater antiquity than Janus, whose worship was said to have been introduced by Romulus before that of the Sabine sun-god Sol. He remained thoroughly Roman to the last, without yielding to Greek influences. His temple was simply a gateway, facing east and west in the neighbourhood of the Forum. Janus was originally among the nations of Italy the god of heaven and of the sun, as Jana was the goddess of the moon. Therefore he was considered the father of all springs and rivers. As god of light and of the sun he was all-seeing; and hence it resulted that at a time when men were still somewhat clumsy in the representation of deities, Janus was represented by means of a single head with double face, to indicate that light or the glance of the sun penetrates on every side. Gradually, however, this was forgotten, and the later Romans believed they had found their old sun-god again in the Greek Apollo. Now there was left remaining only an obscure remembrance of the old god of light. Where heaven's light shone there was felt the power

of Janus, and so every aperture for light, every gateway, therefore also the door, was named after the god
" Janus " or " Janua." Each morning the priests addressed their first prayer to " the Father of morning,"
Janus, and so each day of new moon was consecrated to
him, because then the new light made its appearance. But
the month which after the shortest day again betokens
the return of light was called in his honour *Januarius*,
and it bears his name to this day. In order, however,
that the beginning of the year might be of good augury
for the following time, people were wont to give one
another pleasure through all sorts of little presents
and good wishes—a usage which has also survived to
our times.

Because with the appearance of light a new time
begins, Janus was gradually treated as god of beginning. Every gate denoted entering and exit, and every
entrance into and departure from the door denoted a
separate division of human action. Thus Janus himself became in like manner the porter or agent of all
activity. But because each division of action represents the point of separation between the present and
the future, it was believed that the double face of Janus
denoted gazing into the past and the future. Now
men thought of Janus before other gods at the beginning of the sacrifices, and generally at the beginning
of every transaction, even of war. It was not till the
beginning of war that the temple of Janus was opened,
and it was not closed till the end of the war. The
closing of the temple of Janus was with the Romans
rather a pious wish: for only twice throughout the
existence of the Roman Republic—viz., after the end

of the Second Punic War, and under Augustus after
the battle of Actium—did this closing take place, and
even then only for a very short time. When Augustus
once more closed the temple, it was about the time at
which Christ was born. Paganism had well-nigh ceased
to be a living force, and a new and a purer religion
was destined to rise upon its ruins.

> " From haunted spring, and dale
> Edged with poplar pale,
> The parting genius is with sighing sent ;
> With flower-inwoven tresses torn
> The nymphs in twilight shade of tangled thickets mourn."
> MILTON, *Hymn on the Nativity.*

INDEX.

A CATALOG OF SELECTED
DOVER BOOKS
IN ALL FIELDS OF INTEREST

A CATALOG OF SELECTED DOVER BOOKS IN ALL FIELDS OF INTEREST

CONCERNING THE SPIRITUAL IN ART, Wassily Kandinsky. Pioneering work by father of abstract art. Thoughts on color theory, nature of art. Analysis of earlier masters. 12 illustrations. 80pp. of text. 5⅜ x 8½. 23411-8

ANIMALS: 1,419 Copyright-Free Illustrations of Mammals, Birds, Fish, Insects, etc., Jim Harter (ed.). Clear wood engravings present, in extremely lifelike poses, over 1,000 species of animals. One of the most extensive pictorial sourcebooks of its kind. Captions. Index. 284pp. 9 x 12. 23766-4

CELTIC ART: The Methods of Construction, George Bain. Simple geometric techniques for making Celtic interlacements, spirals, Kells-type initials, animals, humans, etc. Over 500 illustrations. 160pp. 9 x 12. (Available in U.S. only.) 22923-8

AN ATLAS OF ANATOMY FOR ARTISTS, Fritz Schider. Most thorough reference work on art anatomy in the world. Hundreds of illustrations, including selections from works by Vesalius, Leonardo, Goya, Ingres, Michelangelo, others. 593 illustrations. 192pp. 7⅛ x 10¼. 20241-0

CELTIC HAND STROKE-BY-STROKE (Irish Half-Uncial from "The Book of Kells"): An Arthur Baker Calligraphy Manual, Arthur Baker. Complete guide to creating each letter of the alphabet in distinctive Celtic manner. Covers hand position, strokes, pens, inks, paper, more. Illustrated. 48pp. 8¼ x 11. 24336-2

EASY ORIGAMI, John Montroll. Charming collection of 32 projects (hat, cup, pelican, piano, swan, many more) specially designed for the novice origami hobbyist. Clearly illustrated easy-to-follow instructions insure that even beginning papercrafters will achieve successful results. 48pp. 8¼ x 11. 27298-2

THE COMPLETE BOOK OF BIRDHOUSE CONSTRUCTION FOR WOODWORKERS, Scott D. Campbell. Detailed instructions, illustrations, tables. Also data on bird habitat and instinct patterns. Bibliography. 3 tables. 63 illustrations in 15 figures. 48pp. 5¼ x 8½. 24407-5

BLOOMINGDALE'S ILLUSTRATED 1886 CATALOG: Fashions, Dry Goods and Housewares, Bloomingdale Brothers. Famed merchants' extremely rare catalog depicting about 1,700 products: clothing, housewares, firearms, dry goods, jewelry, more. Invaluable for dating, identifying vintage items. Also, copyright-free graphics for artists, designers. Co-published with Henry Ford Museum & Greenfield Village. 160pp. 8¼ x 11. 25780-0

HISTORIC COSTUME IN PICTURES, Braun & Schneider. Over 1,450 costumed figures in clearly detailed engravings–from dawn of civilization to end of 19th century. Captions. Many folk costumes. 256pp. 8⅜ x 11¾. 23150-X

PERSPECTIVE FOR ARTISTS, Rex Vicat Cole. Depth, perspective of sky and sea, shadows, much more, not usually covered. 391 diagrams, 81 reproductions of drawings and paintings. 279pp. 5⅜ x 8½. 22487-2

DRAWING THE LIVING FIGURE, Joseph Sheppard. Innovative approach to artistic anatomy focuses on specifics of surface anatomy, rather than muscles and bones. Over 170 drawings of live models in front, back and side views, and in widely varying poses. Accompanying diagrams. 177 illustrations. Introduction. Index. 144pp. 8⅜ x11¼. 26723-7

GOTHIC AND OLD ENGLISH ALPHABETS: 100 Complete Fonts, Dan X. Solo. Add power, elegance to posters, signs, other graphics with 100 stunning copyright-free alphabets: Blackstone, Dolbey, Germania, 97 more–including many lower-case, numerals, punctuation marks. 104pp. 8⅛ x 11. 24695-7

HOW TO DO BEADWORK, Mary White. Fundamental book on craft from simple projects to five-bead chains and woven works. 106 illustrations. 142pp. 5⅜ x 8. 20697-1

THE BOOK OF WOOD CARVING, Charles Marshall Sayers. Finest book for beginners discusses fundamentals and offers 34 designs. "Absolutely first rate . . . well thought out and well executed."–E. J. Tangerman. 118pp. 7¾ x 10⅝. 23654-4

ILLUSTRATED CATALOG OF CIVIL WAR MILITARY GOODS: Union Army Weapons, Insignia, Uniform Accessories, and Other Equipment, Schuyler, Hartley, and Graham. Rare, profusely illustrated 1846 catalog includes Union Army uniform and dress regulations, arms and ammunition, coats, insignia, flags, swords, rifles, etc. 226 illustrations. 160pp. 9 x 12. 24939-5

WOMEN'S FASHIONS OF THE EARLY 1900s: An Unabridged Republication of "New York Fashions, 1909," National Cloak & Suit Co. Rare catalog of mail-order fashions documents women's and children's clothing styles shortly after the turn of the century. Captions offer full descriptions, prices. Invaluable resource for fashion, costume historians. Approximately 725 illustrations. 128pp. 8⅜ x 11¼. 27276-1

THE 1912 AND 1915 GUSTAV STICKLEY FURNITURE CATALOGS, Gustav Stickley. With over 200 detailed illustrations and descriptions, these two catalogs are essential reading and reference materials and identification guides for Stickley furniture. Captions cite materials, dimensions and prices. 112pp. 6½ x 9¼. 26676-1

EARLY AMERICAN LOCOMOTIVES, John H. White, Jr. Finest locomotive engravings from early 19th century: historical (1804–74), main-line (after 1870), special, foreign, etc. 147 plates. 142pp. 11⅜ x 8¼. 22772-3

THE TALL SHIPS OF TODAY IN PHOTOGRAPHS, Frank O. Braynard. Lavishly illustrated tribute to nearly 100 majestic contemporary sailing vessels: Amerigo Vespucci, Clearwater, Constitution, Eagle, Mayflower, Sea Cloud, Victory, many more. Authoritative captions provide statistics, background on each ship. 190 black-and-white photographs and illustrations. Introduction. 128pp. 8⅞ x 11¾. 27163-3

LITTLE BOOK OF EARLY AMERICAN CRAFTS AND TRADES, Peter Stockham (ed.). 1807 children's book explains crafts and trades: baker, hatter, cooper, potter, and many others. 23 copperplate illustrations. 140pp. 4⅝ x 6.   23336-7

VICTORIAN FASHIONS AND COSTUMES FROM HARPER'S BAZAR, 1867–1898, Stella Blum (ed.). Day costumes, evening wear, sports clothes, shoes, hats, other accessories in over 1,000 detailed engravings. 320pp. 9⅜ x 12¼. 22990-4

GUSTAV STICKLEY, THE CRAFTSMAN, Mary Ann Smith. Superb study surveys broad scope of Stickley's achievement, especially in architecture. Design philosophy, rise and fall of the Craftsman empire, descriptions and floor plans for many Craftsman houses, more. 86 black-and-white halftones. 31 line illustrations. Introduction 208pp. 6½ x 9¼.   27210-9

THE LONG ISLAND RAIL ROAD IN EARLY PHOTOGRAPHS, Ron Ziel. Over 220 rare photos, informative text document origin (1844) and development of rail service on Long Island. Vintage views of early trains, locomotives, stations, passengers, crews, much more. Captions. 8⅞ x 11¾.   26301-0

VOYAGE OF THE LIBERDADE, Joshua Slocum. Great 19th-century mariner's thrilling, first-hand account of the wreck of his ship off South America, the 35-foot boat he built from the wreckage, and its remarkable voyage home. 128pp. 5⅜ x 8½.
40022-0

TEN BOOKS ON ARCHITECTURE, Vitruvius. The most important book ever written on architecture. Early Roman aesthetics, technology, classical orders, site selection, all other aspects. Morgan translation. 331pp. 5⅜ x 8½.   20645-9

THE HUMAN FIGURE IN MOTION, Eadweard Muybridge. More than 4,500 stopped-action photos, in action series, showing undraped men, women, children jumping, lying down, throwing, sitting, wrestling, carrying, etc. 390pp. 7⅞ x 10⅝.
20204-6 Clothbd.

TREES OF THE EASTERN AND CENTRAL UNITED STATES AND CANADA, William M. Harlow. Best one-volume guide to 140 trees. Full descriptions, woodlore, range, etc. Over 600 illustrations. Handy size. 288pp. 4½ x 6⅜.   20395-6

SONGS OF WESTERN BIRDS, Dr. Donald J. Borror. Complete song and call repertoire of 60 western species, including flycatchers, juncoes, cactus wrens, many more—includes fully illustrated booklet.   Cassette and manual 99913-0

GROWING AND USING HERBS AND SPICES, Milo Miloradovich. Versatile handbook provides all the information needed for cultivation and use of all the herbs and spices available in North America. 4 illustrations. Index. Glossary. 236pp. 5⅜ x 8½.
25058-X

BIG BOOK OF MAZES AND LABYRINTHS, Walter Shepherd. 50 mazes and labyrinths in all—classical, solid, ripple, and more—in one great volume. Perfect inexpensive puzzler for clever youngsters. Full solutions. 112pp. 8⅛ x 11.   22951-3

PIANO TUNING, J. Cree Fischer. Clearest, best book for beginner, amateur. Simple repairs, raising dropped notes, tuning by easy method of flattened fifths. No previous skills needed. 4 illustrations. 201pp. 5⅜ x 8½. 23267-0

HINTS TO SINGERS, Lillian Nordica. Selecting the right teacher, developing confidence, overcoming stage fright, and many other important skills receive thoughtful discussion in this indispensible guide, written by a world-famous diva of four decades' experience. 96pp. 5⅜ x 8½. 40094-8

THE COMPLETE NONSENSE OF EDWARD LEAR, Edward Lear. All nonsense limericks, zany alphabets, Owl and Pussycat, songs, nonsense botany, etc., illustrated by Lear. Total of 320pp. 5⅜ x 8½. (Available in U.S. only.) 20167-8

VICTORIAN PARLOUR POETRY: An Annotated Anthology, Michael R. Turner. 117 gems by Longfellow, Tennyson, Browning, many lesser-known poets. "The Village Blacksmith," "Curfew Must Not Ring Tonight," "Only a Baby Small," dozens more, often difficult to find elsewhere. Index of poets, titles, first lines. xxiii + 325pp. 5⅝ x 8¼. 27044-0

DUBLINERS, James Joyce. Fifteen stories offer vivid, tightly focused observations of the lives of Dublin's poorer classes. At least one, "The Dead," is considered a masterpiece. Reprinted complete and unabridged from standard edition. 160pp. 5$\frac{3}{16}$ x 8¼. 26870-5

GREAT WEIRD TALES: 14 Stories by Lovecraft, Blackwood, Machen and Others, S. T. Joshi (ed.). 14 spellbinding tales, including "The Sin Eater," by Fiona McLeod, "The Eye Above the Mantel," by Frank Belknap Long, as well as renowned works by R. H. Barlow, Lord Dunsany, Arthur Machen, W. C. Morrow and eight other masters of the genre. 256pp. 5⅜ x 8½. (Available in U.S. only.) 40436-6

THE BOOK OF THE SACRED MAGIC OF ABRAMELIN THE MAGE, translated by S. MacGregor Mathers. Medieval manuscript of ceremonial magic. Basic document in Aleister Crowley, Golden Dawn groups. 268pp. 5⅜ x 8½. 23211-5

NEW RUSSIAN-ENGLISH AND ENGLISH-RUSSIAN DICTIONARY, M. A. O'Brien. This is a remarkably handy Russian dictionary, containing a surprising amount of information, including over 70,000 entries. 366pp. 4½ x 6⅛. 20208-9

HISTORIC HOMES OF THE AMERICAN PRESIDENTS, Second, Revised Edition, Irvin Haas. A traveler's guide to American Presidential homes, most open to the public, depicting and describing homes occupied by every American President from George Washington to George Bush. With visiting hours, admission charges, travel routes. 175 photographs. Index. 160pp. 8¼ x 11. 26751-2

NEW YORK IN THE FORTIES, Andreas Feininger. 162 brilliant photographs by the well-known photographer, formerly with *Life* magazine. Commuters, shoppers, Times Square at night, much else from city at its peak. Captions by John von Hartz. 181pp. 9¼ x 10¾. 23585-8

INDIAN SIGN LANGUAGE, William Tomkins. Over 525 signs developed by Sioux and other tribes. Written instructions and diagrams. Also 290 pictographs. 111pp. 6⅛ x 9¼. 22029-X

CATALOG OF DOVER BOOKS

AUTOBIOGRAPHY: The Story of My Experiments with Truth, Mohandas K. Gandhi. Boyhood, legal studies, purification, the growth of the Satyagraha (nonviolent protest) movement. Critical, inspiring work of the man responsible for the freedom of India. 480pp. 5⅜ x 8½. (Available in U.S. only.)   24593-4

CELTIC MYTHS AND LEGENDS, T. W. Rolleston. Masterful retelling of Irish and Welsh stories and tales. Cuchulain, King Arthur, Deirdre, the Grail, many more. First paperback edition. 58 full-page illustrations. 512pp. 5⅜ x 8½.   26507-2

THE PRINCIPLES OF PSYCHOLOGY, William James. Famous long course complete, unabridged. Stream of thought, time perception, memory, experimental methods; great work decades ahead of its time. 94 figures. 1,391pp. 5⅜ x 8½. 2-vol. set.
Vol. I: 20381-6   Vol. II: 20382-4

THE WORLD AS WILL AND REPRESENTATION, Arthur Schopenhauer. Definitive English translation of Schopenhauer's life work, correcting more than 1,000 errors, omissions in earlier translations. Translated by E. F. J. Payne. Total of 1,269pp. 5⅜ x 8½. 2-vol. set.   Vol. 1: 21761-2   Vol. 2: 21762-0

MAGIC AND MYSTERY IN TIBET, Madame Alexandra David-Neel. Experiences among lamas, magicians, sages, sorcerers, Bonpa wizards. A true psychic discovery. 32 illustrations. 321pp. 5⅜ x 8½. (Available in U.S. only.)   22682-4

THE EGYPTIAN BOOK OF THE DEAD, E. A. Wallis Budge. Complete reproduction of Ani's papyrus, finest ever found. Full hieroglyphic text, interlinear transliteration, word-for-word translation, smooth translation. 533pp. 6½ x 9¼.   21866-X

MATHEMATICS FOR THE NONMATHEMATICIAN, Morris Kline. Detailed, college-level treatment of mathematics in cultural and historical context, with numerous exercises. Recommended Reading Lists. Tables. Numerous figures. 641pp. 5⅜ x 8½.
24823-2

PROBABILISTIC METHODS IN THE THEORY OF STRUCTURES, Isaac Elishakoff. Well-written introduction covers the elements of the theory of probability from two or more random variables, the reliability of such multivariable structures, the theory of random function, Monte Carlo methods of treating problems incapable of exact solution, and more. Examples. 502pp. 5⅜ x 8½.   40691-1

THE RIME OF THE ANCIENT MARINER, Gustave Doré, S. T. Coleridge. Doré's finest work; 34 plates capture moods, subtleties of poem. Flawless full-size reproductions printed on facing pages with authoritative text of poem. "Beautiful. Simply beautiful."—Publisher's Weekly. 77pp. 9¼ x 12.   22305-1

NORTH AMERICAN INDIAN DESIGNS FOR ARTISTS AND CRAFTSPEOPLE, Eva Wilson. Over 360 authentic copyright-free designs adapted from Navajo blankets, Hopi pottery, Sioux buffalo hides, more. Geometrics, symbolic figures, plant and animal motifs, etc. 128pp. 8⅜ x 11. (Not for sale in the United Kingdom.)   25341-4

SCULPTURE: Principles and Practice, Louis Slobodkin. Step-by-step approach to clay, plaster, metals, stone; classical and modern. 253 drawings, photos. 255pp. 8⅜ x 11.
22960-2

THE INFLUENCE OF SEA POWER UPON HISTORY, 1660–1783, A. T. Mahan. Influential classic of naval history and tactics still used as text in war colleges. First paperback edition. 4 maps. 24 battle plans. 640pp. 5⅜ x 8½.   25509-3

CATALOG OF DOVER BOOKS

THE STORY OF THE TITANIC AS TOLD BY ITS SURVIVORS, Jack Winocour (ed.). What it was really like. Panic, despair, shocking inefficiency, and a little heroism. More thrilling than any fictional account. 26 illustrations. 320pp. 5⅜ x 8½. 20610-6

FAIRY AND FOLK TALES OF THE IRISH PEASANTRY, William Butler Yeats (ed.). Treasury of 64 tales from the twilight world of Celtic myth and legend: "The Soul Cages," "The Kildare Pooka," "King O'Toole and his Goose," many more. Introduction and Notes by W. B. Yeats. 352pp. 5⅜ x 8½. 26941-8

BUDDHIST MAHAYANA TEXTS, E. B. Cowell and others (eds.). Superb, accurate translations of basic documents in Mahayana Buddhism, highly important in history of religions. The Buddha-karita of Asvaghosha, Larger Sukhavativyuha, more. 448pp. 5⅜ x 8½. 25552-2

ONE TWO THREE . . . INFINITY: Facts and Speculations of Science, George Gamow. Great physicist's fascinating, readable overview of contemporary science: number theory, relativity, fourth dimension, entropy, genes, atomic structure, much more. 128 illustrations. Index. 352pp. 5⅜ x 8½. 25664-2

EXPERIMENTATION AND MEASUREMENT, W. J. Youden. Introductory manual explains laws of measurement in simple terms and offers tips for achieving accuracy and minimizing errors. Mathematics of measurement, use of instruments, experimenting with machines. 1994 edition. Foreword. Preface. Introduction. Epilogue. Selected Readings. Glossary. Index. Tables and figures. 128pp. 5⅜ x 8½. 40451-X

DALÍ ON MODERN ART: The Cuckolds of Antiquated Modern Art, Salvador Dalí. Influential painter skewers modern art and its practitioners. Outrageous evaluations of Picasso, Cézanne, Turner, more. 15 renderings of paintings discussed. 44 calligraphic decorations by Dalí. 96pp. 5⅜ x 8½. (Available in U.S. only.) 29220-7

ANTIQUE PLAYING CARDS: A Pictorial History, Henry René D'Allemagne. Over 900 elaborate, decorative images from rare playing cards (14th–20th centuries): Bacchus, death, dancing dogs, hunting scenes, royal coats of arms, players cheating, much more. 96pp. 9¼ x 12¼. 29265-7

MAKING FURNITURE MASTERPIECES: 30 Projects with Measured Drawings, Franklin H. Gottshall. Step-by-step instructions, illustrations for constructing handsome, useful pieces, among them a Sheraton desk, Chippendale chair, Spanish desk, Queen Anne table and a William and Mary dressing mirror. 224pp. 8⅛ x 11¼. 29338-6

THE FOSSIL BOOK: A Record of Prehistoric Life, Patricia V. Rich et al. Profusely illustrated definitive guide covers everything from single-celled organisms and dinosaurs to birds and mammals and the interplay between climate and man. Over 1,500 illustrations. 760pp. 7½ x 10⅝. 29371-8

Paperbound unless otherwise indicated. Available at your book dealer, online at **www.doverpublications.com**, or by writing to Dept. GI, Dover Publications, Inc., 31 East 2nd Street, Mineola, NY 11501. For current price information or for free catalogues (please indicate field of interest), write to Dover Publications or log on to **www.doverpublications.com** and see every Dover book in print. Dover publishes more than 500 books each year on science, elementary and advanced mathematics, biology, music, art, literary history, social sciences, and other areas.